The
GARDEN
and the
GUN

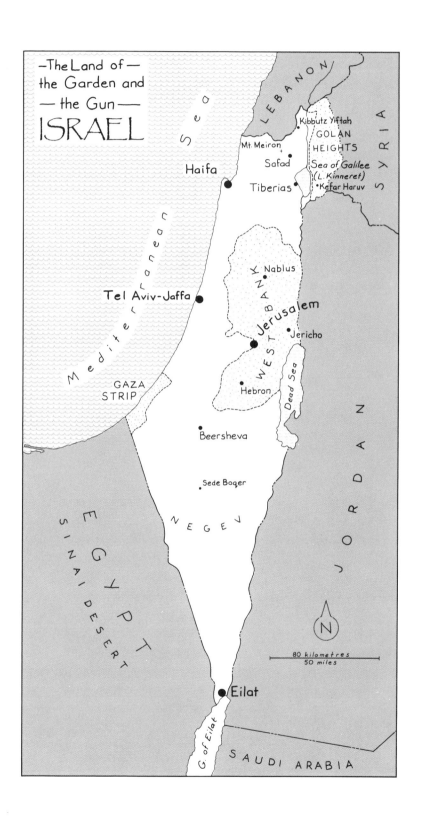

—The Land of—
the Garden and
— the Gun—
ISRAEL

LEBANON

SYRIA

Mediterranean Sea

Kibbutz Yiftah
GOLAN
HEIGHTS
Mt. Meiron
Safad
Sea of Galilee
(L. Kinneret)
Haifa
Tiberias
•Kefar Haruv

Tel Aviv-Jaffa

Nablus
WEST BANK
Jerusalem
Jericho

GAZA
STRIP

Hebron
Dead Sea

Beersheva

JORDAN

Sede Boqer

NEGEV

E G Y P T
SINAI DESERT

N

80 kilometres
50 miles

Eilat

G. of Eilat

S A U D I   A R A B I A

The GARDEN and the GUN

A Journey inside Israel

Erna Paris

LESTER
&ORPEN
DENNYS
PUBLISHERS

FIRST EDITION

Canadian Cataloguing in Publication Data

Paris, Erna, 1938-
   The garden and the gun

ISBN 0-88619-121-1

1. Israel - Description and travel. 2. Israel - Politics and government. I. Title.

DS107.4.P37 1988   956.94'054 C88-094273-8

Front cover photo by M. Milner/Sygma

Design by Craig Allan

Printed and bound by Metropole Litho Inc.

Lester & Orpen Dennys Limited
78 Sullivan Street
Toronto, Canada   M5T 1C1

To my parents,
Christine Lipkin Newman and Jules Newman,
with love and gratitude

Also by Erna Paris

Stepfamilies: Making Them Work

Jews: An Account of Their Experience in Canada

Her Own Woman: Profiles of Canadian Women

Unhealed Wounds: France and the Klaus Barbie Affair

Acknowledgements

I spent a whole summer debating the pros and cons of writing about the dilemmas of Israel today and in the end two people helped convince me to go ahead: the first was my husband, Tom Robinson, who is the bedrock of my life and can always be counted on for pointed, no-nonsense advice; the second was my publisher, Malcolm Lester, who reminded me during the course of a lunch that "People always respect honesty." That simple truth had somehow escaped me during my summer of hand-wringing.

Once I made my decision, the research became one of the most interesting, vivid adventures of my life, and it would be impossible to list all the people who helped me along the way. In particular, Shira Herzog Bessin, former director of the Canada-Israel Committee, was exceptionally helpful in her even-handed description of social conditions in Israel, and I am grateful for the contacts she set up on my behalf. Patrick Martin of the Toronto *Globe and Mail* opened his Israel file and gave me dozens of sources—which is not something writers always do for each other. Michael Marrus of the University of Toronto and June

Callwood both actively encouraged me in this project, as did my good friend Louis Greenspan, of the Department of Religion at McMaster University. Louis also took time from his busy schedule to read the manuscript in an early draft. I am especially grateful to Janice Stein, Professor of Political Science at the University of Toronto, for agreeing to review the manuscript for me during her summer holiday, and to my brother, Peter R. Newman, for reading and commenting on the kibbutz chapters. However, none of these readers is responsible for any errors that may have occurred in the text—or for my interpretations, needless to say.

In Israel I wish to thank Aliza Factor of the United Kibbutz Movement for arranging my visits to Kibbutz Yiftah and Kefar Haruv, and Rabbi David Refson for allowing me to live temporarily at the women's yeshiva, Neve Yerushalayim. Hanoch Smith, Allan Shapiro, Danny Rubenstein, and Avraham Burg, among others, helped clarify aspects of Israeli society; and my friends Lila and Bob Julius and Yossi and Devora Oreg opened their homes so I could rest during a somewhat gruelling two months. But my most profound thanks must go to all the people who allowed me to share their lives, however briefly. Those with official positions and recognizable roles in Israeli and Palestinian society, including kibbutz leaders, will find their names in the text of this book. In some cases I changed the names of ordinary people who agreed to speak freely, in an attempt to protect their privacy. There are no composite characters and every conversation was either recorded electronically or noted immediately afterwards.

I am grateful to my daughter, Michelle, for sharing part of the Israel journey with me: in particular, the difficult visit to Yad Vashem; and to my son, Roland, for allowing me to incorporate some of his own travel experiences in Israel. My family and loyal friends of old vintage—Tom, Jill, Victor, Maxine, Peter, Renée, Ruth, Eric, David, and Alison—helped me find the title *The Garden and the Gun* for the mere price of (several) bottles of wine and a morsel of food. Thanks to my agent and friend, Lucinda Vardey, for her consistent support; to Janice Bearg, director of promotion at Lester & Orpen Dennys; and to my excellent editor, Gena Gorrell.

As a final note of appreciation, I wish to thank the Canada Council Arts Awards program for its generous financial assistance.

Contents

Arrival   1

Jerusalem Beginnings   9

The Kibbutz   22

Tamar and Yeshayahu   33

Morning   39

The Border   49

The Last Day   61

Kefar Haruv   69

The Yeshiva   84

The Neve Way   98

The Conversion   105

The Wedding   113

Shabbat   120

Mrs. Meirovitch and Mrs. Neiman   132

Memory   141

Yad Vashem   153

Menachem   159

Son of the City   176

The Face in the Mirror   191

A Day on the West Bank   208

The Politics of the Messiah   222

Kiryat Arba   238

Questions and Answers   249

The Award Winner   263

The Prophet   268

The Road to Sede Boqer   277

Epilogue   289

Bibliography   291

CHAPTER ONE

Arrival

The security for Pam Am flight 114 from Paris to Tel Aviv left me feeling nervous. The police were there all right, outfitted with their rifles and bullet-proof vests, but my checked baggage went through the most perfunctory of X-ray scans. The hand luggage security was even more lax. A cheerful agent joked with her colleagues of grenades in suitcases—while my bags slid past without as much as a sideways glance.

None the less, flight 114 seemed filled to capacity. Seated not far from me was a family of Italian Jews, the men wearing skullcaps. The paterfamilias buckled his seatbelt and brought out a Hebrew text, which he began to study intensely. An elderly American behind him, also wearing a skullcap, complained loudly about his seat and the placement of his suitcase, then settled in for the journey with his own Hebrew text. Despite a common acquaintance with classical Hebrew, these men could not communicate, for generations of their families had been born and died on opposite sides of the world. But here on a flight to Tel Aviv, the long decades, perhaps an entire century, shrivelled to nothingness; here they were neighbours again, as their ancestors had been, reading prayers in the same ancient language.

A family of Jews from Argentina sat several rows away. Their children, two little girls of eight or nine, entertained their dolls with old Spanish songs. A lost branch of my own family went to Argentina from Russia in 1905; after the revolution failed, my mother's father, following a period in prison, escaped to an "America" that turned out to be Canada. Had he gone to South rather than North America, I and my children would also have sung ancient Spanish songs to childhood dolls, absorbing the ethos of a Latin world. As it happened, my family was imbued with the Anglo-Saxon values of a British-Canadian education. In one generation, my father and his siblings exchanged the Orthodox synagogue of their parents for a Reform temple that taught its children neither the ancient teachings of the Talmud nor the new creed of Zionism, but a passionate humanism in the name of history and the Jews.

On Pan Am 114, we spoke a babel of tongues. Some of us were clearly on a pilgrimage to the resurrected Land of the Jews, a magical place whose biblical contours filled the mind. Others were headed, more prosaically, to the troubled and troubling land situated in the powder keg of the world.

The beautiful girl sitting next to me studied herself intently in a hand mirror. She was from New York. A year before, she had graduated from high school, and now, after a brief trip home, she was returning to Jerusalem to complete a one-year program in Jewish Studies before beginning university in the United States. Her school in Israel—for American students from religious families—was "quite isolated", she said.

"Were you upset during the recent violence?" I asked.

She looked blank. "I don't really know what's going on," she replied. "I don't read the papers or anything and everyone around me is American." She applied her make-up with renewed vigour.

"Do you think you'll stay in Israel?"

"Definitely not. No way." She laid down her mirror and turned to stare at me. "None of us wants to *stay* there...but we really love it anyway. Oh yeah, it's just great in Israel."

The American across the aisle was concentrating so hard on his text that his glasses fell continually off the end of his nose. From time to time he emerged into consciousness to complain about the food, the seat, or the orange juice before disappearing again into his studies. His wife sat in patient silence beside him, isolated for the duration of the journey.

I was a passenger on this plane because I wanted to experience Israel directly, beyond the propaganda and counter-propaganda that depicted that country either as a reincarnation of Paradise whose leaders could do no wrong, or as the abode of war-lusty evil-doers who could do no right. I was, if labels were called for, a humanist who had been educated in the Reform tradition, with a deeply felt commitment to Jewish history and an equally deeply felt commitment to human rights. The latter had, in fact, grown from the former.

I was here because I hoped to glimpse the reality of Israel, beyond the dreams and fantasies, beyond what I had begun to think of as a country of the mind.

In the country of the mind, "Israel" stretches back into a mythic past of religious and secular history. For almost two thousand years—since the destruction of the Temple in Jerusalem in A.D. 70 and the dispersal of the Jews throughout the world—the Orthodox yearned together for the end of exile and the coming of the Messiah who would lead them to Eretz Yisra'el, the Land of Israel. Then, in the late nineteenth century, an Austrian Jew, Theodor Herzl, produced a revolutionary vision, the birth of Zionism: a dream of a secular Jewish homeland, a nation like any other, in which Jews would be free at last from king, Cossack, and czar.

Around the same time, a Ukrainian Jew called Ahad Ha'am added a new wrinkle. He taught that in order to survive, Jews needed to strengthen their "national spirit" as exemplified in the teachings of the prophets, which meant the expression of their traditional morality. The Jewish spirit depended on reason and national ethics and not religion, he said. His belief that a Jewish state would be the *end* result of a Jewish spiritual renaissance, and not the beginning, made him an adversary of Herzl's more political Zionism, although both desired the creation of a Jewish homeland in Palestine.

Ahad Ha'am's vision enjoyed wide popularity among left-wing Zionists and Diaspora liberals, but there soon emerged a competing, more militaristic view. In the 1920s another Ukrainian Jew, Vladimir Jabotinsky, promoted the idea of a Jewish state in Palestine on both sides of the Jordan, with continued Jewish immigration to achieve a majority there and a permanent garrison of troops for defence.

All these ideologies had rivalled one another from the very beginning: the religious ideal of the return to Zion; the coming of the Messiah; the Jews as "a light unto the nations"; the political refuge; the Jewish national state. But what relation had any of these to the real Israel? Living in Canada, it was impossible to know.

So I was coming as a stubbornly curious, old-fashioned traveller. Walking shoes broken in, knapsack packed, modern accoutrements of tape recorder and other assorted paraphernalia at the ready, I hoped to explore the vagaries of settlement and ideology forty years after the revolution.

The seatbelt sign lit up. The American girl beside me repaired her make-up diligently. The Italian brought out a small, leather-bound Hebrew Bible. He read briefly, then continued to move his lips in prayer as the plane prepared to touch down in Israel. Across the aisle, a passenger of the secular persuasion read Shirley MacLaine's *Dancing in the Dark*. I caught my breath and looked out over the dusk-shrouded terrain. Believers, non-believers, seekers, adventurers, and pilgrims, we readied to meet the Holy Land.

The air was balmy. Palms trembled in a gentle wind. In the half-light of evening, a waiting crowd pressed against security barriers, calling noisily to friends and family. Strangers smiled warmly. A young man dressed in army khaki and wearing a knitted skullcap asked what flight had arrived. Three Arabs in *keffiyeh* headdress stood together, significantly apart from the crowd.

Also standing a short distance away were several bearded Hasidic Jews dressed in long, black cloaks and hats, with forelocks and full beards. A young-old man, his fringe of black and white phylacteries hanging below a frock that derived from another century and a vanished world, contrasted strangely with his baby daughter. She was a small, pink ball of fluff in her made-in-U.S.A. quilted snowsuit.

I climbed into a *sherut*, a shared taxicab, to wait until enough passengers arrived to make the driver's trip into Jerusalem worth while. Outside the car, an argument erupted.

"You know you're in Israel when the arguments start," explained the portly Israeli sitting next to me, in a pleasant, matter-of-fact voice.

"What's it about?" I asked.

"Well, if you really want to know, the Orthodox guy is refusing to get into a car with a woman." He shrugged helplessly.

Within five minutes I knew that my neighbour had been born in Vienna and had survived the Holocaust, a fact to which he merely alluded in passing. He had come to Israel after the war, then rejoined relatives in Los Angeles. In 1980 he had visited Israel, met a woman, married, and stayed. This was where he belonged, he told me. Where all the Jews belonged.

"Have family here?" he asked, with the directness of one who has just told all and expects something in return.

"No. I'm just travelling around for a few months."

Silence. What could this possibly mean? "Think you might stay with us?"

"I'm not really planning to."

"Why not?" His question hovered demandingly between us.

Next to the driver sat a reserved American clutching a book called *The Holocaust: How to Teach It*. The conversation in the car became more and more animated, in both Hebrew and English, but he did not participate. The Orthodox (who had boarded in spite of my presence) was a Russian emigrant. In a reversal of the usual order, he had first gone to the United States to study with a famous Lubavitcher rabbi, then immigrated to Israel. Although he was descended from generations of secular Russian Jews, he was now ultra-religious.

The Israeli from Vienna struck up a conversation with a young American medical student—about Miami Beach, of all places. Their families, they discovered, attended the same synagogue there: Young Israel, it was called. Their families lived on neighbouring streets. The Israeli's name was Avi; his brother-in-law was an optometrist and his niece was also specializing in eyes. The student's name was David; his uncle was in general practice and he himself was training to be a surgeon. As darkness blanketed the passing landscape, Israel began to feel like Miami on the Mediterranean, as comfortably familiar as childhood memories in Toronto. I could hardly remember where I was.

We reached Jerusalem. The cab roamed the darkened streets, then stopped at the hotel where I had booked for a few days until I could find an apartment. Here, the same partnership between the utterly strange and the familiar prevailed. The radio in my room emitted wailing Eastern sounds that properly located Israel in its geographical setting, but the hotel dining area looked like what we used to call a "rec room" when I was growing up. The walls were panelled and the tables were of the bridge family. The cavernous space echoed with the animated voices of tourists on package deals from the United States, Australia, Argentina, and Europe, all of whom were bravely eating a meal of brownish avocado filled with oily potato salad, and barley soup, overcooked beef, soggy carrots, and a wiggly red dessert.

Seated alone at my table, I seemed to be attracting attention.
The *maître d'hôtel*, a stocky, balding man with a friendly face
upon which perched a pair of broken hornrimmed glasses, asked
solicitous questions. Did I have family in Israel? In other words,
what was I doing here? His colleague, Joseph the waiter, hovered
about like a fussy grandmother.

"Don't you like the food?" he asked.

"Thank you. I'm not very hungry."

"Are you with a tour?"

"No, I'm alone."

"Family here?"

"No."

He too paused, wondering about a woman alone in a hotel
dining room, hesitating over what might be required of him.

"Care to go out later?" he ventured.

"No, thanks. I'm a bit tired."

He shrugged. All tacks had been exhausted in an effort to place
me. No tour, no family, and apparently not here for sex.

He moved across the room and whispered something to a
second waiter. In a flash, Naim stood beside me.

"You're from Toronto?" he gasped. "I was married to a girl
from Toronto for a year and a half. We've been divorced for nine
years now. Well...welcome to Jerusalem!"

Naim had met his wife over breakfast ten years earlier, in this
very hotel, and the appearance of another woman from Toronto
was momentarily overwhelming. "I feel as though heaven sent
you to me!" he proclaimed. I nodded mutely, taken aback by this
enthusiasm.

"With a tour?" he asked.

"No. I'm a writer," I blurted out, worn down by this question
with its layers of meanings stacked within like painted Russian
dolls.

The news catapulted him into a shocked silence. He peered at
me curiously, and I seized the opportunity. "Where do you live?"
I asked.

"East Jerusalem. Near the Damascus Gate."

Good. That meant he was probably a Palestinian.

"I need a guide," I said.

He looked a little dubious. "I have friends in East Jerusalem...." His voice trailed off. There was clearly something he wanted to ask. He scanned the room as if seeking advice, but his colleagues were all preoccupied and at work. Only the *maître d'* was watching, with obvious displeasure. Why was his waiter talking so intently with a guest?

Naim turned to me abruptly. "Are you a Jew?" he asked.

He looked embarrassed and uncomfortable. What was I to make of this question?

"Yes, I am."

Now that he had his answer, he relaxed. "I have friends for you to meet, but if you want to hear the truth, don't let them know you are a writer or a Jew," he warned. "They are just ordinary people and they are very afraid to see their names in the newspaper. Be a teacher. And say you are a Christian. They won't talk to you otherwise."

"I'll let you know," I replied. "Good-night."

"Good-night." He looked at his boss, who was glaring at him from his station at the door.

I returned to my room. Over the radio, a muezzin wailed in mournful, foreign tones that spoke of a strangeness I did not know.

CHAPTER TWO

Jerusalem Beginnings

My new apartment was of the basement variety, but in a beautiful section of the city. Yemin Moshe was a small, residential suburb situated on a hillside in a park behind the famous King David Hotel. In July 1946, towards the end of the British Mandate in Palestine that followed the First World War, members of the Irgun—the military arm of the Jabotinsky Revisionist Movement—planted a bomb in British offices, killing about eighty British, Jewish, and Arab civil servants and wounding about seventy others. I used to know one of the men who had been involved in that attack. In spite of having risked his life to wrest Israel from the British, he later moved to Toronto, gave up on ideologies, and devoted himself to the more immediate world of real estate development. He was just as successful at making money as he had been at urban terrorism. His wife, I recall, wore an ankle-length leopard coat.

Yemin Moshe was now an upscale community of renovated townhouses built from the same glorious, golden Jerusalem stone that was everywhere in the city. Red geraniums hung in lush profusion from stone balconies. Sculptors and other artists lived here and their works graced some of the doorways.

From the top of the stone steps that climbed the hill beside my new home, I could look directly east to the walls of the Old City and some of the most sacred monuments in the world. The Church of the Dormition of the Virgin dominated the mountain on the spot where Mary, mother of Jesus, was said to have died. To the right of the monastery glistened the black dome of the tomb of David—king of Israel in the tenth century B.C. Jerusalem had been, and still was, David's city. It was David who proclaimed it the capital of Israel, David who developed the city, built its fortifications, constructed its buildings, and decided to house the Ark of the Covenant there. During his time, Jerusalem became the spiritual as well as the political capital of the Jews, and it remained the spiritual capital during the long millennia of exile from Israel.

In a splendid historical irony, the building that housed David's tomb also housed one of the most sacred of Christian monuments: the hall where Christ and his disciples celebrated Passover together at the Last Supper. Here in the Holy City, where men had fought each other in the name of God and empire since the beginning of history, and continued to do so, the religious monuments of the Jews, the Christians, and the Moslems stood cheek by jowl in an uneasy peace.

In 1948, during the War of Independence against the Arabs who opposed the emergence of the Jewish state, Jewish and Jordanian fighters rained bullets on each other from the opposing heights of Yemin Moshe and the Old City across the way; and for years afterwards, Yemin Moshe remained a dangerous place. Surprise sniper attacks were frequent until 1967, when Israel conquered Arab Jerusalem and the Jordanian West Bank, and every door of every home was outfitted with locked iron bars. The bars were still there.

I found it impossible to forget war and suffering here. The serene Old City walls, their ancient stones resplendent in the golden morning light, housed angry Palestinians and tense, watchful soldiers who patrolled the narrow streets. My own upstairs neighbour was crazy, I was warned. At our first meeting she greets me angrily, her hands on her hips. The front door, the iron prison bars, must be locked all the time, she charges. Have I let in an Arab? Her accusation strikes me with the force of a slap. Her son was killed in the '67 war. She does not want me here, a stranger intruding upon her constant grief. Every morning she carefully sweeps the dirt from her steps onto mine.

Miriam, my landlady, brought a lamp, a rug, and some flowers from her garden to make me feel at home. I made tea and we sat down together. She was fortyish and tall and attractive, with the carriage of a woman born to or married to privilege. Miriam had come to Jerusalem from Johannesburg, South Africa, more than twenty years earlier. She had come, she said, because apartheid appalled her. The day she left her country of birth, she tore up her passport and threw it at the last official person she encountered.

Her father never forgave her. "You can disapprove," he said, "but you stay and try to change things." Miriam disagreed.

Now that things had turned so ugly in South Africa, she was planning one last trip "home" during which she would try to memorize the familiar landscape and say goodbye to people she believed she would never see again. After more than two decades, the pain of having belonged—of still belonging—to that desperate land remained as raw as ever.

If being a South African white was an embarrassment Miriam shed early, being an Israeli required a new mind set altogether, especially now that her children were growing up. Her eighteen-year-old daughter had just entered the army. A few days earlier she had phoned home to say she had finished basic training and was about to be sent to the West Bank to guard women prisoners.

"What'll I do?" she had asked her mother fearfully. Just weeks before, she had been a schoolgirl. Now she would be all-powerful, guarding Arab women, some no older than herself.

Perhaps she would want to avert her eyes in dismay, for she came from a family in which at least one parent, Miriam, thought the Palestinians ought to have—and one day surely would have—their own state.

What Miriam feared most was that her daughter would return from the army hardened to other people's suffering and brutalized by the realities of military life.

"You teach them your values and you hope they remember." It was a pat phrase that concealed more than it revealed. She smiled weakly.

But her real worry was her son, because boys went to the front lines and girls did not. If the past forty years were any indication, the chances were high that he'd end up there sooner or later. Having children in this country was a bit like producing cannon fodder.

"It's something we know and have to live with." Another bland remark, a fragile veneer of ordinariness stretched across a chasm of fear. The tension wrinkled her forehead and pulled at her mouth. I heard her emotion and could say nothing in reply. Mute and feeling helpless, I thought of my own son, just nineteen and brimming with hope for a future he was certain he would live to see.

Not long before, Miriam had been driving in the car with her boy, and like most fourteen-year-olds he had begun to criticize his mother for something or other. Miriam suggested that when he was grown up and a father he might want to do things differently, but until then.... It was the old story we've all heard from our parents and passed on to our kids when they got on our nerves. But Miriam's son replied differently than children elsewhere might do. He reminded his mother—calmly, she said—that not every boy in Israel grew up. What with six wars in less than four decades, he already knew he was playing a lottery.

"It was like a stab in the heart to hear him say that, but he seemed to take it more for granted than I did." She stared at the floor for several seconds. "The children grow up so early here. They don't have a childhood. It breaks my heart. I guess that's why we spoil them. We are afraid for their lives."

Miriam had given a considerable amount of thought to the circumstances of her life in Jerusalem. She was a booster ("I wouldn't *dream* of living anywhere else"); but quickly honest when challenged. "No one plans ahead much in this country," she said bluntly. "We live for the moment, we don't save much, we just spend, spend, spend. I'm like everybody else, I also live for the moment. It's not that I'm always thinking something might happen to one of us, it's just sitting there, in the back of my mind, all the time. I've become a fatalist, the way soldiers talk about bullets having their name on them."

She finished laying the rug, and arranging the plants she had so generously brought to make me feel at home in her little apartment. "Let's go swimming one day!" she said, changing the subject abruptly. Her voice was suddenly cheerful, the protective armour back in place.

"Great!" I watched her as she carefully made her way down the steps to the parking lot.

Beneath the tough skin of this city there coursed an underground river of sorrow.

Rafi Horowitz, the man in charge of accrediting foreign journalists, was the most casual official I had ever encountered. His clothes were rumpled and his open-necked shirt hung out over his pants. We were immediately on a first-name basis.

"Why do journalists think they need permission around here?" he asked petulantly. "This is a free country, you know. You don't *need* a press pass. You planning to attend press conferences? No? So forget it! Go anywhere you like."

"I thought I might like to see an army training camp."

"Impossible. Security, you know. That's our first consideration."

"What about the Palestinian refugee camps? Will the army prevent me from going in?"

I had said the wrong thing. Rafi's face took on a sombre cast. He had been leaning forward, talking to his friend Erna. Now he leaned back and pushed his chair away.

"That's not our domain. UNRWA [the United Nations Relief and Works Agency] will take you around the camps and tell you their sad stories." His voice tightened with disdain. "I already told you, security is our main consideration. We're at war, remember that. Not officially, but indirectly." He glared at me angrily.

So the status quo was described as "war". Funny, it had not occurred to me that a failure of "peace" automatically meant one was engaged in "war". There had been "wars" in 1948, 1956, 1967, 1969–70, 1973, and 1982. What was going on now, in 1987, seemed substantially less than "war", at least from the outside. Rafi's comments would make interesting baggage to carry with me into the West Bank.

Upstairs in the Beit Agron press building was the office of Captain Elise Shazar, spokesperson for the civil administration of the Occupied Territories. Her space was as shabby and deliberately casual as that of Rafi Horowitz on the floor below. Two dust-covered, paper-strewn desks filled most of the space in the small room, one occupied by Captain Shazar, the other by a male colleague who was sniffing a Helena Rubinstein sample perfume bottle with unabashed, childlike curiosity. He dabbed a little under his chin, then caught my eye, embarrassed. At home, in a more reserved, more controlled society, I might have imagined him to be a homosexual. Here I did not. It was becoming apparent that personal contact in this society was direct and immediate, that curiosity was not repressed, and that frankness was the rough coinage of social intercourse. I smiled at the officer. I was a bit of a sniffer myself.

He smiled back.

"Captain Shazar around?"

He indicated a young woman in her late twenties who was talking animatedly on the telephone in the next room.

"She'll be here in a minute," he said, waving me off.

Some while later, Captain Shazar made an appearance. She readied herself to be interviewed, finding a semi-comfortable spot on a broken wooden chair. Drilling started outside the building, or was it inside? Neither of us could hear the other without effort. But once she was engaged at her job—public relations—the comic aspects of the shabby office, the perfume bottle, the broken chair, and the drilling that shook the floor beneath us ceased to matter. Captain Shazar was a smooth professional. The relationship between the Israeli military and the Palestinian population on the West Bank and in Gaza was utterly banal, she suggested, and benign, too. Unemployment was down, children were in school, income was up. Everyone felt more or less satisfied with a less than perfect situation. Any other questions? She smiled a practised smile.

Captain Shazar was doing her job well, but the yawningly ordinary scene she described did seem at odds with the "war" scenario put forward by her colleague on the floor below.

I left the building and began to walk in a westerly direction towards the central downtown section of Jerusalem. It was mid-afternoon. The sun streamed into the city and glanced off the stones of the low-rise buildings that lined the main thoroughfare. The army was omnipresent, boys and girls doing their compulsory military service, middle-aged men doing their compulsory reserve duty. The predominant colour on the street was khaki, and the object that caught my eye, the ubiquitous M-16 semi-automatic rifle.

The Israeli and his rifle were a striking pair. Soldiers slouched along the street, slouched in bus shelters, and slouched inside fast-food restaurants eating falafels and smoking cigarettes, their guns slung carelessly over their shoulders. But they were watchful, unnervingly (or was it reassuringly?) watchful. They were both startling and strangely endearing, these unmilitary-looking youngsters who belonged, one had to remember, to one of the world's best armies, and a civilian army at that. One also had to remember that almost every Jewish man and woman who passed along this road had once been a member of that army, and that every man under the age of fifty still was, whether he happened to be on duty today or not. The true scope and centrality of the army was apparent in the dress of the so-called civilians. Since every male owned a green, army-issue jacket, and since the air that day was cool, every male on the street was wearing a green, army-issue jacket. Why buy an extra jacket for one's off-duty life? This jacket was the outward sign of a basic truth: to be an Israeli was, quite simply, to be a soldier, regardless of whatever other identities one might assume in the course of a lifetime. It was to be on duty, or ready for duty. It was to know, as my landlady's young son already knew, that one's true future was as unstable as the wind that blew through the cedars lining King David Street.

Was it the all-pervasive presence of the army that accounted for the general disdain for dress in this capital? Men and women, in uniform or out, were attired as though they were camping in the woods, without a trace of the sexual self-consciousness that is at least minimally present on the main streets of most big cities. Sensuality seemed curiously absent from the streets of Jerusalem. Men rarely looked at women, even surreptitiously, and women did not look at men. Perhaps co-ed military service during late adolescence produced a buddy-buddy relationship between the sexes. Perhaps the significant and visible presence of Orthodox Jews and their sexual prohibitions effectively flattened the atmosphere. Perhaps, like the army, the communal, kibbutz origins of Israeli society encouraged a desexualized contact. Whatever the reason, the distinct lack of sexual tension in the air set Jerusalem apart.

The large number of Arab workers in the city probably added to this phenomenon. As far as one could see, they were doing all the manual, unskilled labour. Arabs were the street cleaners, sweeping the gutters with straw brooms. They were the garbage collectors and the construction workers.

An Arab worker in Jewish Jerusalem knew enough to keep his eyes straight ahead. Just being Arab was potential trouble enough in a place where people lived on the knife-edge of their nerves, knowing that a false step, a booby-trapped package, or an unfortunate choice of city buses could unleash disaster.

The streets were quiet in spite of the hour and the bright sunshine, but Steimatsky's book store on Jaffa Street was crowded with browsers. I pushed my way in, Israeli style. Elbows were an important commodity in this land, I was beginning to understand, and I was sharpening mine as weapons of basic survival.

Steimatsky's was impressive, with a range of scholarly and popular books in Hebrew, French, and English, and a wide spectrum of international newspapers and magazines. The people milling about, elbows *en avant*, were serious readers who were doing their reading right here in the store. And who could blame them? Prices were atrocious: fifty dollars for an average-length hardcover.

"This is expensive!" I ventured to a saleswoman.

"So what do you expect, five cents?" Her English was perfect. "We've got a small market here. The costs are high."

This person was not being rude. Her comments were merely the verbal equivalent of sharp elbows. I felt bruised none the less—in my Anglo-Saxon land, strangers do not address each other in such tones—and then, as I turned away, she smiled a smile of perplexing warmth and familiarity. Had we met? Clearly not. Was this warmth just the flip side of rudeness?

I bought a newspaper and returned to the street. To my left was the paved mall of Ben Yehuda Street, the centre of Jerusalem café life. At least there was some animation here. Strollers paraded up and down the few blocks set aside for their pleasure, and a few tourists sipped tea and picked at Hungarian poppyseed cakes at outdoor tables. The Israelis lined up at fast-food stalls serving a steady stream of falafels, a delicious, cheap meal of fried chick-pea paste in pita bread. Newspaper vendors hawked their wares, their many editions spread out on the ground around them. News was, understandably, a national obsession. And everywhere the young soldiers of both sexes—and their guns.

I ate a falafel and, like a good Canadian, looked around for a garbage can. There weren't any—too dangerous. Someone could hide a bomb in an overflowing garbage can on this crowded street. Better to throw litter on the road. I would have to remember that this golden city where people strolled, did business, and sipped coffee in outdoor cafés could also be a dangerous place.

Suddenly a loud noise sounded, a startling bang. I stopped, spun around, looked to the sky. Nothing. The Israelis hadn't paid any attention. The only people looking as worried as I were other foreigners.

We exchanged sheepish glances. There were obviously clues we had not understood. Like creatures who hear notes the rest of us are deaf to, the practised Israelis on Ben Yehuda Street could distinguish between the sounds of war and peace.

A local newspaper is the fastest route into the vernacular of a society. So the *Jerusalem Post* that day was a small window into a still unfamiliar world. It was a window worth peering into, if only because it had been a while since I last felt like Alice in Wonderland.

A small story on page two reported that Menachem Begin, for-mer prime minister and leader of the right-wing Likud party, had recently compared his mentor, the bellicose Vladimir Jabotin-sky, to Moses, Aristotle, Maimonides, and Leonardo da Vinci. In a Christian society, I reflected, he might have included Jesus Christ in his list of notables. On another subject, it was revealed that pirate cassettes seized in Gaza the previous day included a "chanted version of the Torah portion of the week". Michael Jackson I could understand. But the Torah? On the black market?

On the behaviour of local politicians, the *Post* reported the following:

> Knesset members are in a very combative mood. Yesterday, Haim Ramon (Labour) and Yehoshua Matza (Likud) were busy trading insults—"idiot" and "disgusting hypocrite" were the mildest of them— only three days after Geula Cohen (Tehiya) and Charle Biton (DFPE) came to blows....

Feuding politicians were not a rarity anywhere, but male and female elected representatives hauling off to punch each other did seem a little excessive. Was this an important feature of gender equality that had escaped the attention of feminists at home?

Unsurprisingly, the two chronic problems of the nation captured most of the space: ongoing hostility between Orthodox Jews and secular Jews (the latter seemed to include all the non-Orthodox); and violence and counter-violence in East Jerusalem and the West Bank.

On the first front, the religious political parties were continuing to agonize over the fact that Shoshana Miller, a convert from Christianity to the liberal, Reform branch of Judaism, was to be officially registered as a Jew, according to a ruling from the High Court of Justice. In this latest scene from the strange "Who is a Jew?" controversy, in which the "Jewishness" of converts was examined and pronounced upon by the rabbinical authorities, artillery was being aimed at the entire Reform movement, which was considered illegitimate by the Orthodox. A Hasidic activist claimed that there were 80,000 non-Jews in Israel who were actually registered as Jews. Conspiracy and scandal surrounded this revelation. The rabbi had submitted to the Interior Committee of the Knesset (Parliament) a list of 3,000 false registrants, "with addresses". This matter was hushed up for political reasons, he said, but non-Jews had "infiltrated" the ranks of the secular and the Orthodox, and some had actually "confessed" that they were not truly Jews according to religious law.

The social problems of a nation that had never separated synagogue and state were beginning to shimmer into focus.

Then there was the other intractable problem. Only days earlier, Palestinian terrorists had knifed two young Jews from the Musrara quarter, a working-class Moroccan district of Jerusalem that borders the Damascus Gate of the Old City.

A local restaurant owner complained that business was down; in five months there had been eight stabbings and no one wanted to come near the Old City any more. After the knifing murder of a *yeshiva* (religious academy) student in the Old City, enraged Jewish residents had rampaged through the narrow streets, shouting, "Death to Arabs!"

The *Jerusalem Post* reporter interviewed two youths. " 'We've got to kill all the Arabs,' said the younger without hesitation, his face devoid of anger or any other expression. He was standing within five metres of an Arab driver when he said that, but did not seem to relate to him." The other youth was reported as having a different outlook: " 'We just say those things, but we never do them,' he suggested. 'We don't have any alternative except to live with them.' "

If anyone was able to spread oil on the troubled waters, it would be Jerusalem mayor Teddy Kollek. Kollek was a one-man dam holding back the flood waters; indeed, the metaphor was a commonplace. "After Kollek, the deluge," Jerusalemites were fond of saying, their admiration mixed with apprehension—for it was widely feared that Kollek, who was in his seventies, would not seek another term in office.

"We've got to learn to live with this, " said Kollek in reply to a question about the stabbings. "This is our Via Dolorosa. If it happens again, we will just go on, and likewise, if it keeps happening after that. That is the way we will conquer the city."

"The mayor repeated the last phrase again, as if measuring the slogan against the reality," wrote the reporter.

Was such despair an accurate reflection of reality, I asked myself.

I returned to my apartment to rest. Tomorrow, I would begin my own explorations.

CHAPTER THREE

The Kibbutz

Kibbutz. "The single most powerful cultural force of the entire Zionist enterprise," wrote Amos Elon in *The Israelis: Founders and Sons*. The pioneer men and women of the kibbutz believed themselves to be a symbol of the "new Jew", he wrote, "strong, hardy and courageous as the 'diasporic' Jew was not."

During the first decades of the twentieth century they came in successive waves to Palestine, which was then an outpost of the Ottoman Empire. They were utopians, dreamers, and revolutionaries in revolt against a Diaspora society of authoritarian rabbis, vicious czars, and devastating pogroms. They were romantics and True Believers, men and women who had been influenced by the European liberation movements of the nineteenth century and who yearned for a "perfect" communal society of Jews in a Jewish homeland.

They were also very young—teenagers, for the most part, in rebellion against their parents and their parents' values. They worked fourteen-hour days and held compulsory "discussion groups" long into the night. They changed their names in a zealous desire to strip themselves of their former identities. They drained malaria-infested swamps and built roads through desert terrain where for thousands of years only camels had walked.

Many could not bear the terrible hardship of their new life and returned to Russia, Lithuania, or Poland. A few who had nowhere to go committed suicide. But a minority did survive the early years and they succeeded in founding a new society.

By the mid-1930s the kibbutz settlements had become defence outposts in the battle against the British and the Arabs, and their members had become "soldiers" on a front line. This was not a difficult transition, for their utopian beliefs readily accommodated ideals of patriotic heroism. The young pioneers had expected to live in peace, but failing that, they agreed to fight. They didn't have too many choices. There was no going "home" by 1935.

"Ideology played the greatest role in the development of the modern Israeli psyche," wrote Amos Elon. "The feeling of having no alternative was the second-largest factor."

The central bus station in Jerusalem was crowded with soldiers and other travellers, most of whom seemed to be munching on falafels. I lined up behind a sign that read, "Tiberias". From that ancient city on the Sea of Galilee, I planned to rent a car and drive north to the Lebanese border, to Kibbutz Yiftah; for if settlement and border defence were what Israel was about when the new state was proclaimed in 1948, then Yiftah, which was born in that very same year, was the place to begin my own explorations.

We boarded the bus. A soldier eyed my tape recorder suspiciously, then came over to check it out. Music played from the driver's radio, followed by the hour signal. News time: a sacred ritual in a country where hourly bulletins had too often been replaced by warnings of attack, and calls for national mobilization.

The driver turned up the volume. Passengers already *reading* the news put down their papers to listen. The announcer spoke of the Demjanjuk war crimes trial, which had just opened, and of Dr. Mengele, the former doctor-experimenter at Auschwitz, whose death had recently been confirmed. I looked at my fellow passengers with renewed interest. I needed to remind myself that, unlike any other place I had lived in or travelled to, Israel was a Jewish world where the news headlines spoke of Jewish concerns.

The road bent towards Jericho, slashing through the yellow clay of the desert. In the distance, low mountains rose from the earth like rounded breasts, and brown hills folded in geological creases like the skin of an aged elephant. A surface film of winter-green moss announced the transient presence of water.

It was in Jericho that Joshua fought his famous battle between 1500 and 1200 B.C., and took the city for the ancient Israelites. To the south lay the Dead Sea; and beyond, the mountains of Moab from which Moses viewed the Promised Land. But such events took place in quite another age. Today Jericho lay in the occupied West Bank—where tensions were high. The bus driver pressed his foot to the floor. It would be harder for rock-throwers to hit a vehicle that was hurtling along at a speed I preferred not to contemplate.

Men in keffiyeh headdress drove tractors, or crouched along the roadside smoking cigarettes. Women in embroidered dresses bent over crops, or carried loads on their heads. Groups of Arab schoolchildren headed home for lunch to stone and clay huts set among the fields. The sand-coloured structures faded into the sand-coloured desert.

Here and there old military bunkers looked towards Jordan.

A Bedouin encampment sprawled alongside the highway, the huts capped by thatched roofs from which television antennae sprouted. Their front doors were made from recycled tin. An unpaved, sandy path ran through the village, and abandoned tires and oil drums lay in disorder about the grounds. A dirty, half-naked child stared at the passing bus.

Not five hundred yards away, a new Jewish settlement perched on a hilltop in a cluster of modern, four-storey buildings. This was a dormitory suburb for that other Israel, only minutes away over the now invisible Green Line, a post-1967 demarcation between Israel and the West Bank that was now largely ignored.

Not twenty minutes out of Jerusalem and we had listened to news about one war, passed roadside reminders of another, and observed the incongruous juxtaposition of unequal peoples.

The road north from Tiberias climbed steeply on a narrow, badly maintained surface which was lined with large weeping willow trees. Poorly banked hairpin turns brought me within inches of buses, trucks, and other vehicles, all travelling at breakneck speed. Even the view was distracting. The Sea of Galilee glittered below in the sunlight, the wilderness of the Golan Heights rising from its eastern shore. On the other side of the highway stretched the mountains and green valleys of southern Lebanon.

The farther north I drove, the more army trucks crossed my path. Soldiers hitch-hiked along the highway and a jet fighter zoomed through the overhead blue. Two army helicopters circled above like vultures.

Lebanon. I found it hard to imagine that this pastoral beauty was home to some of the ugliest, most savage internecine fighting in the world. Recently, the inhabitants of a Palestine refugee camp not far from here had been reduced to eating domestic animals, then rats. A woman and her child committed suicide to avoid being forced into cannibalism.

I was driving towards "war". It was there, just over the mountain ridge.

Kibbutz Yiftah grew out of war. Its founders were members of the Yiftah Brigade of the Palmach, the elite shock troops of the Haganah, a paramilitary Jewish defence force that fought both the British Mandate and Arab nationalists from the mid-1930s until the War of Independence in 1948.

The Palmach embodied the ideology of the new Jew: strong-bodied, proud, and committed to a future homeland; and their fame spread beyond the borders of Palestine. (In my Toronto Sunday School, we imagined tanned teenaged boys with muscled arms and hairy chests singing loudly as they fought back the hordes.)

The early Zionist settlers had dreamed a fantasy of "empty land" in Palestine, and the reality of conflicting claims for the same territory came as a shock. Their romantic idyll suffered further with the publication of the British White Paper in 1939. As far back as 1917 Britain's Balfour Declaration had pledged support for a Jewish homeland, but the White Paper favoured Palestinian nationalism and sought to limit Jewish autonomy. Worst of all, it restricted levels of Jewish immigration to Palestine and included a devastating hint that such immigration might actually cease altogether a few years down the road.

As Europe shuddered with early war tremors and Jews were blocked in their efforts to reach the shores of Palestine, the Zionist settlers took up arms in earnest. The fighting took place on two fronts. Some Palmach units defied the British by spiriting illegal immigrants into the kibbutz settlements, while others fought the Arabs.

In April 1948, twenty-eight men from the Yiftah Brigade died while defending a section of the Lebanese border against the Arabs. When the war was over and the new State of Israel proclaimed, eighty survivors of the brigade pledged to maintain a civilian-military defence of the region. Kibbutz Yiftah was the result.

The idea of a civilian army—at Yiftah and elsewhere—was fundamental to the new nation. The birth of the State of Israel, with its ideals of peaceful settlement, agriculture, and the "normalization" of the Jews, was accompanied by the birth of the Israel Defence Forces (IDF). The new army absorbed both the Palmach and the Haganah.

The "garden" was at the heart of the dream; it promised settlement and the regeneration of Jewish life. But the gun was also at the heart of the dream—as a guarantor of a radical new vision. The "new Jew" would be strong, not weak; powerful, not powerless; physical, not intellectual. He would transform himself and in doing so bring to an end two thousand years of Diaspora history.

Yoram was waiting at the bottom of a narrow secondary road that snaked up a steep hill to Yiftah. I followed his car to the kibbutz, which perched strategically on a mountain ridge only a few hundred yards from the Lebanese border. Yiftah looked to me like a summer camp for adults. A barn-like, wooden dining hall was the first building to meet my eye. From the beginning of the kibbutz movement, the dining hall had been the centre of social activity. This was where you met your fellow workers, with whom you laboured daily to open this inhospitable land. This was where you sang rousing songs and danced folk dances to keep morale high. It was where you suffered through interminable meetings to keep your grass-roots democracy oiled and running, where you fought about politics, where you gossiped about the other members of your community. Gossip was an important kibbutz commodity. In a tiny world without an established hierarchy of command, fear of being gossiped about kept people in line.

Five hundred people lived at Yiftah, including two hundred and twenty adult members, more than two hundred children under the age of eighteen, newcomers who hadn't yet decided whether they were prepared to commit themselves to a communal life, soldiers posted here as part of their army duty, and volunteers from outside the country who exchanged their labour for room, board, and a tiny remuneration.

Landscaped flower beds graced treed, sandy "streets" that linked the kibbutz houses: identical small, white boxes with tiny front yards. Everyone rode a bicycle. A young woman from the children's house pushed a large baby cart containing four or five sleeping infants.

There was something strangely "familiar" about this environment. Had I seen so many pictures of kibbutzim that I had unconsciously absorbed their contours? I thought not. What Yiftah resembled at first, superficial glance was the camp where I had spent my childhood summers. The winter-green hills of northern Israel in no way recalled the lakes and forests of Ontario, but the small houses, the dusty paths, the absence of cars, the communal dining hall, the gossip, the sing-songs, and the everlasting meetings where policy and problems were argued out on a daily basis, all touched a distant chord of remembrance. Even the kibbutznik dress was familiar. Jeans and work clothes, no make-up, no nonsense. Good. I too was dressed for work, in jeans, a hand-me-down plaid shirt from my daughter, sneakers, my husband's sports socks, and a bomber jacket surreptitiously borrowed from my son.

My guide was a strong-looking man in his late forties with an intelligent command of English. He had been born in Hungary. After the war, his father returned from Bergen-Belsen, one of the few surviving Hungarian Jews. Between 1947 and 1949 his father headed the national Zionist federation of Hungary, so Zionist ideology was an integral part of family life. When the Russians returned to Hungary in 1956, Yoram decided to get out. There was never any question in his mind about where he would go.

Yoram had arranged a schedule that would introduce me to every aspect of kibbutz life, he said. I would start by meeting a couple who were among the original founders of Yiftah. He hesitated, then shuffled a bit on his feet. He wanted me to understand something first, something about the kibbutzim in general.

"When you walk around Yiftah and look at where we are, you will realize what Israel is all about," he said mysteriously. He shuffled some more. "But that's a cliché, I guess. There is so much banality about the kibbutz...."

"Why do you live here and not in Tel Aviv?" I asked, guessing that he was trying to tell me about himself. I had already picked up the message that, for Israelis, "Tel Aviv" was a generic as well as a particular term. Besides referring to the city, it also meant *decadence*. "Tel Aviv" was the antithesis of those rural values upon which Israel was founded. The "new Jew" of early Zionist ideology was supposed to escape from his European urban condition and the paved ghettos of his ancestors. He was supposed to build a nation, to cultivate the land, to defend its borders. He was *not* supposed to sit in cafés in large cities and pretend he was in Paris.

Yoram told me a story. He had lived in Tel Aviv for many years, and just before the Yom Kippur war in 1973 he had won a contract to set up a small business enterprise in Rio de Janeiro. So he moved there in the summer of 1973, planning to buy a house and bring his family over.

In October the war broke out. Two days later, Yoram had liquidated his affairs and was on his way back to Israel.

"I realized how dangerous it was that more than 80 per cent of our population lives in Tel Aviv, Jerusalem, and Haifa. I realized that if you are a Zionist living in Israel, it's important *not* to live in Tel Aviv." He looked at me intently. I was meant to absorb this lesson.

"We are a border line here, along with the other kibbutzim just down the road from us. Together we are defending the border. *That* is what our country needed and still needs. Not more people living in Tel Aviv."

Yoram was a militant defender of an early form of Zionist ideology that went beyond the usual claim that Jews everywhere owed it to themselves to immigrate to Israel because the outside world would sooner or later throw up a new Hitler to destroy them. In Yoram's Zionism, moving to Israel was not enough. The Israeli could not afford the luxury of urban life when the country remained under siege (if not in reality, then at least in the minds of its citizens). Even a lifetime of active and reserve army service was not enough.

Yoram continued the lesson with another cautionary tale. Several years earlier some friends had emigrated from Israel to Canada, where they had established themselves in Montreal. Not long ago they had returned on a visit. The woman was wearing a large Jewish star on a chain.

"I never take it off," she told Yoram. "But sometimes I hide it inside my shirt."

Yoram peered at me closely. "I'm telling you this to illustrate the difference between the Jewish person in Israel and outside Israel," he said pointedly. "It's like a cousin of mine in Hungary. He's well established there and a loyal Hungarian and all that. He believes it is possible to be Jewish and Hungarian, just the way the Jews of Germany thought it was possible. I, personally, do not believe this. During the last few months he is afraid to write me because they are asking questions again about connections with Zionist things. So he does not write. If this is not hiding your Jewish star inside your shirt, I don't know what is."

My mind strayed to my companion in the taxi coming in from the airport and his question: "Why will you not stay here?" I had felt uncomfortable then as I felt uncomfortable now.

I excused myself. I wanted a shower. "Of course, of course, we will have *much* time," Yoram said quickly. "Your house is just down the road."

The house where I was to stay belonged to a woman whose husband had been killed during the 1982 war in Lebanon. He had been forty-two years old and on a month's tour of duty. For years the community mourned him. Finally they sent his widow and children to live in Tel Aviv, ostensibly so she could study, but in reality so she could meet another man. In the tiny extended family of the kibbutz, where everyone knew everyone else with a numbing familiarity, there were no marriage prospects for middle-aged women.

The house contained a living room, a small kitchen and eating table, a bathroom, and two tiny bedrooms. Her winter jacket was still here and her books were on the shelves. The kitchen cupboard was stacked with jars of tea and coffee.

I closed the door behind me and caught my breath.

I had stepped into the remains of her life, this woman close to my own age whose husband had been killed just over the ridge. I touched a towel in her bathroom, fingered shampoo and conditioner bottles, and looked at her children's drawings on the walls. Hidden behind this terrible ordinariness, tragedy filled the intimate spaces of her home.

A knock sounded at the door. Yoram was there, large in the evening light. We crossed the kibbutz to the dining hall, following the dusty paths. Dozens of people headed in the same direction said hello and smiled a welcome. My presence was decidedly not a surprise. Anyone who had not been apprised of my visit in advance had certainly learned of my arrival within minutes.

Dinner was self-serve and copious, a typical Israeli choice of dairy products and salads. No one dawdled over the meal. In the old days food was a device for staying alive (all other attitudes to eating being bourgeois and decadent), and it probably still was. Eating quickly left more time to exchange news and gossip with friends. Evening meetings had been convened and reluctant committee members needed to be nudged into attending.

Old people, middle-aged couples, teenagers, and young families with children sat on benches at long tables. The teenagers lived apart from their parents and sat separately from them. The foreign volunteers also sat separately; they were quite obviously not included in kibbutz life.

Yoram introduced me to Tamar and Yeshayahu Gavish. Yeshayahu was one of the twenty or so originals from the Yiftah Brigade who still lived at Yiftah. He was a short, sensitive-looking man in his early sixties. His wife, Tamar, looked weather-lined and intelligent.

The talk at our table turned to kibbutz life. It seemed to be a perennial subject.

"This is the 'blah, blah, blah,' " said Yoram, turning to me. "People talk each other to death here. It's a leftover from all the 'discussions' of the early days, a tradition."

"What sort of people decide to live on the kibbutz?" I asked. "Aside from those who are born here."

"People who can live a group life," Yoram replied. "It's like an orchestra. The individuals may not be geniuses, but the orchestra plays together beautifully. Anyone who is a genius leaves. The kibbutz cannot handle geniuses."

"We have a few professors in the kibbutzim," interjected a woman on the other side of the table.

"A group of professors could never form a kibbutz," snorted a man wearing kibbutz work overalls.

The idea of a professors' kibbutz caused much merriment. Although the kibbutz movement had produced the intellectual elite of Israeli society and had the best school system in the country, "intellectuals" were apparently considered unfit for kibbutz life and inimical to the ideology of the "new Jew". "Intellectuals" were the people the Zionist pioneers had left behind in the religious schools of the European ghettos.

The gap between the negative idea of the intellectual and the reality of the kibbutzim as the cradle of the Israeli intellectual elite was the first but not the last contradiction I would encounter at Yiftah.

CHAPTER FOUR

Tamar and Yeshayahu

Tamar and Yeshayahu Gavish were members of a founding generation whose values (it was said) were currently being eroded. The latest buzz talk about the kibbutz movement was that "kibbutzniks" no longer subscribed to the socialist, communal ideology of their parents. Critics called the kibbutzim "country clubs for a privileged class of Ashkenazic [European] Jews" and oases of material comfort for a tiny per cent of the population. They had lost their meaningfulness, cried the town folk—especially the Sephardic Jews, who came from Arab countries and saw themselves at the bottom rung of the economic and social ladder. This charge was echoed by religious Zionists, who had staked a claim in the Occupied Territories and begun to call themselves the true successors to the ideology of settlement and defence. Kibbutzniks didn't even do their own labour any more, they accused, but hired poor Sephardic Jews, or Arabs, to do it for them.

Both Tamar and Yeshayahu were born in Palestine, of parents who had emigrated from Russia in the early 1920s. Their parents belonged to the generation that feverishly hoped to transport the revolutionary ideals of 1917 to a Zionist Palestine; these were the pioneer visionaries who broke the land, drained the swamps, and struggled incessantly with despair.

As a teenager, Yeshayahu joined a Labour youth movement and studied in an agricultural school. The ideology of the youth group focused on the land: new agricultural techniques were being devised and taught, techniques that would eventually "green the desert" of Israel and attract world admiration.

But in 1946, as boatloads of dispossessed Holocaust survivors were turned back from the shores of Palestine to holding camps in Cyprus, Yeshayahu and his friends traded the classroom for the ranks of the Palmach. He and his fellows in the Yiftah Brigade fought the Arabs at the Nebi Yusha fortress overlooking the Hula valley, on the border of Israel and Lebanon, with heavy loss of life. Yeshayahu was captured by the Lebanese army and spent seventeen months in prison in Beirut.

Tamar was born in 1929 on one of the earliest kibbutzim in Palestine, and raised in the "children's house" rather than in her parents' home. Her father was a farmer—a socialist-Zionist farmer. He experimented with crops and was known throughout the community. He taught his daughter to drive a tractor and to work various other pieces of farm machinery. But although he had abandoned his parents' religion, left the country of his birth, and chosen to live the most arduous life imaginable, when he had children of his own he could not resist the pull of tradition. At the heart of the Jewish-socialist revolutionary experiment in Palestine, he taught them Torah.

Tamar's mother believed that the revolutionary concept of the children's house was the very best way to raise children and build a new society. Tamar had a happy childhood, she said, but as an adult she wanted more, especially when it came to family.

"For me it was not enough to love only the kibbutz," she told me. "In my parents' day the needs of the country were so great that no one could be exempt from physical labour. My parents and their generation gave their entire lives to the country. But I wanted a more human life.

"One day—I was already grown up—I asked my mother, 'How could you leave me in the children's house?' I have never forgotten what she replied. She said, 'In those times we didn't ask those questions. Perhaps your great-granddaughter will ask you, 'Did you hate your children? How could you let them go into the army?'

"So I finally understood—because I also do not ask myself this question. My children are needed in the army. And that is all."

"I also have the same ideals as my parents," interjected Yeshayahu. "The same hard work, the same sacrifice to build something. But my children feel this less...."

"The criterion is still the same, that you live not only for yourself and not only for today," cut in Tamar. "With this as a guide, we are very much like our parents. The tension between personal welfare and group welfare has always been at the heart of the kibbutz, but this was not a problem for my mother, the group always came first for her. It is less clear-cut for me and much less so for my children."

Tamar served coffee at a small table in their kibbutz house. The furniture was plain and practical. A television set occupied one corner and, as in every house at Yiftah these days, there was a private telephone.

Yoram sat with us, serving as interpreter when necessary and offering explanations.

The Gavishes were important people at Yiftah. They had both served as secretary of the kibbutz, the elected administrative head of the commune. Being secretary was a leadership position not everyone wanted. It was the most powerful job on the kibbutz but, like everything else, it was completely voluntary. On the kibbutz, no one got paid for anything.

Being secretary meant being responsible for making decisions about who would work where and who could attend school—personal decisions that might alienate some of the people you lived with. And it wasn't as though you could go home from the office and forget about them until the next day: the man or woman whose life you were considering would be your dinner companion in the dining hall every night. And now that the ideology of selflessness was being questioned as never before, it was becoming harder and harder to be a leader. The structures of collective decision-making remained the same, but there was less general acquiescence among the membership.

In the early years things had been different. The Yiftah founders lived in tents and later in wooden houses. When Tamar and Yeshayahu married, Tamar's uncle gave them a radio and her parents gave them a cow. It was the first radio and the first cow in the north of Israel.

"We talked about everything. *Everything* was a discussion," Yeshayahu said with a laugh. "We talked about socialist theory and how to build a well, about our cultural needs, about the farm we were trying to develop. And we wrote everything down for the future. We imagined ourselves as a model for the whole world—not less." They smiled at each other, remembering.

"Why did you settle here in the north?" I asked.

"The farther you were from Tel Aviv, the more Zionist you were," Yeshayahu replied.

"Sure," Yoram jumped in excitedly—we were on his favourite subject. "When we danced the hora we chanted, 'We are going to settle Ein Gedi,' and other remote border places. It was a kind of incantation. People were young and militant and happy to be together."

"You had to listen to the songs," interjected Tamar. "You can't find songs today like fifty years ago. We sang about the earth, the homeland, a new house, a new town...."

I was listening to the "good old days" refrain in its kibbutz incarnation—the nostalgia for a past not so very long ago, when youth, physical strength, and idealism dictated certitudes about the future. The force of the ideology remained such that Yoram could speak of the early years at Yiftah as though he had been present, although in reality he did not choose kibbutz life until 1973.

Such was the transcendent power of the dream.

For almost two decades, Tamar worked in the children's houses and in the kitchen of Yiftah. Yeshayahu worked in the apple orchard and in the youth movement of the national kibbutz organization.

"So women work with children and food and men work in the fields. Does this ever get discussed?" I asked, warming to one of my own favourite subjects. The kibbutz ideal had promised equality to women, but work was usually stereotyped according to sex.

"Every day and all the time. We used to fight about socialism, now we fight over feminism," replied Yoram. They laughed uproariously. "There are women today who want a greater variety of work," he added. "They're ready to accept the assets of equality, but not the burdens, like getting up at 3:00 a.m. to feed the chickens. They want to be equal, but God forbid they should ever achieve it. I do think that women do women's work better than men. And most want to do it."

I remembered a university course in introductory logic, something about circular reasoning. If it's "women's work" of course men can't do it, by definition. If it's simply "work", then who does it becomes a legitimate question for discussion.

"In the final analysis, the women are more effective than the men," Yoram went on. "One of the most crucial decisions we ever made was to allow children to sleep at home with their parents. It was the women who brought about this change with their votes."

Everyone nodded.

Not until they were in their forties did either Tamar or Yeshayahu pursue personal interests. Then she studied social work and he studied social psychology, both subjects being a formalization of skills they had acquired from communal living. After graduating, they began work outside Yiftah—without remuneration, of course—for the kibbutz movement.

"There was always an inner struggle between the self and the group," mused Yeshayahu. "For years I asked myself why I didn't leave the kibbutz to study in the United States or Canada. I told myself I could go. But then I asked myself, 'Who will build this place?' After much inner conflict, I decided to build. I was over forty before I could allow myself something personal, the right to study."

Night was closing in. They looked tired.

I returned to my borrowed house and lay in the bed where they had conceived their three children, the man who had died in a savage war fought just over the ridge, and the woman who had been sent away by this community to remake her life if she could. Between their sheets, I felt closer to the precarious life of Kibbutz Yiftah than any amount of "discussion" would allow. Their family, my family.... Devastation felt very close. I held my breath and listened to the noises in the night.

CHAPTER FIVE

Morning

Early the next morning I set out to explore the kibbutz with Yoram as my guide. It was a quiet, sunny day. Insects buzzed and birds sang; the grassy lawns and flowerbeds of Yiftah refracted particles of sunlight under the spray of a dozen water sprinklers.

Overhead, an airplane roared by—a niggling reminder of geopolitics.

The kibbutz was encircled with barbed wire to which vicious-looking dogs were chained at intervals of several yards. They bared their teeth and lurched at the car as we drove along an outside ring road.

I had been puzzled by a promotional booklet on the kibbutzim put out by one of the kibbutz movements. The barbed wire was the very first thing they wanted the reader to know about. "The barbed wire that surrounds our kibbutz symbolizes our history and sense of purpose," announced the article.

I understood the first part of the sentence; the kibbutz (like the rest of Israel) had needed to protect itself from the beginning. But did barbed wire really represent the kibbutz's "sense of purpose"? The wire looked to me like a sorry reminder of a sorry reality: kibbutzniks could not live freely and in peace.

The answer, such as it was, had come a few paragraphs down. "The Holocaust in Europe strengthened the resolve of [the] Jewish settlers.... Many left the barbed wire of the concentration camps that closed them in and found the barbed wire of a people able and willing to defend themselves and their communities."

Barbed wire, in other words, was a positive thing, a symbol, a source of veritable pride. Here again was the heart of the vision: the heroic and toughened "new Jew" who turned the barbed wire of shame into the barbed wire of self-defence. This was the "sense of purpose" of the kibbutz and of Zionism itself: the transformation of the old Jew into the new.

There was something unutterably sad about the glorification of barbed wire.

Yiftah cultivated 250 acres of orchards and 500 acres of field crops including apples, pears, wheat, cotton, kiwi fruit, passion fruit, and mushrooms. Apples were the major crop. Four local kibbutzim jointly operated a processing plant in which an automatic eye sorted apples into water channels according to colour and weight. This system was developed in the late 1970s and, like so much advanced agricultural technology, was first put into practice in Israel.

Yiftah also operated an important factory for the production of drip irrigation systems for both the local and the export market. Drip irrigation, which delivers water to individual plants drop by drop to minimize evaporation, was also developed in Israel; indeed, it was the central innovation for the development of the country. And there was nothing old-fashioned about either the style or the functioning of these operations. Production at the drip irrigation factory was controlled by an IBM central computer with eight terminals. Income ran into millions of dollars.

The third major money-maker, a chicken-feed plant, was entirely automated and needed only minimal supervision.

In short—Yiftah, like most kibbutzim, was a modern, agro-technical, collective enterprise whose members lived a comfortable, middle-class life. As usual, however, the reality of swift social and economic change had surpassed the ability (or willingness) of human beings to follow suit.

Yiftah had an ideological problem with success. The kibbutz movement had been founded upon the idea that men and women would toil on the land. A direct tie to personal labour was supposed to revolutionize human relationships. So it was understandably hard to maintain a "pioneering" ideal now that a computer was overseeing a multi-million-dollar irrigation industry, while a mere three people kept tabs on an automated chicken-feed factory and the "eye" sorting the apples belonged to a machine.

Another problem was the issue of outside labour. Revolutionary socialists did not hire people to toil on their behalf; only dirty capitalists did that. Yet, understandably, few kibbutzim had been willing to limit the size and nature of their industrial production—and hence their standard of living—for the sake of ideological purity.

In language reminiscent of North America in the 1930s and 1940s, when political rhetoric had a recognizable ring, the kibbutz movement promotional booklet attacked the issue head on:

> We make some unusual demands of a factory. It should be small and efficient enough so that our members can work it alone without the need of hired laborers. We don't want to grow into rich bosses making money off the labor of others; we want to be independent and we want every worker to know that he is an owner, not a salaried hand making money for the boss.
>
> Sometimes, though, our factories are too successful and too demanding of labor and some kibbutzim have decided to hire outside workers. Many of us think that bringing outside workers to the kibbutz contradicts our values....

It is not easy to live up to our ideals of ourselves and each kibbutz must, in the long run, make its own decisions and live by them.

The men and women working in the Yiftah apple plant were not kibbutz members but Sephardic Jews from a neighbouring development town. This presented problems, said Yoram—general problems, whenever it occurred, throughout the country. The question of inequality between Ashkenazic and Sephardic Jews was a simmering one. The two groups had evolved differently over their two-thousand-year dispersal, and the elementary fact that they were all Jews did not mean that they shared a culture. Furthermore, many Sephardic Jews believed they had been treated as a second-class nation within a nation since their arrival in Israel in the 1950s.

For many years Yoram had worked with a hired hand from Kiryat Shemona, just up the highway. The man earned a salary and raised a family. And yet—

"He hated us," said Yoram. "Maybe it was envy, but his hatred and his anger were terrible."

All the same, Yoram had little patience with the purists who worried about whether this or that innovation on the kibbutz was ideologically correct.

"If the kibbutz is doing a good job, it shouldn't have to apologize for not living as though it were thirty years ago. For me the old concept of the kibbutz changed a long time ago. We use the same name for something completely different. But ideas change more slowly and people lie to themselves. It's too bad.

"Okay, from an ideological point of view the use of outside labour is against socialist ideas. But all this is ancient history. Even before industrialization, they had to hire outside people to work the orchards. But the self-deception...."

He looked away so I would not see the disdain written on his face. "The main self-deception concerns the volunteers. They too are paid—not very well—but what is worse, for some members, is that they do not come to the kibbutz out of ideological motivation. People deceive themselves that the money they are paying these workers is not a salary.

"Can you believe we still get heated discussion in the general assembly about whether to hire an outside electrician? Some people fight as though they are fighting for their lives. They say they are fighting for the life of the kibbutz, that if we hire the electrician the kibbutz will cease to exist. We always have to have the fight. And the electrician is always hired."

He was agitated and a glimmer of ambivalence about this life for which he had abandoned everything showed through. We walked on across the grassy fields, past the lawns, the flowers, the houses. Disturbingly ugly pieces of sculpture rose here and there—female bodies with bird heads. A bird figure pecked aggressively at the swollen belly of a pregnant woman.

Was this the artistic expression of a kibbutz? The ideal community that was to revolutionize the future?

Yoram looked uncomfortable. "The sculptor is a disappointed member," he said with a dismissive wave of his hands. "He doesn't like what is happening to the kibbutz, or what the kibbutz is doing to itself.

"It's really better to live on a kibbutz and not be a member," he added in a low voice. "You avoid all the problems and have the advantage of living in a beautiful place. Non-members are not dependent on the kibbutz about whether they can travel, or study, or anything else. In many ways I am like an adolescent in this society. I can't make my own decisions, I don't have my own money, I am dependent on the recommendations of a committee, even if they do have to be approved in a general assembly—" He stopped short. Perhaps he was revealing more than he wished.

"On the other hand, as a member I can say, 'This is mine, all this is mine!' " He waved his arms and turned in a full circle to the orchards, the fields, the factories, the beautifully landscaped terrain. Orange bird-of-paradise flowers grew in beds at our feet. Lush tropical gardens decorated the fronts of the houses, with tall rubber plants, cactus, and palms.

"I can hardly express this in words," he said quietly.

Yiftah began to change fifteen years ago, when the general assembly decided that children would sleep at home with their parents. From that day on the kibbutz was family-centred in a way it had never been before, overturning the ideas of the early kibbutzniks like Tamar's parents, who had been convinced that they had discovered the most progressive, scientifically advanced, successful way of raising children.

In reality, the early pioneers were not particularly interested in children. Children meant family, and family was what they had escaped from: the hidebound religious family of the ghetto and the Russian Pale of Settlement. Children meant that women might be trapped again in the lives of their mothers and grandmothers. The young pioneer women of Palestine wanted equality. Besides, every hand was needed in the fields.

"Let's face it, the kibbutz wasn't built for children, but to make us free," a kibbutz old-timer told child psychologist Bruno Bettelheim in 1964, when he was researching his book *Children of the Dream*. "By this she meant nothing abstract, but the freedom to live in such a way that no kibbutznik, male or female, would lose any of the emotional satisfactions gained from a life devoted essentially to each other rather than to their children," Bettelheim explained.

Ironically, the radical experiment in child-raising became the most innovative enterprise of kibbutz life.

One of Bettelheim's most interesting conclusions concerned sexual repression. Far from encouraging erotic interest, group child care (including communal showers) forced children to repress sexual impulses as inappropriate. Bettelheim believed a family incest taboo was unconsciously extended to the larger "family".

General repression, he said, was necessary in order to "get along" on a day-to-day basis. Tact and submission to the group soon became necessary survival tools in a tiny community where one depended upon one's fellows for absolutely everything.

Yiftah children entered the baby house for daycare at the age of six weeks, and they stayed with the same group of peers until late adolescence, when they left the kibbutz to enter the army. Everyone hoped they would return to kibbutz life as young adults, but there were no guarantees.

At the baby centre, three two-year-olds were having a bath in a plastic tub, playing happily with water toys. In the next room, six children aged two and a half to three were playing doctor.

"Are you a doctoress?" Yoram asked a tiny girl, using the Hebrew gender ending.

"No," she replied emphatically. "I'm a doctor."

"The doctor here is a man," explained Yoram somewhat ruefully. "She has no idea of a woman doctor."

The young teacher clearly loved the children in her care.

"She is committed to them," Yoram said proudly. "She will stay with the same group from the age of six months until they are six years old and leave for the first grade."

"Aren't all the child-care people committed?" I asked, surprised.

"Not really. Most women only stay on this job for a year, even though it's not too good for the children."

"Can't the kibbutz insist that people stay on this job longer than others—for the sake of the children?" I asked.

"The kibbutz can't insist on anything," Yoram reminded me gently.

The young teacher had been born on a nearby kibbutz and raised in the children's house.

"I feel different from people who have lived with their parents," she acknowledged. She seemed very shy—unlike the majority of kibbutzniks I had met so far, who were completely at ease with conversation ("discussions") and with other people.

"Maybe I'm not too close to my parents," she continued. "Perhaps I'm really closer to the group I grew up with and to the adults who looked after me. I think the new way is better for the children and for the parents. I have a baby and I want him home with me at night so we can have more closeness between us."

Across the field, at the pre-school nursery, twenty-two children between the ages of three and six played noisily outside. By North American standards, they had very little equipment and very little supervision.

"In America, the teachers would be saying, 'Don't do this, don't do that,' " commented Yoram.

Their teacher was tidying clothing inside the house. "These children are freer with each other and that makes me freer in my dealings with them," she said. She had worked in Haifa previously, which was her point of comparison.

"Free" meant fewer controls, and politeness, for example, was not emphasized. Initially, the ideology of the kibbbutz had considered such things to be Old World bourgeois affectations.

What children *did* need to learn was the co-operative values of kibbutz life. As early as kindergarten, they began to clean their own children's house and to live in what was called a "self-service" world. They worked in their house gardens and were taken on trips around the kibbutz. They knew what their parents did and from the early grades they worked a few hours every week on a special children's farm. Through teaching and observation they learned constantly about nature.

Starting at age six, the children left Yiftah to attend a communal school several miles down the road. The school was run by five local kibbutzim for their own offspring. (An extreme left-wing kibbutz refused to send its children here and ran its own operation.) In recent years students from the neighbouring development towns had been attending the kibbutz high school, but "mixing" of this sort was a relatively new phenomenon. The kibbutzniks were, as Amos Elon put it, a "rural aristocracy".

It was lunchtime, dining-hall time, time for Yiftah to break from work and socialize. I wanted to meet the teenagers, those who had grown up together in the children's houses.

Yoram introduced me to three eighteen-year-olds who were having lunch together, two girls and a boy. They were friendly and spoke excellent English. There were fifteen of them from their children's house, Miriam said. They had been together since babyhood and this was their last year before going away to the army. Rafi was considering doing a year of service in another kibbutz before his army duty.

"Are you afraid of entering the army?" I asked him.

"Oh no," he replied quickly.

"We just take it for granted," said Dvora.

The girls said they were bored with the kibbutz, but they weren't sure why.

"Well, one reason is the lack of privacy," suggested Dvora. She wanted more "space" for herself. There was too much "peer pressure", she said, and pressure from other people.

"From whom?"

She chewed on the ends of her long, brown hair. "From my parents and their friends. It's not that they say anything. I just know I could make them feel bad if I quit school, or something like that. I'm not going to quit school. I just feel that there's pressure."

"I don't really know the older generation," interjected Miriam, "except that I know when they're looking at me and disapproving of me. I don't see my parents much any more. Maybe I'll see them walking along the path with their friends. I wouldn't like any of them to think badly of me."

I was struck by the plurality of "parents" in their speech. Their own mothers and fathers were seen as part of a group—a parental group that might disapprove of them—just as they themselves were part of a group.

"Will you come back here after the army?" I asked.

There was some uncomfortable laughter at my question—and some thoughtful hair chewing.

"This is such a small place," ventured Dvora. "The army is where we'll meet people from all over the country. I can't really decide whether I want to come back until I see life on the outside."

"Would you feel guilty if you didn't come back?"

"Oh yes, because of my parents and their friends. They would disapprove."

At eighteen the main reason for wanting to get out was sexual. As Bettelheim had suggested, the experience of growing up together, without privacy, was anti-erotic. The males of their age were like brothers, said Miriam. So were the older boys they had known all their lives.

"What would you do differently if you were bringing up children here?" I asked them.

They talked a few moments in Hebrew before answering. "We would have more space in the children's houses so the children could have privacy," said Dvora, speaking for all three.

It was the needs of the individual versus those of the collectivity again, that constant tension at the heart of kibbutz life. Their parents and grandparents had dreamed of a society in which privacy and individualism would no longer come between human beings. This new generation was telling them that thoughts and dreams need a quiet room.

CHAPTER SIX

The Border

Yossi was going to take me along the border of Lebanon, the border just over the ridge. He was the senior army officer in charge of civilian security here, not just for Yiftah but for twenty-nine small kibbutzim and *moshavim* (co-operative farms) that hugged the Lebanese boundary. His job, he said, was to stay awake so that others could sleep. It was to keep a cool head so that a population that lived behind barbed wire could carry on as normally as possible.

"What characterizes Yossi and the others who do this work is a quiet way of doing things," explained Yoram. "Any information that something is wrong gets to the rest of us when it is necessary and not before, so we can lead a normal life. Especially the children. They tend to react with more anxiety."

Yossi nodded agreement. He had carrot-red hair, a red moustache, and gentle green eyes that belied the experience of two wars and the years spent overseeing this border.

The beginnings of Yossi's life mirrored the beginnings of Israel itself. His parents were Holocaust survivors from Poland.

When their ship filled with refugees reached the coast of Palestine, it was intercepted and sent to Cyprus, according to the prescriptions of the 1939 White Paper. Yossi was born there, in 1947, in a British holding camp. The family was rescued by the Haganah and spirited into Palestine just prior to the creation of the state.

We set out in a car marked "Yiftah" in bold Hebrew letters and drove through terrain of startling beauty. Rounded mountains curved under a blanket of spring green. Pools of water reflected the morning sunlight from the bottom of deep gorges.

The quiet was total, a countryside quiet broken only by the occasional low whirr of an overhead jet. It was almost impossible to reconcile this natural loveliness with the reality of Lebanon, with terror, civil war, and fratricide.

In recent weeks the Iranian-backed Hizballah group (also known as the "Party of God") had intensified its campaign of attempted infiltrations into Israel, and Israel was quietly beefing up the South Lebanese Army that was its ally. The last time bombs had actually landed on the Israeli side was just prior to the Lebanese War, said Yoram. At Yiftah they had watched the explosions from the veranda of their dining hall, one kilometre away. The target had been Kibbutz Minara, just along the road, but no one was hurt.

Once, during the 1960s, Yiftah was attacked directly. Terrorists stole into the kibbutz at night and put a bomb in one of the houses. In the morning it exploded. The bomb was noisy but defective, and no one was injured; in fact, the man in whose house it was didn't even wake up, although everyone else in the kibbutz did. This became a Yiftah joke, the sort of battlefield story soldiers laugh at for comic relief.

On another occasion, Yossi and his colleagues informed the local population that a group of terrorists had crossed the border. A state of emergency was declared. The men on duty moved to their posts and everyone else entered the underground bomb shelters.

"In just a few minutes we were all transformed into soldiers," said Yoram from the back seat of the car. "Everyone has done basic training and army service and everyone has weapons in the house, so at very short notice a place like Yiftah can become an additional force for the army. We *are* the army."

"People here don't really feel danger too much," added Yossi. "They are just like people in Tel Aviv. They can't see anything."

"Can't see anything?"

"It's not like in Metulla, which is right flat on the border. They see the military cars all the time, and they see into the other side, right into Lebanon. The settlements on this road are only a kilometre or two from the border but people can't see it—it's over the hill. So they don't think about it. It's all psychological. They're like the people in Tel Aviv, they know what's happening in Lebanon from the newspaper and the television."

"Like I told you," interjected Yoram, "the quality of our daily life depends on how calm the officers in charge of border defence are."

Kibbutz Yiftah lost two of its members during the Lebanese War: the man in whose house I was living and a young man of twenty-one. The youth died just days before his tour of duty was to end. He and his group walked into a trap and all of them were killed.

Two deaths were a heavy burden for the kibbutz to bear. "It has left scars," said Yoram. "Especially because those who were left behind are always present. We see the widow and we see the parents. They are our family."

The burden was heavier because Yiftah had opposed the war. Opinion in Israel was divided along political lines; in general, Likud supporters defended the invasion of Lebanon and Labour supporters did not. Yiftah members (like the vast majority of the kibbutz movement) were solid Labour voters, or even further to the left in their views.

"From our point of view, invading neighbouring countries is a mistake, to put it mildly, " said Yoram, leaning forward from the back seat. "In the long run the whole thing was tragic, and the fact that two people died from such a small community makes it even more tragic."

"It's easy to talk so many years later, but now we can see that Lebanon really is a crazy country," interrupted Yossi. "Not just with us, but between themselves. They are not liars, but it's different there. You can write an agreement, they sign, everyone signs, then the next day it's like nothing happened. I can understand that they try to attack us—but not each other. If they can't make peace with each other, how can they make peace with us?"

"I don't think there will be peace." Yoram's voice was definite. "It will go on and Israel will be sort of sympathetic to the South Lebanese Army, which is on our side as far as keeping peace around this region is concerned. But South Lebanon is not all of Lebanon and I don't see things getting better."

Yoram leaned back. He had nothing more to say. Yossi stared grimly at the road ahead, and I gazed across the border—at the delicate beauty of olive trees shimmering in the quiet afternoon.

The road passed by Kibbutz Malkiah. Barbed wire and defence look-outs faced towards Lebanon. Behind, on the "safe side", fruit orchards spread over acres of ground.

Danger was a relative thing. When new soldiers came to the area on their tour of duty, the local kibbutzniks always told them that their children went places other people might consider dangerous. Not right to the border, but along the road we were travelling now, for example.

"Why do you allow that?" I asked, startled.

"Because *we* don't think it's dangerous," replied Yossi. "My mother lives in Haifa. Every time something happens in this part of the Galil, she telephones me. Now I call her first. Sometimes I can say I read it in the paper the same as she did."

I thought of a trip I had taken some years earlier to the volcanic islands of the Aeolian Sea. The fisherman who ferried us out had visited the mainland only once in his life. Although the volcanoes of his birthplace smoked and spurted constantly, and occasionally erupted causing destruction and death, he was not afraid. Danger? What danger? His family had lived there for centuries.

"What do you tell the children about where they live?" I asked Yoram.

"The truth."

"What is that?"

"We are near the border. Sometimes it can be...." He paused a long while, searching for the right words. "Sometimes there can be dangerous conditions. You have to know what to do."

The car climbed a steep hill. Over the border, a Lebanese village clung to the hillside about one kilometre into the self-proclaimed Israeli "security zone".

"See that house?" Yossi was pointing at a building very close to the border.

"The villagers used to live all together in the village on the hill over there. After the war in Lebanon, they started to build their houses closer to the border of Israel. For security. Even though the fence is electric and there are mines everywhere. It's so crazy in there that they are actually safer near us."

Before us stretched a fenced-in strip of no man's land known as the Good Fence, a corridor through which Lebanese who needed hospitalization in Israel, or had family there, could pass if they received security clearance. Israel had the best medical care in the Middle East and people were admitted to its hospitals from all over the Arab world.

A huge tank was backing up towards us, its engines roaring, its gigantic wheels spewing earth and dust. Young Israeli soldiers shouted orders. The security system protecting the Fence had broken down. It was being repaired as quickly as possible.

For the first time, I felt the military reality of this border: the menace of the tanks, with their protruding guns, and the dozens of armed, uniformed soldiers.

As we continued along the road, a patrol flagged us down.

"Where are you from?"

"Yiftah."

"I can tell by your faces," laughed the young soldier with casual jocularity. "Say hello to Itzak!"

"Itzak used to live on his kibbutz and now he lives at Yiftah," explained Yoram. "They were in basic training together."

It was a very small world.

Yossi stopped the car to point out a beautiful valley on the Lebanese side. He seemed excited.

"Almost forty years ago, cowherds from Yiftah and shepherds from the Lebanese village used to sit together here, by the stream. Our fields used to extend this far, to the olive trees there."

I peered into the valley. A few olive trees shook silvery leaves at the wind. Wildflowers grew in the field.

"Here is the cow-fence. See?" Yossi seemed inexplicably thrilled.

"Two years ago I took two of the old cowherds from Yiftah into Lebanon to meet their old friends," he said. "I could take them because of my officer's pass. We all met and they talked about the peaceful times they had together. Then they came to visit *us* through the Good Fence. I took many pictures. It was very happy for everyone.

"I have so many good friends in Lebanon," he continued. "One day I was visiting a friend. He had a broken wooden plough in his yard. I thought I would like it as decoration, to show my children the old ways of farming. So I asked him for it. He said no, so I said, 'You don't need it. Give it to me,' but he still refused.

"A week later he came with a new one and he said, 'You can't use the broken one. I've brought you a new one you can use.' "

Yossi's face shone. For him Lebanon was not alien territory, nor were "Arabs" his enemies. Although he was in charge of civil defence, of the symbolic "barbed wire" that protected the border population, for him Lebanon remained a warm and familiar place of memory. This dangerous, volatile border was, quite simply, home.

We were passing Moshav Avivim. Some two decades ago, terrorists attacked a schoolbus filled with children from this village. All were killed, just yards from their home and literally before their parents' eyes.

The most shocking part of the attack was that the killers did not even need to enter Israel. They hid behind a hill, a tree, and a few rocks on the Lebanese side of the road. From a mere few yards away, they lobbed their bombs into the bus.

The tree, the hill, and the rocks remained in place, of course. The children's parents also stayed, rooted to the very place of their tragedy. For twenty years the terrible landmarks had met their eyes as they travelled the only road to anywhere.

The barbed wire of Avivim extended sharp spines towards the road and the border, just yards away, but here the heroic ideology of strength and defence had failed. Israel may have had the best jet fighters in the sky, but this silent strike reached its target effortlessly.

Steps away along the roadside was a makeshift memorial erected by the parents of a nineteen-year-old soldier. In 1971, snipers shot at him from the Lebanese village on the hilltop where Yossi's friends lived. Like the tree and the rocks, the village on the hill remained unchanged and peaceful-looking.

We got out of the car to look. "May God avenge his blood," the inscription read.

A quotation from Isaiah. In the Christian land of my birth, nothing so graphic, so raw, so direct, would appear on a marker. There was nothing attenuated about this grief, this rage that called out for retribution.

We were quiet as we returned to the car. Nothing was merely as it seemed. The border road hid death and shadowed secrets. My little house at Yiftah hid death behind a careless veneer of shampoo bottles and children's drawings. The moshav on the hill hid death behind its flowering orchards. The very stones and trees that lined this road hid death. And the picturesque Lebanese village high on the hill beyond.

We drove towards the old British police station of Nebi Yusha where the Yiftah Brigade of the Palmach triumphed over the Arabs in April 1948, at the cost of twenty-eight Jewish lives. The Hebrew name for this place was Metsudat-Koah—"The Stronghold of the Twenty-Eight".

The twenty-eight men were buried alongside the fortress wall in a communal grave. An explanatory plaque in both Hebrew and English detailed their feat, and designated each man by name, military number, and age. Most were teenagers.

Yoram and Yossi stood stiffly, privately, visibly struggling to contain their emotion. For several moments none of us spoke.

"It's as though time has stopped on this hill," Yossi said softly. "They were so young. It was so long ago, but for me they always stay young." He singled out a name from the list. "This one had a song written about him. He has become part of Israeli folklore."

"Why him?"

"He was brave."

Children from all over Israel were brought here on pilgrimage. Bar mitzvah ceremonies were held here. The religious and the national had become one: the youngster was consecrated to God and the nation at one fell swoop.

"It's a surprise for the children," explained Yoram. "We bring them from Yiftah every year. We tell them we're going to a movie. Their parents come here to wait. Last year we told them we had a little problem and we had to stop at the station. When we arrived, they were given clean white shirts and candles. It was night and they all walked to this wall with lighted candles." Yoram paused thoughtfully. "We want them to remember."

Memory is crucial to the Jews. The memory of the destroyed Temple in Jerusalem kept hope alive over two thousand years of dispersal. The memory of the Holocaust in Europe is invoked in homage to millions who were murdered and in the hope of averting a similar catastrophe. At this border station, memories of blood and heroism were nurtured to keep alive images of the beginning of the state. But when a bar mitzvah ceremony took place at a martyrs' monument, when the destroyed Temple and the nation state merged, a potentially explosive mix of religion and politics began to brew.

Significantly, it was not the war in Lebanon that they remembered here. The two men from Yiftah who died there would not enter the ·realm of folklore. An alternative memorial was needed to mark that tragic period, one that bypassed the forms of conventional patriotism.

I watched Yoram and Yossi fight back their tears with sympathy, but a persistent, niggling thought insinuated itself all the same. How long could a drive for peace survive in a society whose emotional referent points were of battles and blood, I wondered. What price had been paid for forty years under siege?

At the kibbutz that evening, I visited a young couple with a small baby. Sara and Avi were in their early thirties and among the youngest married members at Yiftah. What with four years of military service followed by several years of post-secondary training and a travel or rest breather of a few months, most Israelis were close to thirty before they commenced their adult lives.

Sara and Avi's house was filled with the sweet, moist smells of fresh baking. Most people took their meals in the dining hall, but sweets were baked at home. Women prided themselves on cakes and pies made from the fruit of the kibbutz orchards.

In spite of Yoram's assurances that Israelis on the Lebanese border were calm, cool, and collected about geographical reality, Sara, for one, was openly frightened.

When I asked her how she felt, she laughed nervously and glanced at her husband.

"I am very afraid to be living at the border. Especially now that I have a child. Every minute I think about what will happen if the Arabs come in."

Her husband turned towards me. "I know you travelled today with Yossi to the border and he told me that you feel safe now."

News at Yiftah had wings. "I didn't feel unsafe before I went," I replied. "I don't live here."

"Yossi said you now realize everything is normal here," he persisted.

Sara cut in. "It's the boom at night," she said breathlessly.

Avi looked surprised at this admission blurted out so quickly to a stranger. "Sometimes there are explosions in the evening," he explained. "Usually it's the Israeli army doing manoeuvres, but you can never tell."

"Most of the women feel the way I do," Sara insisted. "The worst moment is when the alarm goes off."

"How often is that?"

"Once in six months, once in a year, once in three months—you never know," said Avi. "It's quiet now. During the Lebanon war it was more often, but I was in Lebanon then."

Avi had been subject to what he called "confusions" since his service in Lebanon. At night the young soldiers on the front lines had needed to talk. These were boys of eighteen, nineteen, and twenty who had not seen combat before—no one had seen *this* kind of combat before, said Avi—and they were deeply disturbed.

"We were fighting civilians! These children, ten, twelve, fourteen years old, they were out there firing rockets. What do you do if you see a child with a hand grenade? Maybe he's fourteen or fifteen, but he's still a child. He's climbing on your tank and he wants to throw it in. What do you do?

"There's no answer. The men put women and young children out into the streets and shoot from behind them. Or they shoot at you from the fifth floor of a building and then you see women in the window. Can you point a gun? Can you fire?

"We didn't ask our soldiers what they did. How could we?"

Avi had suffered a breakdown of sorts.

"Have you recovered?"

"Yeah," he said slowly. "I'm lucky to be alive."

Avi and Sara were not Zionist idealists. They were members of a new generation of Israelis who were choosing kibbutz life for reasons more closely related to economics than to anything else. When times are tough in Israel, the kibbutz is a good place to be. The kibbutz provides each and every one with a house and spending money. It feeds and clothes its members, looks after their children with quality daycare, and sends many people to university.

Conventional wisdom held that kibbutz life was wonderful for young children, their parents, and the elderly, because community living and daycare answered so many of their needs. It was a less happy arrangement for adolescents, who strained against its limits, and for the middle-aged, who were without money at a time when their children had grown and they were theoretically free. Middle-aged kibbutzniks suffered much ambivalence. If ever they were to leave this world and start again, this was their last chance.

Avi had followed several of his army buddies to Yiftah and stayed there. Sara was a Sephardic Jew from a nearby town who had been employed as paid, outside labour at the kibbutz apple-processing plant. Although they missed having money, other benefits kept them at Yiftah. Sara was getting an education at kibbutz expense—she was studying to be a kindergarten teacher (a skill she was expected to put to use in the kibbutz). In the meantime, their child was cared for in the children's house, their laundry was done for them, and their meals were prepared.

But none of this had anything to do with Zionist ideology; in fact, both Avi and Sara felt positively alienated from the workings of kibbutz democracy. Leadership did not tempt them. ("There's very much responsibility," said Avi.) Their principal worry about leadership was the criticism, that invisible stick that kept kibbutzniks in line. "Kibbutz members are very critical," Avi said. "And once you're in duty, all eyes are on you."

Indeed, they were so removed from the governing structures of their society that it had not occurred to either of them to seek help for an annoying problem they faced. They could not go out together in the evening because there were no babysitters. On the kibbutz, you were not allowed to exchange money for services, so teenagers were not interested in the job. Sara's mother sometimes came from Haifa for important occasions, but that was rare.

The original idea of the children's house had been to liberate adults from these practical concerns, but with Yiftah children now sleeping at home in their parents' houses, "family" had once again become a constraint. Tellingly, neither Avi nor Sara nor any of the other young couples at Yiftah had considered asking the kibbutz leadership to find a solution to their dilemma.

"I know they don't care," said Sara with utter certitude. And that was that.

CHAPTER SEVEN

The Last Day

Every morning, about 125 Yiftah children left for the co-operative elementary and high school in the valley below. Yoram's wife, Eliza, and I drove down the winding road to Kefar Blum to visit the school. Eliza was the elementary school librarian. Coming to Yiftah had not been her idea at all, and she hinted that she had never quite adjusted. "If people are just sitting around talking about nothing in particular, it's very hard to fit in," she confided. The "in group" was born to the kibbutz, or arrived early in their lives. Coming late was like being an immigrant.

Several buildings were spread about the landscaped school grounds. Sculpture and pottery made by the children decorated the outside walls.

In the staff room, the teachers drank coffee and prepared for the day. Most were women in their thirties and forties. They wore slacks, flat shoes, and bulky sweaters to ward off the morning cold, and their scrubbed, lined faces reflected weather and experience. The atmosphere in the staff room was informal and *simple* in the way the French use that word, to mean utterly without pretension or device.

There was no reason to believe these women were feminists in any North American or European sense of the word, but they looked the way women were meant to look. They were profoundly attractive, down-to-the-core natural.

The school was entirely up to date. In one room, children learned programming and computer language on seven IBM PCs which had been paid for by the kibbutzim themselves, not by the national Ministry of Education. In language classes, they were being blitzed in English. English was taught widely throughout Israel—more so than Arabic—and the implications of this policy for future relations with edgy neighbours could only be guessed at.

The kibbutz school also provided adult education. The previous night, I learned, there had been a lecture on the role of women on the kibbutz. "There was practically blood on the floor," laughed my guide, a former American called Milty who had lived on Kibbutz Kefar Blum for several decades.

"Women came as idealists, just like the men, but the theory of equality turned out differently for them," he said.

"Is this a serious issue today?"

"Very serious." His grey-flecked, pointed beard complemented mischievous grey eyes that brimmed with humour.

True to kibbutz principles, the curriculum emphasized nature study, and every few weeks, each class went on a specialized trip to a different location. The curriculum also stressed music, drama, and art (by sixth grade children were doing four hours a week in art alone). It was easy to see how kibbutzniks had developed into a cultural elite.

The key to the method was observation and experimentation. Each year nature study began with the vulture, for in the autumn thousands of the dark predators migrate through the skies overhead. Mobiles of vultures hung from the classroom ceiling. In this class of seven-year-olds, the children were encouraged to create whatever it was they were discussing. They did not just read, talk, or draw; they sang songs about the subject, acted it out, and drew murals depicting the story. In one corner of the room, an exhibit built by the children demonstrated the centrality of the tree, of agriculture, of planting. This was kibbutz and Israeli pioneer ideology at its purest.

There were also bomb shelters everywhere.

"What do you tell these children about where they live?" I asked the teacher.

"We discuss it," she said. "Some of the children are very frightened, so I reassure them. I say, 'You are in your country and the army is protecting you. You don't have to worry.'

"We also have regular drills. I explain very carefully that this is just a practice, but some of the children cry anyway. So I tell them that when they know exactly what they have to do in an emergency, they make the soldiers happy. I say, 'You are helping defend your country by knowing what to do.' "

Milty's face grew serious as he listened. "During the Six Day War I spent the entire six days in one of these shelters with a group of children. It was very strange. The kids who usually talked all the time withdrew into complete silence. Others who never talked babbled the whole time through. Some of them had wheezing asthma attacks. It was frightening."

Every week, one hour of classroom time was devoted to a discussion of news. This week, the "news corner" featured a newspaper picture of the mother of a dead soldier. "Don't exchange Palestinian terrorists on the back of my dead child," she pleaded in the caption.

Every day, these little children looked at this picture. From the very beginning of their lives, they were forced to confront the reality of politics, of life and death.

A drama class was acting out aggression—an effective way to cope with the tension of living on this border, I thought, as well as an antidote to the repression brought about by fear of group criticism.

But most important, the kibbutz school kept an eye on the vagaries of Israeli politics. When Menachem Begin and the

Likud party came to power in 1977, the principal built a scaled-down replica of an original kibbutz on the roof of one of the bomb shelters. There was a watchtower, a pigeon coop, a garden area, and a central eating and meeting place where the "cultural committee" met for planning and "discussions". Now that an ideology of territorial expansion and religious orthodoxy was gaining strength in the country, it seemed necessary to show kibbutz children what their origins looked like—and to couple this with a renewed discussion of the ethical values that underpinned the kibbutz movement.

Later in the day, I saw the same policy at work at the kibbutz high school. A newspaper clipping of a crying woman had been tacked up in a prominent spot outside the library. The story explained that her child had become one of the newly religious. The ultra-Orthodox were an emerging power group that threatened the secular values of kibbutz life, and a small minority of the kibbutz children were "returning to the faith".

It was clearly a case of "us" and "them", and the kibbutz educators were mounting a campaign to shore up their values, which they saw as the foundation of the state and of Israeli society. They were, however, under serious attack—in fact, the very idea of the kibbutz was in trouble. A generation or two ago, wide-eyed utopians had escaped the narrow strictures of anti-Semitic Russia and Poland to claim the "empty land" and revolutionize Jewish life. Later, thousands of Holocaust survivors arrived on the kibbutzim to help build the country. "To build" became the key verb of an entire society. A state came into being.

But their children were neither pioneers, visionaries, nor Holocaust survivors. They were, quite simply, Israelis. The land of their birth was not a dream to be swooned over, but a birthright. And the modern kibbutz was certainly not a revolutionary enterprise. Like most institutionalized revolutions, the kibbutz had grown deeply conservative. Young people had trouble finding a niche for themselves in the ranks of a leadership that did not want to hand over the reins. There was no interesting work for women if their ambition stretched beyond teaching, child care, or kitchen and laundry duties.

It was the classic dilemma of the "second day of the revolution", as Yoram put it astutely. Were kibbutz children really to "continue the revolution", they would need to break with their parents, leave the kibbutz *en masse*, and do something completely new. To stay on the kibbutz was to live in a house someone else had built. This painful irony did not escape attention and many of the brightest children—those who had learned the revolutionary lesson best—were the ones to leave.

The other crisis was money. Years ago everyone was poor, said Gad, a man of fifty-eight who had lived at Yiftah for thirty years. But Israeli society had changed, and now people outside had a lot more money. When they came to visit their families on the kibbutz, they left little gifts. This meant that some people had more than others. They could furnish their houses better and go on longer trips. Envy was corroding the egalitarian society. In Utopia, some were more equal than others.

Gad was especially incensed about people who moved to the kibbutz to improve their personal economic situation. Before making the move, they could put all their personal assets into savings.

"When they come to the kibbutz, they get an apartment—free, of course—but they also keep their own money, which they can use outside, or after they leave. So they are actually getting rich here while I am poorer and poorer because I am paying for their apartment, their food, and their education. I have no assets, nothing but the kibbutz. And of course it takes quite a while before they know the work and can begin to produce income."

The problem was so new and so potentially divisive that the kibbutz leadership had not begun to deal with it, he said. No one really knew what to do.

Gad was also angry that several years earlier Yiftah (along with other kibbutzim) had invested in high-risk stocks and lost millions of dollars. That was his money, he said, the fruit of a lifetime. Yiftah had been wealthy. Now it was in trouble. They couldn't even afford a new dining hall.

"Because we all have to live together, no one said anything," he told me bitterly. "To this day, no one has really said anything. In any other situation, people would be accountable. Here they are not." He smiled a scornful smile.

Tamar and Yeshayahu had watched the kibbutz evolve over the decades, but they had not succumbed to bitterness. They—and Yoram—were realistic about the changes brought about by the passage of time.

"The kibbutz is changing and will keep changing," said Yeshayahu. "The real miracle is that it still goes on. I can't be sure when it will finish, but I do think it is a need for some people. Even without ideology, without building a society and without changing the world, this kind of co-operative life is good for some people. Not all, but some."

Tamar agreed. "I think the kibbutz will become more nuclear-family oriented, much more private and more individualistic. And that's fine. People will not live as we did. It will be easier and more comfortable. There is always the difficult line between communal and private life, but I honestly think the second generation has been very influenced by us and our values. Maybe I would like things to go on as they were, but I know change will happen and I want it. Life is better than when I was a child."

Yoram too accepted the prospect of change. "What I hear from the youngsters is that they are dissatisfied with the fact that this is the second day of the revolution. So maybe this means that their values are the same as their parents'. The deep thing is that they also want to create something. They are not satisfied with what was created for them."

Statistically, fewer than half the kibbutz children now chose to share their parents' and grandparents' dream.

Gad was eating alone in the dining hall, at the volunteers' table, deliberately excluding himself from the community. I joined him for coffee.

Yoram pulled up a chair. "Well, Erna, do you think you could live on a kibbutz after what you've seen?" He smiled broadly.

"I'm too old," I said with a laugh. "I've lived independently for too long. You have to get your people young."

He nodded. "Well, what about Israel? Could you live in Israel?"

The Question again. "I'm fascinated by Israel," I said, "but so far it would not occur to me to move here."

Yoram's face darkened with disappointment. "Why not? You're a Jew!"

"I'm a Canadian, a northerner. I was raised in an Anglo-Saxon culture. That's where I'm at home."

I heard myself making a speech. I felt deeply uneasy.

"So you should stay in Canada and foreigners should do the work in Israel? Is that what you want for Israel?"

He was angry. I remembered that when we walked around the kibbutz together, he had said that the battle over outside workers was an anachronistic dispute from the past, a tedious hangover from a rigid, ideological heritage. But he too was caught in the push-pull of kibbutz contradictions, unable to reconcile idea and practice. What he was really saying was a generic "How dare you!"

"I thought I could get some answers from you," he charged.

"You've had answers," I replied, trying to keep my voice down. "You just don't like what you heard."

After a few days as a kibbutznik I was no longer a guest with whom one must be careful and polite. For Yoram, a classic Zionist, all Jews must return "home" to Israel. I was simply refusing to follow my true life's course. I was betraying him and the others.

The old ideas of the kibbutz clashed with reality. An intellectually elite society spurned "professors"; a would-be egalitarian world had relegated women to child care, laundry, and the kitchen; barbed wire symbolized "purpose" and freedom *from* barbed wire; people defended nineteenth-century notions of independent labour while they lived in a high-tech world; no one was obliged to work with children any longer than they would pick apples, although the kibbutz was now as child-oriented as any other sector of Israeli society—and probably more so.

Predictable changes had taken place, but nostalgia, ambivalence, and regret lived on. It was so human. They had dreamed of a "perfect" society, but things hadn't worked out quite that way. What could be harder, I wondered, than to redesign a dream?

I left Yiftah in the early morning light. Everyone waved goodbye. A baby cart containing six or seven plump, tanned toddlers was wheeled by. Gad's wife, Hanna, gave me a Yiftah postcard as a souvenir.

I pointed my car down the mountainside, opposite the snow-capped peak of Mount Hermon at the northern boundary of the country. A bomber shot across the tranquil sky.

An appropriate last image, for what did remain intact from the original Zionist ideology was an unquestioned commitment to border defence. "We are all in the army, all the time," Yoram had stated flatly and accurately. Hanna had put it even more succinctly. "We must be strong to stay alive," she said. "There is no other way to live here."

CHAPTER EIGHT

Kefar Haruv

A steep road twisted up the Golan Heights from the Sea of Galilee below. Rocky outcroppings jutted from cliffs and ancient-looking stones sat, implacable, in wilderness pastures.

Spring wildflowers carpeted the rolling hills in purple, yellow, and green. Soon they would die, and the unrelenting summer sun would suck the clay earth dry as bone-dust.

Large white egrets perched on low branches. This region was part of an ancient migration path between Africa in the south and Europe and Asia to the north, and rare birds were a common sight. Hoopoes were as numerous as crows and eagles. Pelicans and storks had flown these skies for thousands of years, using the only body of fresh water around, the Sea of Galilee, as their referent point. The region had also been a transitional customs point for caravans from the Orient carrying spices and other wonders of the Orient to the marvelling peoples of Europe. The Greeks, the Romans, and the Turks of Byzantine splendour had in turn settled these same strategic heights.

The juncture of continents was marked, as well, by an ancient geographical upheaval. The great Afro-Asian rift had slashed through the Jordan Valley below, creating the startlingly beautiful mountains and valleys of Israel.

At the top of the Golan plateau there was only mountain wilderness. The road forked. Unsure, I turned to the right. With my very approximate sense of direction, I might have been heading straight towards Damascus.

I was looking for Kefar Haruv, a new kibbutz that had been established in 1973, at the time of the Yom Kippur War. Unlike Yiftah, it was populated exclusively by young people: average age twenty-eight, I'd been told. These desolate, wind-blown heights had been their home of first choice. Some of the older members were former Americans: *sixties* people. They had leaped from their anti-Vietnam protestations and back-to-the-earth communes to a pioneer settlement in the newly occupied territories of the Golan.

There it was, at the end of a dirt road. Alan was waiting in a makeshift parking lot, a tanned, lean man with a friendly face. At thirty-seven, he was the oldest member of the kibbutz, and it was his job to integrate newcomers and welcome guests.

I stepped out of the car and felt the driving force of the Golan winds.

"They're constant," Alan said with a laugh. "Always from the east, too."

Alan lived in a little row house with his wife and three children. In the last decade no fewer than eighty children had been born at Kefar Haruv. A hundred adult members lived here as well, and fifty others who were doing their army service or deciding whether they wanted to stay.

Before I met any of them, Alan (like Yoram) wanted to show and explain.

I bent my head against the wind as we walked to the edge of the kibbutz, to a cliff ridge that overlooked the Jordan Valley. Maybe they got used to being blown about like this? Alan seemed oblivious.

But the view below and beyond was breathtaking. To the north, the city of Safad perched on the summit of Mount Meiron, the highest point in the country before 1967.

I knew Safad to be a remarkable place. In the twelfth century the Crusaders defended themselves from its heights. They were followed by the Moslems, who turned the town into the capital of northern Palestine. By the sixteenth century, mystical cabbalistic Jews had made Safad their centre of learning, and at least one rabbi of the day announced that from Safad enlightenment would spread throughout the entire Jewish world.

For a hundred years, from a massive Druse attack in 1833 until the War of Liberation, Jewish Safad suffered through hard times. Although a small population of elderly, pious Jews remained, the Arabs held the strategic positions in the town and controlled its only entrance. When the city was recaptured by the Jews in 1948, those inclined to such thoughts called it a miracle.

To the south-west, the rounded hump of Mount Tabor dominated the landscape: Tabor, where the ancient Israelites had repelled a Canaanite invasion of the surrounding Jezreel Valley; Tabor, where—according to the book of Matthew—Jesus was transfigured before his disciples; Tabor, where in A.D. 66 the Jews of Galilee fortified themselves in a (futile) revolt against the Romans.

Alan spoke with awe of the centuries of history hidden in the mute record of ancient dust.

Snug against the far shore of the Sea of Galilee (also known as Lake Tiberias, or Lake Kinneret) lay the city of Tiberias. And directly below us sat Kibbutz Ein Gev, which was founded in 1937 on the disputed border of Palestine and Syria.

Syrian troops had shelled and shot at Ein Gev from the very ridge where Alan and I stood. The kibbutzniks of Kefar Haruv discovered the Syrian bunker one day when they were digging five or six feet under the ground; they literally fell into a room with three bunk beds, a jacket, a lantern, Syrian money, and ammunition. I climbed down into its hollowed-out roundness and peered through the old gun sightings. There was Ein Gev, lined up perfectly.

The years of living with fear took their toll. After the Israeli occupation of the Golan Heights in 1967, the members of Ein Gev began to breathe more freely and to prune away some of the dense brush they had planted to protect themselves. But one man could not bear to see his "protection" destroyed. He clutched at the trees and screamed hysterically until they were forced to carry him away.

Several metres farther along the cliff edge, the Kefar Haruv settlers had discovered an ancient Roman plantation. Three natural springs fed the soil then and continued to do so now. The Romans had planted almond, fig, and olive trees, grapes, pomegranates, and cactus pear, and new generations of these plants still grew there. Ruins of Roman columns lay by the water source.

Kefar Haruv looked very prosperous to me. The members were in the process of building a new million-dollar dining hall, with an outright grant of $200,000 from the government and the rest in loans from the government and the kibbutz movement. Their laundry operation ran on computerized cards that told the machines what detergent to use. A small tailoring industry in children's clothing had been established.

The kibbutz grew cotton, avocados, almonds, wheat, and tomatoes, but its serious income derived from industry. Here on these windy Golan Heights, they produced plastic water accessory pieces, which they hoped to market all over the world. In co-operation with other kibbutzim, they ran a highly commercial hot spring in the valley below, on a spot that had been a health spa since Roman times. The complex contained ruins of one of the most beautiful Roman baths I had seen anywhere.

The springs were doing well. In 1986 approximately half a million Israelis had enjoyed the mineral waters, and projected income for 1987 was $3 million.

But the pride of Kefar Haruv was a large dairy herd. There were twice as many cows on the kibbutz as there were people, and they produced 2,500 gallons of milk per day at a value of $1.2 million a year.

All Kefar Haruv industry and building installations were largely subsidized, for the kibbutz movement and the government of Israel supervised almost every aspect of life on the kibbutzim. In the early days of Kefar Haruv, this paternalism had caused trouble. The young Americans who founded Kefar Haruv in the early 1970s considered themselves pioneers in the way the original Russian kibbutzniks had been pioneers. They did not like to think of themselves as inheritors of a tradition that had been subsumed by a bureaucracy that told people what to do, what to produce, and what sort of housing to live in.

The tension at Kefar Haruv between the Americans and the kibbutz bureaucracy, and the Americans and their fellow Israeli communards, had not entirely dissipated over fifteen years. English-speakers were under pressure to talk only in Hebrew, and all schooling and group activity took place in that language. At Kefar Haruv, Hebrew was the more fragile language and culture. The Israelis feared being swamped by the American juggernaut—a familiar enough notion to a Canadian, I thought.

Sometimes fine principles just can't compete. That evening, I watched a folk-dancing class in the dining hall. The dancers were all in their early twenties or younger and they laughed with the sharp, brittle sounds of sexual nervousness.

"A lot of Israeli girls move here to meet Americans," a woman explained with utter candour. "They're looking for marriage with a green card so they can move to the United States."

On the other hand, Alan had immigrated here because he was looking for something "pure", he said, something authentic—and that had excluded the established kibbutzim that had a television in every living room. He and his American friends had lived in a commune in Stanford, and they were looking for a kibbutz alternative. This was not because they were Zionists or had an overweening commitment to Israel; it was more because they were children of the sixties and Israel promised possibilities of truly new beginnings. Being Jewish and coming from families that had probably supported the United Jewish Appeal or the Jewish Agency, if only in the most perfunctory way, made the idea of starting a kibbutz in Israel feel more comfortable. They were young, romantic hippies and flower children who wanted to found an ideal commune, people who thought they could escape the rat race of American materialism in the most radical way of all. They were also imbued with the spirit of the American frontier, and when you came right down to it, there wasn't one square inch of land in the United States that could pretend to equal the challenge of the Golan Heights, where they would actually be *required* to tote guns on the wind-swept hills. It was Israel as viewed from California: John Wayne and Abbie Hoffman rolled into one irresistible fantasy.

"I was basically naive," acknowledged Alan, "and I don't think I understood anything of the politics of the Golan, or the Occupation, or anything of what was happening in Israel. When I look back, our idea was basically to start a new place with our own ideals and with a group of people who had no preconceptions about what they were going to do, except that they were motivated by their beliefs. When we first came here, we found one guy ahead of us. He invited us into his tent and, you know, just the thought of someone actually living here.... Well, he had to cut down some olive trees to have a fire. He gave us a couple of cigarettes, American cigarettes, and a little bit of coffee. And then he just told us to go and look at the cliff. It was solid wildflowers and open fields. And there was this tremendous view. It really made an impression, there's no doubt about it.

"We were all products of our time, we were the generation that wanted to escape and get away from established things and go back to the land. The Golan was as basic as you could get. It was pure, I mean completely undeveloped. Maybe it sounds like a cliché today, but when you lived it, when you were a part of communes and alternative lifestyles, the ideas were all fresh."

We were drinking coffee in Alan's house with Sid and Sandy, his wife. They were both from Boston and had both studied sociology—leftist sociology, sixties style. They had come to Israel independently, lived on different kibbutzim, and met on a kibbutz-sponsored horticultural course. Sandy had already learned to her chagrin that American feminist ideas of women's equality meant little in kibbutz society, and that women with children were pressured to devote themselves to communal child care on a continuing basis, whatever their personal interests. After intense effort, she had been fairly successful in helping to turn horticulture into a "female" job on her own kibbutz.

They both listened intently as Alan described their generation.

"The Israelis make jokes that *we* are the Americans who took the sixties seriously, at least the going back to the land and everything else that was talked about then," said Alan. "All the others became—"

"Sell-outs," interjected Sandy. "Like Jerry Rubin."

"Sell-outs, yeah," parroted Sid. "You should meet Roy," he suggested. "He's the guy who got many of us interested while we were still in the States. He was really inspired and he was only seventeen. He's a really strong personality. Can be violent, too. Punched someone not too long ago."

I wanted to meet Roy, but I also wanted to meet the man he had punched. On a kibbutz populated by former American flower children, what sort of person punches and what sort of person gets punched?

Mike, the latter, would say only that he "detested" Roy. Mike was from Toronto, my home city. He was passive. Nothing had worked for him in Canada: not school, not work, not family life, not friendship. He had been in danger of losing his grip on whatever rudiments one needs to get a handle on life in North America. So he had moved to Israel—to a kibbutz, the one society where, in return for labour, other people will grow your food and cook it, clean your clothes, care for your children, and generally look after your needs. In this way the kibbutzim perform an important social function: they care for that minority of people who have trouble in a capitalist society where everyone is on his or her own.

I made arrangements to meet Roy the following day and returned to the little house they had prepared for me. It was furnished with great care (and not inexpensively) by its owner, a young Dutch woman with a small son. Pictures of this beloved child adorned the walls.

On her bookshelves was further evidence of a time warp on the Golan Heights. Jack Kerouac's *On the Road* rubbed jackets with *Siddhartha* and *Steppenwolf*, both by Hermann Hesse.

I fell asleep listening to the wind and thinking about Gulliver's magic travels into worlds of blunted time.

In 1968, Roy was fifteen years old and already involved in "the struggle": the California farm workers' struggle led by Cesar Chavez. Roy's middle-class family lived in Culver City, California, where his mother was a housewife and his father an aeronautical engineer. Airplanes occupied the imagination of the entire family. His mother and father both flew small planes, and Roy learned to fly before he learned to drive.

The impulse to fly had never left him. On the Golan, he hang-glided over cliffs whenever he had a free moment, floated like an eagle over the Sea of Galilee. The very urge to move from California to the Golan, and to carry others along through the sheer force of his personality, was not unrelated to flying, I thought.

Roy was thirty-four, lithe and energetic-looking, and he ex-uded a tightly coiled sexual energy. He lolled uncomfortably on the grass outside his house, looking apprehensive about this tape-recorded encounter.

An infant wail sounded from inside. Eight days before, Roy's wife had given birth to their third child, a daughter. "That's the most awesome experience a person can go through," he said, relaxing a little. "I've always liked the idea of building new things."

It had all started with the farm workers. Somebody in Roy's group of young volunteers made the connection between New Left ideology, farming, and the kibbutzim of Israel. Weren't they left-wing over there? Right on! Didn't they live collectively, do without profit and material motivation in their lives? Didn't they defend themselves against their enemies, as did Cesar Chavez and the farm workers, the Yippies, the Students for a Democratic Society, the Panthers, and all the other groups spawned by the Age of Aquarius?

Somebody asked Roy to find a kibbutz representative to speak to them. He did: an Israeli who worked in Los Angeles promoting one of the kibbutz movements, a spirited, adventurous, macho kind of guy who appealed to the excited teenager who was looking for a place to fly solo.

"He said, 'Listen, if you really want to know about kibbutzim and are interested in the workers' struggle, go to Israel.' This made perfect sense to me. My grandfather had come from Russia. He was a socialist and in the 1920s he had thought of moving his family to Palestine. Then the Depression came and they never did go."

So that summer—he was then sixteen—Roy spent two months in Israel, on Kibbutz Hulda. He lived with Israeli kids his own age and was "adopted" by a kibbutz family he admired intensely.

What impressed him most were the old people. They seemed different from old people in California.

"They had a sort of fire in them," Roy recalled. "They had a way of talking to each other and sharing things. You could see that they had undergone a lot together. These were people who had come out of Russia, some before the First World War. Just the way they would bring food to each other...."

He stopped to remember. "They were eighty-five, ninety years old and they were out there at 4:00 a.m. picking apples and pears. They had gone to war together, buried their children together, seen their children marry each other. And they seemed so much more alive than the old people I had seen in Los Angeles, who were kind of sitting around waiting to die. At least that's the way it looked to me when I was sixteen. I thought that it would be a good thing to be able to experience a challenge like this and look back and say my whole life didn't revolve around how I was going to pay the next mortgage payments or compete with my neighbour about getting the next model of Plymouth.

"It wasn't really the Jewish thing, just that the pieces sort of fit together, you know: Israel, the land, the kibbutz, the Jewishness. It was a very organic kind of thing."

Roy went back to Kibbutz Hulda the next year, and it was then that he began to think about "building something new", a kibbutz on the Golan. This was 1971 and the Golan Heights had been under Israeli occupation for only four years. The area was undeveloped, rugged, potentially dangerous. Deeply appealing, in other words.

So he went home and began to research the possibility of putting together a group of young people to immigrate to Israel. He wrote a letter which was widely circulated and which reflected the impulses that moved him: idealism, adventure, individualism, danger, the creation of something absolutely new.

Although all this "building" was to take place in a besieged country halfway around the earth, the prospect seemed somehow familiar. Roy's values were, of course, archetypal American frontier values; in fact, the entire back-to-the-earth movement was, at bottom, an updated version of the frontier ethos. The sixties could only have originated in the United States, where a revulsion against "amoral" technology and an apparently senseless war was translated into a nostalgia for authenticity, for direct human relationships, for physical challenge, and for pioneering virgin land with only horoscope, native wit, and almanac at hand.

Furthermore, the kibbutz project was "Jewish"; for youngsters in their teens and early twenties it was psychologically easier to plan an adventure in a place that was presumably acceptable to their parents. A proposed commune in Algeria might not have met with the same success.

Roy's letter was a remarkable document for one so young; and it was infused with a passion for goodness:

> We are committed to actively engaging ourselves with the social problems and conflicts in Israel. Each member of our Kibbutz will spend a certain amount of time outside the Kibbutz working in one or more facets of social work and development.... We will work to establish a mutually helpful social, cultural, and economic interaction between ourselves and the neighboring Druse Tribesmen and Arabs. In dealing with our neighbors, we do not expect them to assimilate and adopt our ways, and we do not plan to adopt theirs. We are striving for a relationship that will create dignity, respect, and friendship.

The group would "take a firm stand" on conservation. Roy hoped they would reforest the Golan with the black oaks that had been wiped out by the Turks a century earlier. He also wished to encourage "professionals and artists", who would engage in "advanced studies".

Just who would shovel out the barn or plant or harvest was not entirely clear, since it looked as though everyone would be busy with finer things.

Eventually the kibbutz bureaucracy had to take Roy and his group seriously. Without help, they had put together the largest North American *garin*, or youth group, since the creation of the State of Israel. And they were bringing sixty people who could and would serve in the Israeli army.

Roy arrived in Israel in June 1973. Four months later he collided with reality.

When the Yom Kippur War exploded in October the group was evacuated from the Golan plateau, where Kefar Haruv was being built, to an older kibbutz in the Jordan Valley. One day Syrian soldiers arrived within a mile of where Roy crouched, hidden in a bomb shelter.

His voice dropped in the telling. Before 1973, the mood of Jews inside and outside Israel had been cocky and self-assured. The Arabs were scared, people said. They'd never try anything again.

But then there was war again, and the fields were suddenly filled with bodies. Hundreds and hundreds of dead soldiers—Israelis and Syrians—and burnt-out tanks.

"It was like a horror movie," Roy recalled in a soft, distant voice. The image, as he remembered it, was entirely appropriate for a youngster just arrived from Movieland.

There were further shocks ahead. This was the period of the Ma'alot massacre of children, the terrorist assault on the town of Kiryat Shemona on the Lebanese border, the beginnings of the Lebanon crisis that would climax almost a decade later, in 1982.

He did his basic army training in 1974.

"Were you opposed to fighting in Vietnam, but in favour of fighting here?" I asked.

"Well, yeah," he replied. "It was a question of survival. You felt that these people were planning our demise, that they would take us and our friends and families and destroy us.... That was not the case with the war in Vietnam. It was very hard to cling to a pacifist ideology...."

I thought of the widow at Yiftah; of the psychology of "seeing" or "not seeing" the source of potential danger only yards away over the border ridge; of my own uneasiness on that Lebanese boundary. I appreciated what Roy was saying. To arrive in Israel in 1973 was somewhat less abstract than demonstrating against the Vietnam war at Berkeley, or exhorting Mexican farm workers to defend their rights. Especially if you were still a teenager.

Roy's romantic ideology of frontier individualism expanded easily to accommodate defensive war, just as Zionism had easily embraced the Haganah and the Palmach a quarter of a century earlier. But the fact that he and his friends were sinking roots into occupied territory did not seem to be an issue to him. The Golan was not the West Bank or Gaza; there were villages of Druse Arabs, but the Golan was not heavily and visibly populated with Palestinians.

By the spring of 1974 the commune of Kefar Haruv had sprung into being, and a developing conflict with the native Israelis who made up 60 per cent of the kibbutz's population had to be addressed. Unlike Roy and the other Americans, the Israelis were not rebel adventurers. Hilla, for instance, the first secretary-general of the kibbutz, was "continuing a family tradition," she said. Her *parents* had been the adventurers. The Israelis on Kefar Haruv were "second day of the revolution" people, like the younger generations at Yiftah. But Roy saw himself as a first-generation pioneer. He felt inwardly superior to these more passive Israelis, as he saw them. He identified with the original "crazy people", the Russians who had defied their Old Country parents and settled the wilderness of Palestine.

Wild West cowboys did not follow "family traditions". Did the Lone Ranger have a mother?

In 1985, Roy went home to the United States for a visit and the local rabbi in Culver City asked him to address a group of teenagers about life in Israel. So he tried to tell them about what the kibbutzniks of Kefar Haruv had achieved on the Golan Heights, in a desolate, rock-pitted, moonlike landscape. How they had turned it into a place where they were now raising children and growing crops and producing cattle. How they had sweated their guts out, but were now prospering. He tried to tell them about the caravan routes that had criss-crossed the Golan between Mesopotamia and the Mediterranean Sea, and how it was possible that the Golan had been occupied by more armies than any other piece of land on the earth's surface. He wanted to tell them of the political struggle now going on, and how at Kefar Haruv they saw themselves as the focal point of the major political powers of the world. "The whole thing is centred on a bunch of settlers here," he told them.

"It was going great, then one girl raised her hand and said, 'Aren't you worried that you're not going to be a success?' You know, join a corporation, get a title for yourself. The Reagan generation. Then another said, 'Yeah, I know about all that. My father protested at Berkeley.'

"It really set me back. They weren't like kids any more. Something had been eroded from them. It made me feel that I had really travelled the distance, a psychological as well as a physical distance, and that I really could never go 'home' again."

America had changed, but Roy and his friends at Kefar Haruv had not. They were still more American than Israeli and probably always would be. At bottom, they were still sixties people and not Zionists.

Most sixties people who stayed in America adapted sooner or later. They got jobs, acquired Visa cards, and had children who grew up to be as square as boxes. It was the price of living through change, at home. But things were different on the Golan, there you could be a hippie American and a pioneer Israeli at the same time.

The Big Chill had come to America, but safe in his cocoon on the Golan Heights, Roy would stay warm for ever.

I returned my car to the Hertz office in Tiberias, but then I was unable to find the bus station, so I asked a woman in a small, open-air shop to direct me. She shook her head to indicate that she did not understand me, and made a clicking noise with her tongue.

A young man with dark hair and a growth of new moustache offered to help. The bus station was just a block or so away, he said. He would walk me there.

"Where you from?" he asked, making polite conversation in halting English.

"Canada."

"Oh!" He brightened. "I just came back yesterday from the United States. New York City, New Jersey."

"Did you like it there?"

"Very, very much. I would like to live there. I don't like to stay here in Israel. Too many wars and too many Arabs. There is no future. But I have to have a reason to leave."

"What sort of reason?" I asked.

"Marriage is the best," he replied earnestly. "The best way to get a green card is to have a wife or a girlfriend."

"Is that what you went there for?" I asked, incredulous.

"Yes. But I didn't find. I have to love. If I do not love, I will not go."

"Yes, yes, of course." We walked in silence for a moment.

"Tell me," he said, turning in my direction. "Are you married?"

"Ah, yes, I am."

I heard an apology in my voice. After all, he *had* helped me find the bus station. The least I could do, it seemed, was marry him and take him to Canada.

He looked terribly disappointed.

We reached the bus station. "Well, goodbye," I said, "and good luck!"

He smiled a sad little smile, then fixed me with a meaningful glance. Perhaps I was meant to ruminate on my loss.

I boarded the bus for Jerusalem and we waved to each other through the window.

For some Americans, the Promised Land was in Israel. For some Israelis, the Promised Land was in America.

CHAPTER NINE

The Yeshiva

If the kibbutz movement was locked in a life-and-death struggle to defend its ideology and its position of social and political supremacy in the country, it had a formidable opponent: the increasingly muscular power bloc of the ultra-Orthodox. Until recently, the *Haredim* ("those who are God-fearing") had been content to live apart from society, without trying to dominate; but new political power was making them more confident than they had ever been, and they were presenting themselves as an authentic alternative to the "evils" of modern Israel.

The Haredim—largely Hasidic Jews—were not especially interested in Zionism or the State of Israel. As far as they were concerned, true Jewish life was the same today as it had been a thousand years ago: the Torah and only the Torah had kept Judaism alive in the past, and would continue to do so in the future. Like their ancestors, they spent their days praying devoutly for the arrival of the Messiah. *Then* they might think about celebrating a Jewish state—but one run according to Torah law.

There were three main streams among the myriad groups of Orthodox Jews in Israel: the Neturei Karta and other Haredim who were indifferent to or militantly opposed to Zionism; the ultra-Orthodox, religious Zionists who had settled the West Bank because they believed the creation of the state was in itself a religious event, and because God had told them the entire "Land of Israel" belonged to the Jews; and the liberal Orthodox, who lived pragmatic day-to-day lives in society, like the majority of the population.

The ultra-Orthodox, non-Zionist Haredim represented a tiny 5 per cent of the population, but their two political parties controlled the balance of power between the mainstream Labour and Likud blocs. In 1987 the Shas party held four Knesset seats and Agudat Israel held two. The other component of the parliamentary religious bloc, the National Religious party (representing an additional 10 per cent of Orthodox *Zionists*), had dropped from twelve seats in 1977 to four, and was expected to lose more ground in the next election. So among the combined 15 per cent of Orthodox Jews living in Israel, the ultras were calling the political shots.

The peculiar "Who is a Jew?" controversy was only the most dramatic of Orthodox demands: it threatened to delegitimize Reform and Conservative rabbis (who were responsible for the disputed conversions) and by extension cast doubt on the authentic "Jewishness" of their congregants.

But the "Who is a Jew?" conflict was not the only concern. On the basis of ancient texts, the Haredim passed judgement on everyday events. Some of their rabbis declared that medical organ transplants were immoral (one rabbi, a member of the Knesset, demanded that a heart surgeon be charged with murder), and after a murderous terrorist attack in 1985 another rabbi proclaimed that God was punishing the Jews for eating non-kosher food. Flexing new muscles, the ultra-Orthodox Haredim burned down

bus shelters carrying ads for bathing suits, ads that looked positively prudish by Western standards. They stoned cars on the
Sabbath, and bombed newsstands selling non-religious papers.

The Haredim did not believe in pluralism (God did not have
opinions), nor did they subscribe to wishy-washy liberalism, a
product of Godless humanism that led to the worst evil of all:
the assimilation of the Jews. If God's laws were the laws of the
land, Israel would become a *truly* "Jewish state".

The battle in Israel between the secular and the Orthodox
had whipped up waves that were beginning to crash into the
Diaspora. In 1984, Canadian rabbi Reuven Bulka wrote a book
called *The Coming Cataclysm*, which was into its second printing
while the original ink was still wet on the page. Scholars held
debates with titles like "Is Liberalism Good for the Jews?", a
question that would have been simply unthinkable just a few
years earlier.

Ultra-Orthodox power was abetted by a "return to religion"
movement that had swelled from a groundstream of disillu-
sionment. Old-style left-wing Zionism in the David Ben-Gurion
mould seemed to be fading; the election of a right-wing Likud
majority in 1977 and the subsequent war in Lebanon had un-
ravelled much of that. And in the Diaspora, the memory of
the Holocaust and the need to teach its lessons had begun to
appear somewhat hollow when promoted as the central content of Jewish life. What remained was what had been there all
along, however neglected: the source of the Jews, the religion of
Judaism.

There had always been yeshivas in Israel for the tiny percent-
age of ultra-Orthodox Jews who wanted to study there, but by
the mid-1980s the new academies for religious returnees were
something else again. They were bridges hastily constructed over
a chasm, a connecting link between the anxiety-ridden world of
the late twentieth century and a pre-modern, absolutist society
that provided comforting answers to life's troubling questions,
and a promise of happiness.

The returnee movement was directed primarily at North American Jews, although a small number of native-born Israelis were also beginning to "convert" to ultra-Orthodoxy. The reasoning went like this: Diaspora Jews have been corrupted by modernity, westernization, and secularism. If Judaism is not to disappear off the map, young Jews need to rediscover their religious roots at the source, in the Holy Land itself. The hope was that the young people who came to study would remain in Israel as members of the Haredi community.

The returnee yeshivas occupied a middle ground amid a plethora of ultra-Orthodox sects. They were not resolutely anti-Zionist, like the Neturei Karta, nor militant religious Zionists. They combined elements of both.

The returnee yeshivas (primarily Aish Hatorah and the Ohr Somayach academies for men and women) generally presented themselves as purely educational institutions. Why not learn something about one's heritage, they asked. A perfectly reasonable question—but in North America, where they recruited many of their students (in New York, Toronto, and Hollywood, of all places), they were sometimes accused of being cults, of having a sub-text to their teaching methods that went beyond the traditional.

Rabbi Noach Weinberg, who founded the Jerusalem Aish Hatorah in 1975, had researched his potential clientele carefully. He was dealing with a generation of 1960s children at the tail end of that era, about the time the Age of Aquarius started to slip over the horizon and the Age of the Stock Market began to rise in its place. Yippies and Weathermen, Black Panther sympathizers and flower children just returned from failed communes in the rain forest, were not yet candidates for Masthercharge and Yuppie narcissism. Some of them were headed for places like Kefar Haruv, but Rabbi Noach had his eye on the others—the less political ones who had experimented with Eastern religions, for example, or sat in the lotus position on clifftops at Big Sur.

"Our students come from a world where there is no Absolute Truth. That makes for very dull minds," he was quoted as saying in the Aish Hatorah promotional brochure.

Rabbi Noach's debating techniques could be devastating to the untutored, often confused young minds he encountered. One ex-student named Ian Slaw provided this report of his first encounter with Aish Hatorah in Jerusalem:

> Reb Noach allowed me to flow with my Marxist rhetoric before moving in deftly for the "kill".
>
> "Do you believe in God?" he asked harmlessly.
>
> As I stammered a positive reply, he was already changing gear.
>
> "What is happiness? What is love? What did Marx say about this? Are YOU happy? Are you satisfied with your life? Do you believe Man can be happy?...What would you say if I told you we had happiness in the Yeshiva? Would you stick around and have a look? If I gave you $10,000 to stick around, what would you say? Isn't happiness more important than money? What d'ya say? Wanna take a look?"
>
> By this time, the room was spinning around madly. Reb Noach seemed to be everywhere. Whatever I said made no difference. He had a one-way ticket inside my head, and every barrier I put in his way, he tore down remorselessly with hard, simple logic....

Between 1975 and 1978, some four thousand young men entered the doors of Aish Hatorah to be confronted by the "powerfully charismatic nature" of Rabbi Noach Weinberg, the brochure continued.

My own son had had a different sort of encounter with Aish Hatorah. In 1985, when he was seventeen, he visited Jerusalem. At the Western Wall of the Second Temple, the holiest shrine in the Jewish world, he was approached by a young American.

"You American?" Roland was asked.

"No, I'm Canadian."

"Know the baseball scores?"

"No."

"You Jewish?"

"Yes."

"Where ya staying?"

Roland was staying in a grotty youth hostel in the Old City.

"Come stay with us while you're here," offered the young man. "It's free."

Roland considered the offer.

"Do you believe in God?" asked the young man, diving straight to the point.

Roland had just finished a semester in Cartesian philosophy and had, he said, been thinking about such things. He did not believe in God, he told his interlocutor; nor did he believe in absolutes of good and evil. Furthermore, he did not agree that he needed God in his life in order to live morally.

"So Hitler was right! So you think Hitler was right!" pounced the young man. This leap of logic came with an alacrity that led Roland to think the conversation was less spontaneous than he had supposed.

They began to debate in earnest.

"You mean you don't even believe in the afterlife?" asked the man. "You think we just die and that's the end?"

Roland concurred.

Each grew angry. "I will buy the pleasures of your afterlife for seven hundred shekels," offered the young man. "If you don't believe, why should you care?"

Roland looked around and noticed that he could buy two Cokes for that price. The man pencilled a contract on a piece of paper.

I, Roland Paris, agree to sell the pleasures of my afterlife to x for 700 shekels.

My son thought this was funny. He signed and the money was paid over.

"If anyone else is interested in shares of my afterlife, tell them to come and see me," he called to the young man, who had begun to walk away clutching his contract.

"It's non-transferable," the man called back.

Roland was mildly surprised that his debating opponent was not laughing, that he was deadly serious. He began to think that there was something spooky about buying and selling souls when one of the two parties actually believed in the procedure and hoped literally to destroy his antagonist with this transaction.

In 1972, Rabbi Noah co-founded the Ohr Somayach yeshiva in downtown Jerusalem, for returnees to the faith, but he left abruptly the following year after an argument with his rabbinical colleagues. One of these, Rabbi Nota Shiller, continued to direct Ohr Somayach.

Rabbi Shiller was handsome and athletic-looking and seemingly at pains to convey that, despite ultra-Orthodoxy, he remained a man of the world. He had lived in Toronto, he said. And he had been an avid fan of the Toronto Blue Jays.

Our smiles became friendlier. We were connected by an authentic bond: major league baseball.

Rabbi Shiller was mildly apologetic. I would have to do my research at the women's yeshiva, Neve Yerushalayim, he said.

"That's fine," I replied.

He smiled a rueful smile of relief. I guessed it wasn't easy to relegate the writer from overseas to the secondary women's institution. Research was genderless, true enough, but women were still women.

In fact, I was genuinely pleased. Female returnees to Judaism would almost certainly have a longer, more arduous road to travel than their male counterparts, which might well make them more interesting. Young women raised in a secular Israel, or in North America or Europe, in the latter half of the twentieth century were already second-generation inheritors of a feminist revolution that had begun to alter attitudes and provide hitherto undreamed-of opportunities. But in Orthodox Judaism, since biological differences defined social and cultural differences, which were "divinely inspired", a woman's only source of status was as wife and mother. What these modern young women needed to learn—and quickly—was submission; how to despise the worldly gains many of their own mothers had struggled to achieve; how to accept a system of absolutes that effectively relegated them to a subordinate role in the life of learning and in the very religious world they had chosen for themselves by coming to Neve Yerushalayim.

Their brothers, on the other hand, automatically advanced their social status merely by attaching themselves to Ohr Somay-ach. Back home these boys would have to prove themselves in competition with women. At the yeshiva, they were immediately and inherently advantaged.

Night had already fallen when I reached Har-Nof, a new suburb of Jerusalem reserved for the ultra-Orthodox. Housing was being constructed on a series of hills. A steep, unlit footpath led up one of these and at the top the lights of Neve Yerushalayim gleamed yellow in the night sky.

I stood quietly for a moment in the surrounding dark, my eyes fixed on the light. With my knapsack slung over my shoulder I felt like a medieval knight errant approaching a castle. As unfamiliar as Israel might be to me, the world that glowed from the top of the hill was a complete unknown.

The evening cold sent a shiver through me. I had exchanged my jeans for a skirt and stockings, so as not to offend, but I wondered whether my red skirt was unforgivably wrong. Black was an ideal one aspired to in this society; the "blacker" one was, the more devout.

I knew little about the world of Orthodoxy, but I was genuinely curious. This was the universe my grandmother had belonged to—and I had loved my grandmother. This was the universe of my ancestors whose root tendrils dug into a past I had never known. This was a medieval cocoon adapted in some small way to the 1980s. Or did the world at the top of the hill seek to adapt the 1980s to itself?

I would live here for a little while, sleep in a dormitory, eat in a communal dining hall, attend lectures, and meet the women.

I climbed the path, stumbling against bushes and stones. I hoped it was not yet 8:00 p.m. A rabbi from Ohr Somayach was scheduled to lecture on psychology and ideology and I had a sense that this thematic conjunction might be central to what went on in the returnee yeshiva community. Rabbi Noach's approach to prospective students as described in the promotional brochure had suggested as much.

Gitty was waiting for me at the top of the hill. She was "house mother" to the girls, a down-to-earth sort of woman with a pleasant, no-nonsense manner.

"Why don't you get settled, then come back to the main hall for the lecture," she suggested, pointing in the direction of one of the residences.

One key unlocked the outside door and a second key opened a small apartment complex. No one was home. A tiny vestibule with coat hooks and a sink led into a narrow hallway which was lined by four bedrooms, each housing three women. At the end of the hall was a communal bathroom.

The rooms were cold and damp and the tiled floors were bare. Unadorned electric bulbs hung from the ceilings. I placed my bag on a narrow bed that had been provided for me in one of the dormitory rooms. Next door, in the bathroom, a thin film of water spread over the floor.

I returned to the designated classroom to await the lecturer. The students began to arrive, carrying clipboards. They looked college age. A few married women arrived from the outside community. They were recognizable by their covered heads; they could not appear in public without a scarf or wig or other covering.

The lecturer appeared. He wore the compulsory black broad-brimmed hat, a black coat, and a stark white shirt. His dark beard was flecked with grey, and large, round glasses perched on his nose.

Within moments it was clear why the discipline of psychology had been chosen as the subject of this lecture. The rabbi's underlying assumption was that contemporary Western society was "psychologized" to its very core. Ideals of behaviour, development, maturity, and responsibility; concepts of normalcy and deviance; all these broadly accepted beliefs were attitudes that sprang from a pervasive social and cultural ideology.

There was some truth to this, but the purpose of tonight's talk was clearly not objectivity. It was, rather, to expose this ideological system as "value-laden", then to posit a better one in its place. The *new* assumptions—Torah verities—were better, by definition, because they were "true", "absolute", and "eternal".

What was wrong with psychology (and, by extension, all Western values), aside from the intrinsic absence of God and revealed truth, was its stress on individualism and its willingness to reconcile "sin". The rabbi's voice grew increasingly loud as the lecture progressed. "According to [Erik] Erikson, maturity, or autonomy, is finding value in one's self without regard to anything else!" he cried. " 'Maturity' is a loaded word. Who is a psychologist to tell us what types of development are valuable and not valuable? And the search for meaning? That is in us all, but it must be real, objective, and true. Not a subjective, narcissistic thing.

"Spirituality is not *feeling!*"

But his real ire was reserved for moral relativism: for the American Psychological Association, for example, which had decided, he said, that homosexuality was not an illness but an alternative lifestyle; for the woman "who seeks an abortion so she can go on a skiing trip"; for the classification of alcoholism as an illness and not a moral choice.

The rabbi's own language was peppered with value-laden terminology. He spoke of "gimmicks" in psychology, and of professional psychologists as charlatans, as "guys who are in it for the money". Psychologists were dishonourable cheaters who fabricated evidence to fit their theories. ("Freudians invent facts," he announced.) "Therapy" (which served only to reconcile people to their vices) was a hoax. Furthermore, it couldn't possibly make people happy because "happiness" was more than personal satisfaction. Happiness was accomplishment, greatness. Like Abraham, Isaac, and Jacob. And Sarah, he added quickly for the benefit of his all-female audience.

Skepticism rumbled through the room. These young women were fresh from undergraduate psychology courses in American universities and from middle-class families that probably lived and breathed the very values that were here under attack.

"These are vast generalizations," countered one of them angrily. The rabbi disagreed firmly. Sometimes truth was unpalatable.

"There are Torah scholars in Jerusalem who are doing psychotherapy who have no background in this," called out a second woman. "If a person needs good therapy, what should she do?"

Here we seemed to be at the heart of the matter. Not religion, and not the exemplary lives of Abraham, Isaac, and Jacob (and Sarah), but old-fashioned, rock-bottom unhappiness. People in difficulty searching for a new way to live. If psychology—the basis for therapeutic help in secular society—was discredited, there had to be a better way. Orthodox Judaism was the better way.

"Therapy is only good advice. Anyone can give this," replied the rabbi, apparently changing track now that the help under discussion would originate from an acceptable source. "Torah psychology also depends on ideology, but if the ideology in question is not debatable and if its values are correct and its world view is the true one, then I will not think it is bad."

This was the old *tabula rasa* style of indoctrination. Erase the old writing. Then ink in the new.

Back in the dorm, a party was taking place. Rachel, my new roommate, had just become engaged and about ten women were cracking open a bottle of celebratory wine. They toasted the future bride with warm wishes, especially for many children. In the ultra-Orthodox sectors of Jerusalem, families of ten are not unusual.

Rachel and her fiancé had met through the good offices of the Neve matchmakers (known as *shadkins*), two motherly women who kept a shrewd eye on the available pool of potential husbands (often boys of nineteen and twenty) at Ohr Somayach. The couple "went out" six or seven times, which meant they sipped coffee and talked purposefully in the lobby of the Jerusalem Plaza Hotel. Since Orthodox unmarried men and women were not permitted to be alone together, they met in public places. And since their discussions went directly to the point—marriage suitability—they were satisfied that a few brief meetings were enough.

"You present your curriculum vitae to the shadkin. Then your shadkin meets his shadkin," laughed Deborah, my other roommate. She was from Chicago and her name had originally been Ann.

Men and marriage were the main subject of discussion at Rachel's engagement celebration. The women all wanted to get married. A few "dates" (more like interviews) and the deed was done. In fact, those who were planning to return to the United States in a mere six weeks or so continued to hope they would become engaged before they left, to someone they had not yet met.

Unlike most Neve women, Rachel had been raised in a traditionally Orthodox (though not ultra-Orthodox) family, and she had come here to deepen her knowledge of Judaism. She was twenty-eight, intelligent-looking and serious. Her course of study at Neve was "at the highest textual level", she said.

But her real reason for being at Neve was marriage. She had tried all the conventional routes back home in the United States: meeting men at parties given by friends, third-party introductions, and so on. It was a waste of time.

As soon as she arrived at the yeshiva, Rachel had made an appointment with the matchmaker, to whom she detailed the kind of man she hoped to meet. He was to be kind and respectful and outgoing—but not too much so, because she herself was a serious person. She wanted someone who had been to college and had a profession, and whose religious commitments were as stable as her own. And he needed to be "mature", she told the matchmaker.

Brian was only the second man the matchmaker had sent her way. The night they were to meet, the girls in the apartment had pooled their best clothes and dressed Rachel up for her interview.

The encounter clicked. "It's a very good way to make marriage choices," said Rachel. "You know you're dating to see if this could be a potential partner in life. So you try to be as relaxed as possible, but you don't play games."

Rachel and Brian had never so much as held hands, and they would not touch until their wedding night. "It is forbidden," she said in her engaging, earnest way. "What this means is that as a dating couple, your prime purpose must be to concentrate on your intellectual relationship, to develop your ability to communicate with each other. It takes a lot of the pressure away. But there is definitely a strong feeling of warmth and a desire to be together, and that too is treasured very much by God, to be expressed at the right time in a person's life."

Her language was so intellectualized that I had difficulty remembering that she was talking about love and sex.

"Are you a virgin?" I asked. I knew I might offend her with such a direct question, yet she was a woman of twenty-eight who had lived twenty-seven of those years in the United States, at a confused time when young women felt pressure to have sex with men they did not love and who did not love them. Was she an anomaly in the 1980s even before she decided to commit herself to the extreme world of ultra-Orthodoxy?

She shifted a little uncomfortably. "Yes, I am," she said. "My beliefs have always been a strong part of my life. And my mother was very strict about those things...." Her voice trailed off and she looked away.

Rachel was so controlled that the permissiveness of North American life must surely have frightened her. Here in the tightly circumscribed world of extreme Orthodoxy, she could finally relax. Here there were common rules for *everyone*—and they had been ordained by God. No upsetting surprises, no worrisome impulses. Here in Jerusalem, a justified universe unfolded as it should.

It was time to sleep. I crawled into a cold bed and spread my winter jacket over the blanket. The lights at the top of the hill went out, one by one, until it was dark. I lay quietly, listening to the prayers of Rachel and Deborah.

CHAPTER TEN

The Neve Way

The basic introductory course of studies at Neve included Jewish Thought, Bible Studies, "Taryag" (the study of the 613 commandments), and an examination of the philosophy of the twelfth-century Jewish philosopher Maimonides. First on this day's timetable was Jewish Thought.

Six young women in their late teens or early twenties awaited the arrival of the rabbi-professor. I joined them in the classroom.

The teacher burst into the room like a gust of air. He was about thirty and he exuded friendliness like palpable radio waves.

The topic of the day was self-confidence, he said. Self-confidence and Jewish Thought.

We were back to psychology, I noted, in its preferred, Jewish version.

"What bad results does a lack of self-confidence have on a person?" he boomed. He stood on his tiptoes and waved his arms with enthusiasm.

"Why, it makes us sensitive to criticism and hyper-critical towards others," he cried. "But! What is *wrong* with having a bad self-image?"

A girl in the front row raised her hand. "It is an insult to God because we are created by Him?" she suggested timorously.

"Because the universe was created for Man! Because everyone should say, For me was the universe created!"

He smiled at the self-doubting young women seated before him. His voice had reached such a pitch of excitement that one of them began to giggle nervously.

"God wants us to live in the present. Maybe you've squandered the last ten years. That does not matter to God. Self-image is how we feel about ourselves today. Yesterday must not deter us.

"In secular society people have choices. Their criteria for success and self-valuing are arbitrary," he continued. "But Torah tells us otherwise, that *everyone* is unique and important."

There was some appreciative nodding at this comforting thought.

"Take the question of intelligence," the teacher suggested. "People can be righteous and happy without a lot of it. Just the other day, I personally was four jokes behind everyone else. Being envious of another person's intelligence is as ridiculous as being envious of the glasses on their nose! I'm me, that's all. And I am happy to use my potential to my best ability."

By this time the students were smiling and relaxed. The rabbi was charismatic and engaging as he quite literally leaped about the room putting forth arguments designed to make his audience feel good about themselves and cared for by a Supreme Being who did not demand that they stand first in their classes at the Hebrew University or Berkeley, who did not judge them on their witty repartee, or rank them in any order whatsoever. A Supreme Being who said that whatever their past failings, only today counted, and that it was never too late to change.

The rabbi paused to observe his class. Then he tackled the most peevish question of all: the status of women.

"Housewives without professional careers sometimes lack self-esteem," he told us, raising his arms and shrugging. "But to raise happy, contented kids is the most creative work in the world. It is an enormous and gigantic task. Why should a woman who is a lawyer think her work is more demanding? Anyone who does not consider that children are the most important thing in life is mistaken.

"Everyone should feel happy and confident with what they are supposed to be doing."

Since there was only one job that women were "supposed to be doing", this class, ostensibly on "Jewish Thought", needed to prepare them to accept that life with joy, not resignation. That this was not an easy task soon became apparent, as did the energy the Neve administration was prepared to commit to the struggle.

Between classes, I leaned against the wall and studied my timetable. "Jewish Philosophy" was next. I wondered whether this would be another forum from which to pound home the gender-coded happiness message.

It was. But this lecture also included another attack on Westernism. Secular thought, it appeared, had come to us from the ancient Greeks: a horrid, physical race that idealized the human body, promoted relativism in moral thinking, and defined knowledge in terms of past learning. "In Greek-based thinking, a person can have a Ph.D. at age twenty-four and be considered wise, even if he never learns another thing," reported the instructor, Rabbi G.

Judaism, on the other hand, taught that knowledge was a state of being, a process. The major problem in the world was "how to describe success and happiness and according to which vision: Greek or Jewish," said the rabbi. No surprises here: Jewish was better.

"Why do only men study these things in detail?" came the inevitable question.

"Questions like this come from the Greek world, the secular world that is based on Plato and Aristotle," answered Rabbi G.

with a scowl. "The main role of men is to think, and of women to act. Man initiates; woman completes.

"Men deal in abstract thought and women express those thoughts in the world," he continued. "Therefore it is obvious that women should learn less than men."

A dissenting murmur swept through the room, but no further questions were asked.

Taryag class brought the first overt attack on the quintessential Zionist experience, the kibbutz.

"There are two types of people on the kibbutz," explained the teacher, "idealists and people who want to be looked after. You're not allowed to leave whenever you want. In other words, you pay a price for what you get."

This observation was followed by a more important message. "It is worth questioning whether certain aspects of kibbutz life are coherent with Judaism," suggested the rabbi. "There's some weird stuff there, like the separation of children from their parents. In Judaism we are directly before God and responsible to God. So the idea of putting other responsibilities before that is detrimental to the primary relationship.

"God has given us free will, the freedom to choose. The kibbutz is a form of life that will always impinge upon this freedom."

Although the students appeared to agree with him, the rabbi tried to neutralize his words. He knew that for many people, "kibbutz" and "Israel" were one and the same thing. "I'm not seeking to criticize," he urged, "I'm just explaining. The kibbutz is just not in conformity with Judaism."

"Have you met Mrs. H. yet?" I was asked by half a dozen women at the lunch break. "She's wonderful, she's *brilliant*, and she has ten children, too."

I couldn't wait to meet this paragon who was so genuinely loved by her students. Mrs. H. was a role model: an ultra-Orthodox woman who remained beautiful after giving birth to ten children and whose mind was as sharp as a razor, they said.

Mrs. H. turned out to be fortyish and youthful-looking. She wore stylish glasses with tinted red rims, and an orange scarf wrapped around a beautifully coiffed wig. She moved energetically and smiled with the assurance of a media star.

The purported subject of her class was Maimonides, but the long-dead thinker received not a moment's acknowledgement. The real subject was, once again, female self-image, and the task of the teacher to convince previously secular young women (perhaps still wavering in their commitment) that the world they came from was error-ridden at the very least, and that religion promised happiness.

"Can women study the Torah?" came the first question. The questioner was assertive and mildly hostile. If she were to choose Judaism as her life, it seemed, she would demand equal intellectual rights.

Mrs. H. replied, "A man who teaches his daughter Torah, it is as though he teaches her something tasteless or lewd. But if she initiates things, it is meritorious. And the 'man' here includes all men," she added.

"Tasteless or lewd? What does that mean?" persisted the student, who I later learned was a political science graduate who had worked as an executive assistant on Jewish affairs for an East Coast American politician.

"It means that woman is less than man is. Therefore she will feminize the text," replied Mrs. H.

At least there was no attempt to conceal the stark message. No one was attempting to hide the fact that "to feminize" meant to sully.

For the rest of the hour, Mrs. H. explained that women's brains were "insight-oriented" and not analytical like men's. Therefore they were inadequate for Torah study. Women's brains were physically different "in lobular size and also in the electrical connection between the two sides," she announced authoritatively. "There is an observable difference that is simply not arguable. One can observe that the side that works with experience is more developed in women and the analytical side is more developed with men.

"Now, doesn't this fact make you think that the sexes don't think alike?" she asked with a flourish.

The students were stumped. What studies might Mrs. H. be referring to? She had neglected to mention the source of her irrefutable knowledge. Since they were not scientists, they could not reply.

I was reminded of an interesting book I had come across some years earlier called *Fads and Fallacies in the Name of Science*, in which the author, Martin Gardner, had demonstrated how it was possible to "prove" much nonsense (such as a flat earth or racial superiority) by developing selected "scientific" theories that were based upon assumed ideological premises. I also happened to remember that legitimate experiments were in fact taking place regarding possible sex differences in human brain function, but that contradictory results to date had not satisfied the scientific community. The only controversy Mrs. H. was prepared to acknowledge was that engendered by misguided "feminists", a term she repeated several times with much distaste.

"A woman who is a lawyer is trashing herself because she is developing the analytical part of herself," she concluded categorically. "Even women who are in the men's world can't be as good as men because exceptionality does not lend itself to top performance in the field."

And that was that. With skilful "analysis" the brilliant Mrs. H., who was herself happily ensconced in a professional career, had "proven" that women were biologically unsuited to analysis and to professional careers.

She swept out of the room majestically, surrounded by a retinue of vaguely troubled but admiring ladies-in-waiting. The difficult task of indoctrination, I was beginning to understand, had been assigned to energetic, charismatic teachers who were adored by their student-disciples.

CHAPTER ELEVEN

The Conversion

My roommate, Deborah, appeared in front of me carrying an armful of books. She looked excited.

"My conversion is this afternoon," she whispered. "Want to come along?"

Somewhat guiltily I stole out of the building, hoping to escape the observant eye of house mother Gitty, who had set me up with a full academic schedule. Deborah did not want anyone to know where she was going.

This was not her first conversion ceremony. Deborah had adopted Judaism in the United States two years earlier, but the Israeli rabbis had their doubts about the initial process and wanted her to repeat it under their supervision. The time and place had just come through this morning.

We set out for the home of Leah Feldman, one of the Neve matchmakers and a kindly mother-figure for most of the girls. She had promised to help Deborah prepare for the event, which consisted of an immersion in the ritual bath known as a mikvah.

We made our way down the path to the main road and the bus stop. It already felt like weeks since I had climbed that road towards the lights at the top of the hill.

Deborah was thirty years old, dark, tall and beautiful. Her eyes were large and brown, and waist-long hair hung down her back in a thick braid. She had been raised as a Catholic in Chicago, but most of her family was Methodist. There was something about her that suggested a black ancestry.

Deborah's pre-conversion life sounded painfully lonely; indeed, she described it as a "void". Her parents had been separated; her father had died when she was twelve; and poverty had forced her mother to ship her off to Detroit to be raised by a grandmother. There were no siblings.

In her early twenties, the "void" had become unbearable. Deborah had returned to Catholicism but found it "unsatisfying". There were too many "leaps of faith", she said.

In the course of her reading, she had discovered the "historical Jesus". From there, she had moved into a study of Judaism.

"It looked attractive," she said, her face softening at the memory. "It caught me emotionally, too. It was just so, so...*obvious* that I had to become a Jew."

We were sitting together on a Jerusalem bus, still in an ultra-Orthodox sector. Black-hatted men bent over religious texts as the bus lurched along the road. Married women with wigs and covered heads got on and off, clutching baskets of market vegetables and what seemed like dozens of children.

Deborah looked directly at me, as if trying to discern whether I understood the compulsion she had experienced and what it had meant to her. I understood a little, but mainly in terms of her terrible neediness. Precisely the way the faculty at Neve understood these things, I mused.

She looked away and was quiet a while. Then she continued. She had studied on her own for several months; then one day she had looked up a local rabbi, gone to his house, and asked to be converted. Just like that. He looked startled. Deborah said to him, "I can't really articulate the process, but I know this is what I have to do. It's an emotional and spiritual imperative."

The rabbi accepted her simple explanation.

Following her conversion, the emotional distance between Deborah and her relatives increased. "To a certain extent this is because I can no longer eat in their houses," she said. "They're not kosher, which means I'm restricted as to how long I can stay there. Sometimes I pack in matzohs and a can of tuna.

"Really, they're very accommodating. One of the silliest things I've ever seen was for my grandmother's ninetieth birthday party. They had it kosher-catered!"

"That's very touching," I said.

"Oh, it was a wasted effort. First of all, I couldn't vouch for the kosherness of the caterer, and secondly, it was the sabbath. I mean, I had spent a full day eating, and boy, I didn't even *want* anything else.

"Of course, there's no way to really resume life with them. Even our conversations are limited now."

There was something chilling about Deborah's description. Her family and her entire early life had been relegated to a past that was "wrong" and irrelevant. They could no longer share a meal, that elemental cornerstone of family communion. They had nothing to say to each other.

We got off the bus and walked along the street. The shops sold religious artefacts and posted pictures of famous Hasidic rabbis in their windows. Deborah stopped to gaze fondly at the photographs. "I want to cry when I see those beautiful faces," she said. "They are like fathers." Like the father she had barely had.

Deborah wanted to become as "black" as she possibly could—as devout, as committed, as Orthodox as a lifespan and her own abilities would permit. She gazed longingly at the displays of religious phylacteries the way other young women might gaze at a window of designer fashions.

Deborah was essentially and deeply conservative. As a Catholic, she had wanted a Latin mass when everyone else was strumming guitars and writing prayer-songs. Indeed, home—the United States—had evolved into a society where she felt out of place. She didn't *want* to work in a career. She wanted to bake bread, she said, and have babies, and that was no longer very acceptable where she came from.

It was better in Israel, especially since she was "uninterested" in politics and therefore undisturbed by events. Zionism was anti-religious, she said, so that too was a write-off—except for the Gush Emunim religious Zionists who had set up settlements in the Occupied Territories. About that movement she was absolutely clear and *very* political.

"Judea and Samaria are an integral part of Israel," she told me in a firm voice. "Jordan took them in 1948 and we just took them back. They attacked and lost, so that's just tough luck, isn't it? I mean, it's as though someone mugs you and you wound them in self-defence and then they try to sue you for damages when they actually committed a criminal act against *you*. It's ridiculous. It violates any sense of order or justice."

Like everyone else at Neve, Deborah wanted to get married; but being a convert was proving to be an obstacle. One young man had been interested in her, but he had thought his parents would not be able to cope. Maybe the new, official conversion this afternoon would help.

We had reached Mrs. Feldman's apartment building. Deborah smiled and bit her lip with excitement, then rang the bell.

Mrs. Feldman was there in a minute, smiling warmly, fussing, and exuding motherliness as she led us to her modest upper-floor apartment. Once indoors, she instructed Deborah on how to prepare for the event, and there was much scurrying about as soap, shampoo, and towels were supplied. Deborah needed to wash her entire body, Mrs. Feldman explained, "to remove anything that was not of the body such as dirt, or a hanging fingernail. Her hair must be washed and combed, and the hidden places of the body cleaned thoroughly."

Deborah disappeared into a steamy bathroom, and I was consigned to the only living-room chair to wait. I scanned the books on the wall shelves beside me. There were Hebrew texts and a number of English-language books on Judaism, especially on the return to religion. I randomly opened a book entitled *The Road Back* by Mayer Schiller. The author was excoriating a Reform rabbi who had published a book in which the following apparently despicable sentence had appeared: "The ultimate commitment of the modern Jew is to rationalism." Author Schiller had set off the word "rabbi" in disdainful quotes.

A second book, called *Israel, Torah and I: Musings of a Temporary Resident*, had been authored by Rabbi Emanuel Feldman, Mrs. Feldman's brother-in-law. I opened it at random too.

"I am worried about Israel and it is the Torah that makes me worry...," Rabbi Feldman had written in 1974. He then described how his views of "Torah first" had elicited the accusation that he was anti-Zionist and anti-Israel. A rabbinical acquaintance had called him "a hater of Israel", an epithet usually reserved for anti-Semites. To make matters worse, the militantly anti-Zionist Neturei Karta had reprinted the book, giving it a dubious stamp of approval.

A third book entitled *In Search of the Jewish Woman* caught my eye; after all, the principal role of Neve Yerushalayim was to transform the secular woman into a *Jewish* woman. This book was blunt about its central concern: the necessary exclusion of women from the world of political, social, and economic power.

> Woman serves to guard Man's humanity; but she can do so only if she is not exposed to the identical temptations....
>
> Wisdom is with those who are modest and hidden, out of the limelight, away from the roar of the crowd, uncorrupted by the power structure.

> Woman has an unclouded view with which to see the truth as it really
> is. Therefore it is understood that modesty is designated as a female
> speciality allowing her to...hold the world back from its headlong
> plunge into spiritual suicide.

I found myself smiling. These were the very arguments that had been used in Canada's Roman Catholic province of Quebec (and undoubtedly elsewhere) in the early decades of this century, in an attempt to keep women from acquiring the vote.

In the final analysis Orthodox Judaism depended upon the acquiescence of women, for family was central to the Orthodox life, and women were central to the family. But just like the Catholic Church, Jewish Orthodoxy was having to confront female rebellion within its ranks—though more in the Diaspora than in Israel. In response, books like this were being written and returnee yeshivas like Neve Yerushalayim had mounted a frontal counter-attack. At stake was the very heart of religious organization.

After an hour and a half, Deborah emerged from the vapours of the bath. Her hair was damp and shiny, and her scrubbed face shone with expectation.

We left the apartment and hailed a taxi in the street. After fifteen minutes or so, the forest of television antennae came abruptly to an end, announcing our entry into an ultra-Orthodox residential section. The car stopped before the building that housed the ritual baths.

It was anything but luxurious. A main entrance opened into a narrow corridor flanked by changing rooms. The ubiquitous cold, tiled floors reappeared. The bathroom was a sickly green and paint peeled off the walls.

Mrs. Feldman and I entered the area of the bare-walled immersion pool where the conversion ceremony would take place. Deborah was already in the water. She wore a cotton robe and stood with her back towards us, facing the Old City of Jerusalem

and the Western Wall. Her dark hair fell wet down the length of
her back. She looked, in fact, like a biblical Jewess.

Three rabbis entered the small room, all bearded, all wearing
Hasidic black frocks and black hats. They lined up beside each
other on one side of the pool; Mrs. Feldman and I lined up on the
other.

"Why do you want to join the Jewish people?" asked one of
them in a kindly voice.

"Judaism has entered right inside of me," replied Deborah
very softly, still with her back to the proceedings. "I tried
Catholicism and that didn't work."

"That's negative," he retorted. "What is positive?"

"This is what is most meaningful in my life," she essayed. Her
voice wavered a little.

The rabbis smiled as one.

"Do you promise to obey all the laws of the Torah, without
exception?"

"I do."

Deborah needed to immerse herself in the water, to be covered
from head to toe. She took a deep breath and tried to go under.
The rabbis had been averting their eyes, but they needed to
ascertain that immersion had truly taken place. They rushed to
the edge of the tank as one and peered in quickly.

Her head had not been under water. This was not good enough.

She tried again. Again the rabbis swooped over to look.

Another failure. This was proving difficult. Deborah could not
swim and water, it seemed, terrified her.

On the third attempt, the rabbis were satisfied that the deed
had been done. They departed quickly so as not to see her emerge
from the water, her wet cotton robe clinging to the contours of
her young body.

Deborah climbed out of the pool dripping and smiling joy-
ously. This was the culmination and confirmation of her choice,
the holy moment that would henceforth inform every act of her
life. I watched with immense interest. I, a Jew by birth, had never

seen a ritual bath, let alone immersed myself in one. This ritual was as remote from the experience of my life as the baptisms that took place daily in the River Jordan with bus-loads of fundamentalist Christians on pilgrimage to the Holy Land. I tried to project my imagination into an Eastern European past of nearly a century ago, to my grandparents' generation and beyond, to a time when the rhythms of Orthodoxy still held sway in my family.

Deborah looked at me with passing curiosity. A radiant smile had illuminated her face. Then she turned away, lost in a private joy.

CHAPTER TWELVE

The Wedding

There were notices all over Neve. Sonya's wedding was at 6:30 that evening. Everyone was invited and everyone was planning to go.

Sonya was twenty-two and from Cape Town, South Africa. She (as was apparent to all) was one of the lucky ones. She had found a husband through the good offices of the Neve matchmaking services.

Her fiancé was studying at Ohr Somayach. He was from Denver, Colorado and, like Sonya, new to the world of ultra-Orthodoxy. This made them an ideal couple, for in the world of the Haredim those not to the manner born were often looked upon with suspicion. Converts, even Jewish converts, would always lack that instinctive, unspoken edge of understanding that is absorbed by osmosis in childhood.

Rachel was dressing carefully for the wedding. Brian, her new fiancé, would be there and this would give them a chance to talk together for a few precious moments and then, for the rest of the evening, to seek out each other's eyes from the edge of the opaque partition that divided the men from the women.

Rachel and Brian met briefly near the hall where the wedding was to take place. They smiled, spoke softly, and smiled again, for they were forbidden to touch one another and this intense communication had to convey what hand-holding, a kiss, or the gentle stroking of the face or hair of one's beloved would signal in the outside world.

Rachel had arranged for me to meet Brian in her company. He was twenty-eight, an economist by training, intelligent and well spoken. We talked of his family. He said he was by now much more religious than they were. He did not tell me that he was a convert, something I happened to have learned elsewhere.

Rachel listened intently, sometimes responding with surprise and pleasure, for she was learning about this man she was about to marry through my questions. They had met only a few times in circumscribed situations. That was the Neve–Ohr Somayach way.

"Before we go our separate ways, can we meet again soon?" he asked her quickly as the three of us entered the hall and prepared to take our respective places on opposite sides of the gender barrier.

Rachel nodded vigorously. Brian turned to leave and she followed him with her eyes. They would not speak again this evening.

Like everything else in non-tourist Israel, the wedding hall lacked style and pretension. The lace-covered partition that separated the sexes ran down the centre of the room with a narrow passageway at one end for exit and entry purposes.

I entered tentatively, not quite knowing what to do. To reach the women's side I needed to pass through a tiny corner of the men's section, and I worried about mistakenly doing something gauche and unforgivable. Was I allowed to look at these bearded, black-hatted, black-frocked men? What if I accidently brushed against one? Would this create a problem for him, or for both of us?

I successfully navigated my way to the women's section and breathed a sign of relief. With a host of unfamiliar prohibitions in operation, it was definitely more comfortable here.

Three or four round tables topped with white and brown tablecloths lined one side of the women's section while a food table stretched along the partition itself. The food was modest, Israeli style. Avocado mixed with egg, marinated beets, coleslaw, a sort of eggplant ratatouille, and rolls. At the back of the room a makeshift "bar" served glasses of tepid orangeade. Guests had carelessly thrown their coats on this bar. No hired "wedding consultant" had produced this affair.

A three-man band played melodic Israeli music at an ear-splitting decibel level. They were bearded and wore *payos* ringlets, locks of hair that fell over their ears.

About fifty women milled about, greeting each other and chattering happily. The married ones wore wigs or head scarves, or both, and almost all of them looked pregnant. Their children were here as well. A baby of about eighteen months toddled by, wearing a navy-blue pin-striped suit.

A middle-aged woman was holding a three-week-old infant.

"Your grandchild?" I asked.

"Oh yes," she replied, beaming at the child. "I'm thrilled. I've had three of them this month."

In the centre of the room sat the bride, flanked by her mother and her sister. Sonya was wearing a white wedding gown with a headdress and a veil that was pushed back from her face. She was dark-complexioned, with large, frightened eyes. According to religious law, she had fasted all this day, and she looked drawn and exhausted.

Her mother, who had just flown in from Cape Town, was expensively and stylishly dressed. Her dress was mauve—this year's colour—and a matching beret sat jauntily on her head. She clutched her daughter's hand and her eyes conveyed a similar fearful expression. Her husband was on the other side of the partition, of course. They were not Orthodox; their daughter had moved into this world without them, and as a relative from a kibbutz confided later in the evening—with an expression of distaste—"No one in the family knew what to expect from this wedding."

I felt deeply for this woman who had travelled here for the wedding of a beloved daughter who now inhabited a remote and inaccessible world.

Women pressed bits of paper into Sonya's hands and she was praying fervently. On her wedding day the bride was thought to be holy and in a position to pray for other people. The notes conveyed requests to pray for sick relatives and friends—as well as the deeply felt desires of the women in this room. There were dozens of Neve girls who would have changed places with Sonya in a minute. They had asked her to pray that they too might find a husband and thus begin to fulfil their destiny as Jewish women.

The music had changed in character. Now the trio was playing a beautiful melody that was traditional for sabbath eve. In Judaism the sabbath is a bride, as the bride is holy. A feeling of expectation filled the room.

The women formed a line on either side of the bride, from her chair to the end of the room. Mrs. Feldman popped up at my side, smiling warmly. She pushed me to the front.

"You must see this properly," she urged, her kind face shining with pleasure, her elbows actively preparing a place for me.

Suddenly the men were entering the women's section, the groom, his brother, and his soon-to-be father-in-law at the head of a disorderly procession. The groom, in a pure white smock, approached Sonya and lowered the veil over her face. They had not seen each other in a week. He smiled happily at her; she smiled back weakly. Sonya and her mother gripped each other's hands even more tightly. The crowd buzzed with excitement.

I found it hard to follow what happened next. The procession of men swept by and Mrs. Feldman materialized at my elbow to steer me outside with the surging crowd. With unerring skill, she created a prime viewing place. The couple and their families were squeezed under the wedding canopy, which symbolized the home the bride and groom would make together. Across the canopy were written the words "Joe and Faye". These were the Tanenbaums of Toronto, a family that has contributed millions of dollars to religious institutions in Israel. The Tanenbaums were apparently present at every Neve–Ohr Somayach wedding. As for the rest of us, we pressed in close, shivering in the February air.

The bridegroom's brother had come from Colorado to represent the family and he too seemed to be struggling with an unfamiliar situation. While the groom was bearded and black-hatted and now belonged to a new-ancient world, his brother looked like a linebacker for the Denver Broncos. His clothes spoke America, as did his loose limbs and his square-chinned, close-shaven face.

The bride's mother—looking tense and unsure, but in control of herself—led her daughter around the groom seven times before Sonya took her place beside her future husband. The ceremony was brief. The rabbis offered several blessings and it was done.

The bride kissed people and the groom kissed people, but still they did not kiss each other. They had never touched and they did not touch now. There was a ritualized moment for that, and several of the Neve girls had spoken to me about it in abashed whispers.

The guests returned to the hall without the bride and groom. The young couple were locked in a private room. Here they would touch for the first time.

An hour passed. We ate coleslaw and drank orangeade. Some people danced.

Then, suddenly, the bride was there, among the women. At the same moment, the groom had returned to the men.

Sonya had eyes only for her mother, and her mother for her. They moved quickly towards each other, blind to the crowd of happy well-wishers that crushed against them. Sonya's lips were parted with emotion and her eyes glistened as she reached for her mother. Her mother, wide-eyed, wept softly. They held each other at arm's length, each looking into the other's face as if to communicate and read the experience of the last hour. Then they fell into each other's arms.

The music got louder and the dancing began in earnest. Sonya was raised on a chair and paraded wildly around the room while on the other side of the partition the men paraded her new husband in the same way. Sonya danced with her mother, her sister, and her friends. Friends danced with each other. The atmosphere was raucous and fun. Masks were brought out; one little girl made the rounds wearing a plastic gorilla head.

I danced too, with the reserve of someone who is enjoying the event but does not belong. Yet this wedding, which was as foreign to me as a Zulu rite, contained familiar elements that caused me to pause. Those remnant symbols that had survived the eighteenth-century Enlightenment and the subsequent westernization of European and North American Jewry were as close to me as my own childhood, my own family, my own wedding. How odd it seemed that I was only two or, at the most, three generations removed from this remote world. And that so many of the young men and women dancing here—as their ancestors had danced in Poland, Lithuania, and the Ukraine—were themselves products of my world, who had chosen to return to an older way of life. Indeed, I happened to know that some of the bearded, black-cloaked young men on the other side of this room were the children of acquaintances in Toronto, modern, secular people like myself, and that several of these very boys had gone to school with my son. Years ago they might have come to my home for milk and cookies after school. Today their counterparts might be sitting in wrongful "Greek-based" university lectures with my son. Yet here, garbed in an ancient dress and committed to an absolute vision of the world and its God-given laws, they inhabited a universe that our forebears, both theirs and mine, had abandoned a century before.

According to their laws, I could not cross the room to speak to them, nor could I shake their hands in warm recollection of days gone by. They were lost to me and I to them.

CHAPTER THIRTEEN

Shabbat

It was Friday, sabbath eve, the magic time. At sundown this evening, families across Israel would sit down to pray and share food together.

Neve girls were farmed out for Friday nights. Local families invited them for the sabbath meal and then to spend the night in their homes, for they could not travel in vehicles on the sabbath.

Gitty had arranged for Deborah and me to visit a family in the ultra-Orthodox sector of Geula, which borders on the equally Orthodox neighbourhood of Mea Shearim.

"Mrs. B. is a great cook," said Deborah longingly as we swayed dangerously in the speeding bus. The food at Neve was quite atrocious—served like slop right out of buckets—and the sabbath meal away was discussed and looked forward to all week.

We made our way up a narrow, ghetto-like street to the home of Mr. and Mrs. B., our hosts for the evening. They were an older couple, in their late sixties or early seventies. Mr. B. had returned to the faith just a few years ago, after a lifetime of error-ridden ways, said Deborah in a whisper.

A short alley led away from the street. A dozen children played there, already dressed for the sabbath in their best dresses and suits. The boys wore skullcaps and ringlets.

A little gate at the end of the alley opened into a small courtyard which, in turn, contained four tiny row houses. Ten children lived in one of these doll-sized homes; twelve lived in another. "That's *nothing*," said Deborah. "A woman down the road here has twenty children."

I became very quiet.

We knocked on the last door. Mrs. B. answered. She was expecting us, she said in a friendly tone.

The house was in fact a cottage, consisting of a tiny entrance hall and a living room with a plain, pull-out couch for their many overnight sabbath guests, a small end table, and three plants. On the other side of the hall was the dining room, which was bedecked, this evening, in its sabbath splendour. A small bedroom, a tiny corridor of a bathroom, and an even smaller kitchen made up the rest.

One hour remained to sunset and an evening cold had settled in. Mrs. B. offered me a sweater and a coat. "Why don't we take a walk?" she suggested.

Deborah demurred.

Mrs. B. and I strolled together through the narrow, congested streets of Geula, listening to the sounds of Yiddish being spoken around us—for Hebrew was a holy language, not to be sullied by common use. Orthodox men were rushing to get home before the neighbourhood whistle sounded, informing everyone that the moment to light the sabbath candles had arrived. Women passed by hurriedly, their long dresses concealing bulging pregnancies, their shaved heads covered by wigs and scarves.

"There's a bit of a scandal going on," whispered Mrs. B. "You see, some of the wigs are actually more attractive than real hair!"

A Hasid approached from behind. Mrs. B. pulled me over to the side of the narrow street so he could pass.

"He's not allowed to pass between us," she explained. "It's too sexually arousing."

I must have looked skeptical.

"The only way to keep men from straying is not to let them have anything to do with women," she continued earnestly. "You know how in America everyone switches husbands and wives. This is a way to prevent it. You know, men think about sex all their lives—and not just the young ones, either." This last piece of information was delivered *sotto voce*.

I thought of several of my friends back home whose husbands never thought about sex at all, to their wives' everlasting despair.

Another man made a wide circle around us, averting his eyes. I was beginning to perk up with this knowledge of my fatal attractiveness. One look at me and long-standing marriages would dissolve in a flash. I was tired and I knew my hair needed a comb, but I had no need to worry—not now, not ten years from now, not ever. My desirability would last for ever.

We returned home. Deborah was waiting, as well as two young men from Ohr Somayach. So was Mr. B.

The whistle sounded and we took our places at the beautifully laid table. Mrs. B. had put out her best white embroidered tablecloth and her gleaming silver. A twisted challah (eggbread) loaf was in its ritual place ready to be blessed and eaten. It was a long time since I had tasted challah. I thought of my childhood, and of my father's mother, at whose home we used to gather as one boisterous, amiable family of cousins, aunts, and uncles every Friday night. I felt warm and strangely happy, as though the people sitting around me were old friends and not strangers, as though I were close to my own loved ones and not thousands of miles away on the other side of the world.

I hadn't counted on Mr. B.

Mr. B. was seventy-one and he looked like a Torah sage. He had a long white beard and a round, full-featured face, and he wore a black hat. During his working life he had been a travelling salesman along the east coast of the United States. During the Second World War he had been in India with the U.S. army.

Until five years before, he had been a divorcé, and a very old hippie. He had lived in New York's East Village and smoked dope and indulged in other nameless vices; he had lived on a houseboat in France and travelled the canal routes of that country. Aimless, aimless.

He told his story with the pride of a reformed alcoholic.

His conversion had come suddenly. One of his sons had been living happily with a Gentile woman for many years, but when they travelled to Jerusalem and visited the Holocaust Memorial, Yad Vashem, he decided to leave her.

Mr. B. flew to Jerusalem to dissuade him. "You can't do this to her," he yelled at his son. "You *love* her."

His son explained. He had been talking to some of the yeshiva people. There was an answer for disaffected Jews, and it was religion—in Israel.

"Dad, why not look into this yourself?" his son had suggested. Mr. B. was ready for something meaningful in his life and both father and son soon became returnees to the faith. Mr. B. married Mrs. B., a widow. His son's Gentile girlfriend converted, and they too got properly married.

It sounded as neat as a pin. Mr. B. looked around the table for a reaction. We widened our eyes in wonderment, nodded vigorously, and made little noises of appreciation.

Mr. B. had embraced Orthodox Judaism with a vengeance. Never having studied anything since he left school more than half a century before, he was delighted with the Talmudic world, although whether he understood much seemed at best doubtful. A twenty-volume set of the Talmud, leather-bound and gold-embossed, looked out from his bookshelf in pristine newness. Earlier I had had a chance to observe that the books that had been read and reread had to do with self-help (Jewish style) and not religion at all. *Gateway to Happiness* was in Mr. B.'s library, just as it was being taught at Neve. In red magic marker, Mr. B. had underlined sections on how to cope with anger.

Before he became a religious Jew, Mr. B. might have directed his anger at an "establishment" that considered him uncouth (he burped at the table and ate before others were served), or a society that relegated him to the ranks of a Willy Loman, plying his trade up and down the Atlantic seaboard. As he got older, selling got harder and harder.

In the world of the Orthodox, however, all such distinctions were erased. A man studied, kept God's laws, and prayed. Before God he was equal to all other men, beyond a class-ridden society that valued people according to how much money they made, or how socially successful they had been. Orthodoxy also accorded him instant superiority over all women: religious women, of course, but non-religious women too. Indeed, the latter were held in even greater contempt than non-religious Jewish men. Neither had recognized Truth—but the non-religious woman who pursued a career in a man's world was unnatural as well as misguided.

Mr. B. did not seem overly pleased to have a female writer at his sabbath table, but it remained to be seen if she had perhaps the one redeeming characteristic. We were not halfway through the chicken soup when the question was asked.

"Where do you stand as a Jew, Esther?"

"It's Erna."

"Well?"

"I was brought up in the Reform movement and I am a committed secular Jew."

His eyes widened a little, his mouth tightened a little.

"A secular Jew? What does that mean?"

A fair question, perhaps, at this table and in this neighbourhood. Six soupspoons came to an abrupt mid-air halt. No one breathed. Six pairs of eyes stared at me.

"It means that I feel deeply connected to the Jewish people and that I am not religious. I've been influenced by traditional ideas of liberal Jewish ethics," I added, hoping vainly to redeem myself.

It was a bit of a speech. Embarrassing. I saw myself in the Kibbutz Yiftah dining hall, vainly attempting to explain my politically incorrect attitudes towards Zionism.

Mr. B. looked taken aback—perhaps because I did not apologize for my Godless state.

"What have you written?" he asked, changing tack.

I mentioned that part of my work had dealt with Jewish themes.

"But from a *secular* point of view, I suppose." The word "secular" plopped out of his mouth like an olive pit. He was squinting at me as though I were the last surviving specimen of a strange and repugnant species.

"Yes, I suppose that's true."

"So? Do you expect me to applaud you?"

I laughed to break the tension and everyone joined in. We had several courses to go yet, and in spite of Mr. B. I was enjoying being here in a Yiddish neighbourhood that resembled the Galician streets my grandparents had emigrated from. I was enjoying Mrs. B.'s chicken soup and, after a week at Neve, looking forward to boiled chicken and carrots, followed by sponge cake and tea with lemon.

The young men at the table were called Nathan and Sandor. Nathan was from Washington. He was twenty-seven years old, aggressive and intelligent, and he had been head of the Jewish Students' Union at a well-known university.

Nathan spoke with unbridled contempt about everyone, Jew or Gentile, who was not exactly like him. The Jewish students at his university were "ignorant", a summer camp he had attended in northern Michigan was "destroyed by the goyim because they didn't want the Jews to have a camp". (Further questioning revealed that there had been an electrical problem that had affected all structures in the area.) The kibbutzim in Israel were a "joke" and their members were "not real Jews".

"Secular Jews are angry at the religious because we have all the power now," he said with a sly smile. "The secular will probably have to leave."

Just before I came to the yeshiva I had met a radio journalist of Iraqi origin. He had been in Israel since the 1950s, had married and raised a family, but after all these years he was now planning to leave. It was the endless war and the endless occupation that had finally got to him, he said, and the growing right-wing tenor of the country. He was especially disturbed by the new breed of American immigrants, the ones who tried to blow up the Dome of the Rock mosque on Temple Mount and who supported Rabbi Meir Kahane in his campaign to drive the Arabs out of Israel. Nathan sounded like one of them; he was a smouldering volcano of hatred.

I tuned in to the dinner conversation again.

Sandor, a quieter, gentler young man of twenty-three, was suggesting that the true explanation for religious-secular hostility was that the Messiah was about to arrive; it was prophesied that before He came, there would be great hatred among Jews. Man did not invent the ways of God, nor could he interfere with His plans. Given the current bitterness in Israel, it was plain that the Messiah would not tarry long.

Nathan and Sandor were both Ohr Somayach students, but one was a political militant while the other preferred to wait for the Messiah to turn the world in his direction.

Mr. B. interrupted. "You probably think I'm not tolerant," he said, "and you are not completely wrong. It's not that I dislike Reform and Conservative Jews as people, it's their rabbis that cause the problems. I *hate* their rabbis."

Everyone looked surprised at the vehemence of this statement.

"Yes, they lie to their congregations. They are *atheists*." A hush fell over the table. "They are despicable men because they are only doing it for the money," Mr. B. continued. "Okay, I was a travelling salesman for the money, but that's something else. These rabbis disgust me. They are homosexuals and atheists."

"How do you know all this?" I asked

"They've slipped off the path," he replied, growing angrier by the minute. During the course of our walk, Mrs. B. had told me her husband had a heart condition. I felt concerned.

"Look where they came from!" he shouted. "They have perverted Judaism!"

He interrupted the course of his invective for another prayer.

The conversation turned to Egypt. I had just enjoyed a weekend visit to Cairo.

"They have no love for the Jews there," muttered Nathan. "And is it dirty!" A murmur of assent swept the table. "They went along with Camp David only so they could get Israeli technological know-how," he added.

Sandor leaped in to change the subject. "Isn't it wonderful how the Torah has influenced all mankind as the embodiment of the Truth?" he professed brightly. "The ideas of body and soul...."

I sallied forth. "The distinction between body and soul was a Greek idea," I announced. "It probably entered Judaism quite late, during the Greek occupation of Palestine."

"*The Greeks!*" Mr. B. looked apoplectic. "They had no true spirituality! The Greeks emphasized the *body*! They *adored* the body, built statues to it! They *worshipped* the physical."

At a loss for words, we buried ourselves in our plates.

Dinner was over and Nathan and Sandor offered to take Deborah and me on a sabbath-eve tour of Mea Shearim. I thanked Mrs. B. for her hospitality, saw the kindness in her eyes, and felt sorry for having upset her husband.

For some unfathomable reason, she seemed to like me. "Would you like to meet the woman next door?" she asked. "She was born here. I could interpret from the Yiddish for you."

I would indeed. She promised to set up the meeting for the following week.

It was dark outside, but the night was clear and starlit. A loud hum vibrated through the air, the sound of generators producing independent electricity. This was necessary, Nathan explained, on the off-chance that some secular Israeli was desecrating the sabbath by manning the electrical station.

We reached the crossroads of Geula and Mea Shearim.

"This is where the guys from the kibbutzim in the north come to desecrate the sabbath," said Nathan. "There's one guy who used to come here on his motorcycle every Friday. He'd just ride around and yell insults at everyone."

The hatred cut both ways. Nathan gritted his teeth and looked ready to punch someone.

Men and boys were returning from synagogue along the narrow streets reminiscent of the lost ghettos of Eastern Europe. The air resounded with voices singing loudly as the followers of this or that rabbi prayed and danced in their yeshivas.

We were looking for a yeshiva with a women's section.

Nathan and Sandor had half reverted to their North American selves—they were walking the streets with women. But we were careful not to brush coat jackets, and when we crossed a group of their fellow students from Ohr Somayach they seemed embarrassed.

There it was—a yeshiva with a section for us. Through a lighted upstairs window, black figures swayed and chanted. A very tall, pencil-thin man looked down, the sharp angles of his body recalling a Picasso line drawing. He saw me below, a woman, watching him. He stopped for a moment, presumably in shock, then he leaned forward, grasped the window curtain in one hand, and partially covered one side of his body. He was angry. Suddenly the curtain was drawn.

We entered a dim stairwell and climbed to the women's section, a darkened upstairs room with narrow, slatted blinds.

I crouched to look. Below, in a brightly lit room, was spread an amazing sight. I was the Little Match Girl peering through a pane of glass at a world of light I was forbidden to enter. I was a traveller in time dropped into a secret universe whose language I did not know and which excluded me today and for eternity.

A T-shaped table covered with a white cloth stretched across the head of the room and down the centre. The old rabbi, or *reb*, sat at the head. Crumb-filled dishes were scattered about him, the remains of his dinner.

Two to three hundred men faced him, paying tribute. They were dressed in black silk coats, black stockings, and fur-trimmed hats, and they all stood on tiered bleachers, swaying and singing at the top of their lungs. I wondered how many hours this had been going on. Some looked ready to fall over from tiredness. Little boys were sleeping on the tables.

After several minutes, the reb stood and moved to an armchair in the corner of the head table. At this signal, the men linked arms and began a snake dance around the room. They bowed forward and backward to each other and to the old rabbi when they passed him. They sang with abandon, their loud, melodious voices rising and falling in waves. For fifteen or twenty minutes they continued with no let-up.

I could have stayed all night, but Nathan signalled from below that it was time to leave. On our way back to Geula he told us a story.

Many, many years ago, Nathan said, the chief rabbi of Mea Shearim had gone out into the street to face a band of wild, shouting Arabs coming on a pogrom. (Nathan made them sound like Red Indians on the warpath, an image he may have been brought up with in the United States.) Well, the reb picked up a gun and went out and took aim. And a miracle happened. He hit the chief Arab between the eyes, and the others ran away.

"The Arabs have always wanted to murder all the Jews," Nathan added darkly.

"You seem interested in politics," I said. "Are you?"

"Sure," he replied. "I'm an ultra-Orthodox, right-wing fanatic." He smiled mockingly. "That's what people think I am and that's what I am."

Sandor tugged at his sleeve. "Shut up," he growled. But Nathan's contempt for "the goyim", "the Arabs", and non-Orthodox Jews knew no bounds.

He planned to stay in Israel, he said, in the full expectation that he represented the future of the Jews.

"Will you stay for lunch?" asked Mrs. B. the following morning. I blurted a quick "No thanks." I felt a strong, almost physical compulsion to escape.

We shook hands and I began to walk as quickly as I could, out of Geula, out of Mea Shearim. My feet picked up speed as I fled. I looked neither left nor right until I reached my own apartment.

Only after a warm bath, a glass of wine, and an evening of Beethoven did I begin to feel myself again.

I awoke exhausted the following morning, disturbed by angry thoughts. For the first time in my life, I had been perceived as essentially contemptible. Only one attribute would have made me a worthwhile human being—to live according to the precepts of the Torah. At the sabbath table in Geula, everything I might have accomplished and every value I held to be worthy was as nothing. Pluralism, independent thinking, equality, compassion that might extend beyond my own group—all were a perversion of immutable Truth. From the viewpoint of Nathan and Mr. B., I was the enemy: an unrepentant, "Greek-corrupted", unnatural female and a travesty of a Jew. Yet the Judaism I had learned to respect as a child had taught that the good life was rooted in an expression of rational morality; that the Jewish spirit depended not on the trappings of ritualized Orthodoxy, but on collective and individual ethics.

We represented two distinct traditions. Theirs preceded the Enlightenment and rejected the rationalism and modernization that had come in its wake, while mine stemmed directly from that radical shift in Jewish history.

In the midst of my reveries, the telephone rang. It was Mrs. B. calling to say that she had arranged a visit with her neighbour, Mrs. Meirovitch, for the very next day.

I accepted, but not without trepidation. I went to the sink and ran a glass of very cold water. The thought of returning to Geula so soon had suddenly dried out my mouth.

CHAPTER FOURTEEN

Mrs. Meirovitch and Mrs. Neiman

At the intersection of Malechai Israel and Rehov Amos in Geula was Gerolitz's bakery and coffee shop, of city-wide renown. Black-frocked men with side curls and imposing beards lined up beside squarish housewives and students on their way home from school. They pushed energetically towards the counter with a proximity that their rabbis would surely have frowned upon.

Behind the little counter, Mrs. Gerolitz dispensed poppy-seed cakes, fresh breads, cheesecake, and, since the festival of Purim was approaching, those three-sided, prune-stuffed delicacies shaped to resemble Haman's hat. Haman was a wicked, wicked man, I sang lustily in my Toronto Sunday School. He would have murdered all the Jews in Persia in the fifth century B.C., had it not been for the interference of Queen Esther, King Ahasuerus's Jewish wife.

In the coffee shop behind the bakery, the visitor was welcome to munch on one of Haman's hats and nurse a cup of coffee all afternoon. On the window ledge sat collection boxes begging contributions for various yeshivas in the neighbourhood, and stacked beside the boxes were piles of Hebrew prayerbooks for the edification of those patrons who might be feeling the need to plug in before continuing on their way. Enjoying Gerolitz's poppyseed cake was no excuse for neglecting the religious life.

A young man and an older one sat opposite me, discussing a text that lay open before them. They spoke together in Yiddish. In my Canadian experience, Yiddish was an anachronism. It was the language of my immigrant grandparents, a generation that never fully integrated into the strange ways of Anglo-Saxon Canada. It was the language their children refused to speak as they strived to become Canadians. It was a language I and many in my generation did not know at all, except for a few pithy words that had passed into English and were being adopted by people who had no idea they were speaking Yiddish.

But in Geula, as in neighbouring Mea Shearim, living one's life in Yiddish was a political imperative. Hebrew was the language of the Torah and it was a sacrilege to profane it on the street. Secular Hebrew was something those Godless Zionists had brought into being—along with their so-called state, which was also a sacrilege. The Messiah had not yet come, and therefore the Jews must wait, not go about proclaiming a secular state and acting as though they were Gentiles.

I walked back up the narrow ghetto street of Rehov Amos to the little courtyard where Mr. and Mrs. B. shared row housing with their Yiddish-speaking neighbours. Mrs. Meirovitch was waiting for me in her miniature house, surrounded by a few of her ten children. Her friend, Mrs. Neiman, was also waiting. So was Mrs. B.

We shook hands. The women assessed me with reserved, appraising glances.

Ein Yiddische meidele? Mrs. Neiman inquired of Mrs. B. I understood the question. It was the usual one in Israel: "Is she Jewish?"

Mrs. B. nodded vigorously. "Oh yes. She's not religious, but she spent a week at Neve Yerushalayim and she came to our house for *shabbat*."

"Did you learn much about religious life at the yeshiva?" pursued Mrs. Neiman in Yiddish. Mrs. B. translated.

"I found my week there most interesting," I replied.

We moved from the tiny corridor into the dining room, which was the only sitting area available in the house. The table occupied most of the space in the room. It needed to seat twelve people on a regular basis, and more if there were invited guests. A child's drawing of the sabbath table was taped to one wall, as were two diplomas pertaining to Rabbi Meirovitch's yeshiva studies.

Mrs. Meirovitch was an intelligent woman with a loud, laughing voice and a strong, peasant body—luckily for her, since constant childbearing was her fate. She was thirty-four years old and by the time she reached menopause she might have produced seventeen or eighteen children. This would be a cause for rejoicing. The lady on the next street had twenty. *Kein ein hara*, they said—against the evil eye—every time the subject of children was raised.

I knew how many children Mrs. Meirovitch had because Mrs. B. had told me, but Mrs. Neiman refused to say. With the evil eye, one simply did not take chances. Mrs. Neiman was in her late thirties. She too was humorous, opinionated, and shrewd.

Mrs. Meirovitch had been born in Romania of poverty-stricken Holocaust survivors who emigrated to Israel in 1956. In line with the immigrant absorption policy of the time, the family had been placed in a development area. But their adaptation was so inadequate that their daughter was removed from them and placed in an "orphanage"—a girls' school for underprivileged children funded from the United States.

Most of the children in this school were Sephardic Jews from Islamic countries, but the school was run along Ashkenazic lines, with what Mrs. Meirovitch called "Ashkenazic values", including the use of Yiddish. There she studied a regular curriculum of subjects including world history, mathematics, and science. But no Hebrew: these were ultra-Orthodox children and everyday Hebrew was taboo.

Not too many years ago—around 1980, she said—a separate school was built for the Sephardic students. Until then, these poor girls had had no one to marry. They had been raised in an Ashkenazic school, in an Ashkenazic culture, and Yiddish was their language, but the Ashkenazic boys wouldn't lower themselves to marry them. "An Ashkenazic would only marry a Sephardic girl if he was handicapped or crippled and couldn't do any better," explained Mrs. Meirovitch. This crude class structure seemed perfectly normal to Mrs. Meirovitch and Mrs. Neiman, who were both of Ashkenazic background.

The children of Geula all went to school in the neighbourhood; in fact, they almost never left the neighbourhood. They learned some "outside" history, some geography, some mathematics, and some science, although a few parents pulled their children out of class so they wouldn't learn the history of other peoples and countries. Girls were taught cooking and sewing, and something called "the natural wonders of the world"—which may have had to do with anatomy, judging by the blushes this admission entailed.

Most girls attended school until grade twelve, but a neighbour just down the road had recently taken her daughter out of school after eighth grade so she could learn housekeeping full time.

English was *definitely* not taught. The rabbis had forbidden it during the British Mandate.

"But the British left forty years ago," I ventured mildly.

"The rabbis haven't changed their minds," Mrs. B. informed me.

The Haredim craved isolation, and they had achieved it. They used a language that was no longer spoken anywhere in the world beyond their few streets, except by the elderly. In this way they "protected" their children.

Why bother with languages? The children of Geula would stay in Geula. Oh, they might cross the street to Mea Shearim or live in B'nai Brak or Safad, the two other strongholds of ultra-Orthodoxy in Israel. But the boys would continue to study Torah, everyone hoped, and the girls would have babies and keep house. So who needed languages?

"Hebrew isn't kosher," Mrs. Meirovitch stated forcefully. "Ben-Yehuda, that man who made it into a so-called modern language, he actually wrote it out on the sabbath!" Mrs. Meirovitch and Mrs. Neiman clucked and wagged their heads with outrage at a probably apocryphal story that had survived the passage of forty years.

"My husband never says *Shalom* to anyone, because you cannot use that word if either of you has dirty hands or is not wearing a hat. Shalom is one of the thirteen names of God. And the Israelis use it all the time!" Mrs. Meirovitch shuddered visibly.

"What about the Israelis? Don't they have a right to be here?"

They looked at me aghast. "Of course! Israel is the place for all the Jews. We were promised that in the Torah. But the State of Israel, that's something else." Mrs. Meirovitch inhaled deeply. "Even the Zionists say the government is no good," she continued. "They're morally bankrupt. They're all goyim."

Then she spat out an ancient Yiddish curse: "They should all be deep in the ground."

Mrs. Neiman wanted to soften her friend's words. "That's not right to say. All Jews can repent and come back to the Torah. They're not goyim, they're Jewish."

"If they don't keep the sabbath, they're goyim," retorted her friend. "There are lots of Jews who don't know anything about being Jews and I feel sorry for them, but those who do know and still don't do anything, they're the worst. Some Jews don't even believe in God. They were religious in Europe, but now they're goyim. Once they became free thinkers, they became angry at people who are still religious. They're the worst."

"I always tell my children that even Jews who are free thinkers can come back. No Jew is a goy," countered Mrs. Neiman.

"My husband was a real anti-Semite before he repented," chimed in Mrs. B. "When he was young, he even went out with a German girl."

A young woman from the ultra-Orthodox community had only one profession open to her, that of teacher. She could not leave the ghetto to work in an office because that would bring her into contact with men and worldly ways. "Anyone who worked would get a bad reputation and then she wouldn't be able to make a good match," Mrs. Neiman explained while nodding wisely. But there were only so many teachers needed in Geula and Mea Shearim.

The answer was sewing. Every woman made all her children's clothing, and some sewed for others as well.

Money was a problem for most people. Mrs. Meirovitch's husband, Rabbi Meirovitch, was an important assistant to the chief Hasidic rabbi in B'nai Brak and was paid a salary, as were all married yeshiva students. The money (most of which was raised abroad) was channelled through the Israeli government. This was becoming a point of growing contention for Conservative and Reform Jews in the Diaspora who had begun to object to seeing their money go to people who did not accept the political State of Israel, refused to speak its language, and more often than not claimed that the Diaspora donors were not authentic Jews.

There was also a government family allowance (which could amount to an important sum with ten children in a family), and grumbling about the Godless political state did not prevent the ultra-Orthodox from accepting this support.

Weddings (and the circumcisions which followed) were the major social events of Geula and Mea Shearim, and there were usually several a week. Mrs. Meirovitch bought presents in bulk. Yesterday she had picked up half a dozen cut-glass candy dishes at less than two shekels each.

Daughters were "married off" at seventeen and boys at nineteen. "Our children never say no," beamed Mrs. Meirovitch.

"They've been prepared for this all their lives. They don't know anything different because they never go out of the district. We have no radios and no television and we don't read the newspaper."

Mrs. Neiman nodded her agreement. "We train the children to do only good things," she said.

"I don't read the newspaper because it's full of dirt," interjected Mrs. Meirovitch. "I just heard about the trial of that Ukrainian guy [John Demjanjuk] and they said it's been on for weeks. I don't want to know the news because I get so frightened. After what happened to the Jews in Europe, and then all those Arabs around us. I don't need to know. Anyway, there's always dirt, gossip and slander. On the radio they have immoral songs and programs. People steal and they talk about it. I don't want my children to learn all that. They might start to use dirty language!"

Mrs. Meirovitch did not want to show me her house, but Mrs. Neiman and Mrs. B. prevailed upon her. So I was shown the tiny room opposite the dining room where six of the children slept. There were beds that slid under beds and folding beds that stood in corners. Each child had one small shelf in the cupboard for his or her clothing and every article was marked with a child's name in indelible ink.

"When I'm in hospital giving birth, this helps my husband know what's what," she explained.

Three more children slept in the dining room; the baby slept with her parents.

There were no toys in sight.

The kitchen was barely turn-around size. Meals for twelve were cooked daily on a little burner set on top of a low cupboard. A doll-sized oven had been placed behind a curtain in the corridor. The bathroom was a tiny space containing a toilet and a tub.

The family was splitting the house at its seams, but they needed to find another place within the same district. Rabbi

Meirovitch wouldn't even *think* about moving to the ultra-Orthodox enclave of B'nai Brak where he worked. It was too "modern", he told his wife. The children might be corrupted there.

But the rabbi was a thoughtful man: twice a year he sent his wife on a holiday to Tiberias. "He says a woman with so many children to look after is like a machine that needs to be oiled," she told me proudly. Mrs. Neiman's husband did not send her on holidays. She looked at the floor disconsolately.

"Mrs. Meirovitch has a wonderful husband," whispered Mrs. B. as we took our leave. "I know I can count on him to help, even though he won't look at me in the street because I'm a woman."

We said goodbye. We had somehow liked each other, across an abyss of centuries. These few narrow streets were the only place on the earth's surface where they could feel completely secure. These were the remnant ghetto paths of a destroyed Eastern European world I never knew. Mrs. Meirovitch and Mrs. Neiman were, I imagined, time-warp recreations of my grandmother as a young woman, of her life and the life of her parents and grandparents for a thousand years into a misty Jewish past. Their earthy arguing, their chauvinism, their pithy wit, their pre-liberal prejudices, their salt-of-the-earth female strength—all of this felt familiar to me, more familiar, in fact, than the new Israelis who now populated the land.

I caught myself short. I was being absurdly sentimental. When Mrs. Meirovitch and Mrs. Neiman "found out" the kind of person I *really* was, they would doubtless relegate me to the ranks of the "enemy". If and when their husbands assumed political as well as religious power, they would deny women like me the right to live as they chose. They would happily transform Israel into a theocracy along the lines of fundamentalist Iran.

Had I been their daughter, Mrs. Meirovitch and Mrs. Neiman would have denied me the right to a Western-style education, just as their own lives had been narrowly circumscribed by their families. This was inadmissible to me, just as my beliefs were inadmissible to them. And yet, on a personal level, we had liked each other.

Back at Gerolitz's bakery, I could not resist temptation. I approached the counter and for the first time in my life I spoke in Yiddish. *"Tzvei beigelech, bitte"*—two bagels, please—was as far as I could go. A small payos-ringed boy behind me giggled, but it didn't matter.

Clutching my bag of bagels, I smiled at the bewigged and befrocked customers lined up behind me. For a fleeting moment I had spoken my grandmother's language.

CHAPTER FIFTEEN

Memory

My daughter, Michelle, is arriving in Israel today to work for a few months as a volunteer on a kibbutz. She will be confronted with the same questions.

"Are you Jewish?"

"Will you move to Israel?"

My children are even further removed from Judaism than I am. Their father, from whom I am divorced, was born in France and is a lapsed Catholic. Their stepfather was born in England and is an atheist by conviction. Their Jewish grandparents were born in Canada and, like many of their generation, chose to abandon the formal structures of religion.

My children recall little of their immigrant great-grandmother with her broken English and her Yiddish accent, except that she always kept candies on her table.

Am I the last to remember?

I hailed a taxi to take me to the airport. En route, we passed the house of Menachem Begin.

"You know Begin?" asked my driver in French, our common language.

"Of course."

"He's very depressed now. Never comes out. Too bad. He's the first prime minister I liked."

"So you like the Likud party?"

"Sure. They love Israel. The others—they do not love Israel. They're traitors. Labour wants to give Israel to the Arabs, but Likud wants to keep it for the Jews. Labour makes me sick. They do *protectia* for their friends, that's the way it is here. If you're Oriental and you don't have connections, you don't get anywhere."

My driver was Sephardic, and he had come to Israel as a child from a remote mountain village in Morocco. It was hardly surprising that he felt alienated from the European elite in the Labour party who had controlled the political life of Israel for the first three decades of the country's existence. With the election of Menachem Begin in 1977, he had felt enfranchised for the first time.

Although he was only a child when he came to Israel, his father had told him over and over again about life in the Old Country, especially about the powerful rabbis. One of them could kill *anyone*, just by willing it, and he could cure people or make them sick in the same way.

He glanced at me, testing credulity, perhaps.

"One day the rabbi went to the King of Morocco and he said, 'If you hurt the Jewish people you will suffer greatly.' The king heard him in his sleep, like in a dream. When the king had this dream three times he became frightened and changed his actions towards the Jews."

"Hmmm," I said.

"I don't really know if it's true or not, but it sounds true," he insisted. "My father told me."

We drove in silence for a few minutes. "You on a tour?" he asked suddenly, turning to stare at me.

"Visiting friends," I said.

"You Jewish?"

"Yes."

He paused a moment. "There should be only Jews in Israel," he suddenly exclaimed. "Those Arabs cause trouble. They work for ten or twenty shekels a day without any benefits or anything, when Jews demand fifty. So people won't hire the Jews. There's a lot of unemployment because of those Arabs. I'd give them anything, just so they'd go away. To Jordan, to Egypt, to Syria, anywhere they like."

My driver loved his car, his only possession, and there was only one man in the entire city of Jerusalem who knew how to fix it properly. This man lived in the eastern sector of the city, and he was an Arab. My driver had been surprised and delighted to learn they both came from Morocco and had lived not too far from one another. He would be lost without this man, he said.

"But he's an Arab and you want to kick him out," I protested.

"Not him!"

He swivelled around in his seat and shook his head at me as though I had said something crazy.

After a brief rest, my daughter and I set out for Tel Aviv, the population centre of Israel and the locus for the raging discontents of the nation. Tel Aviv: city of decadence and sin. Tel Aviv: where *real* Zionists wouldn't dream of settling. Tel Aviv: cosmopolitan metropolis of the Middle East.

Compared to the small-town quietude of Jerusalem, Tel Aviv does have the feel of a big city in a hybrid mix of Europe and the Middle East. The central artery of Allenby Street (named after Lord Allenby, the British commander-in-chief who captured Palestine from the Turks in 1917–18) was dusty and congested. Street vendors hawked a myriad of newspapers, falafels, and transistor radios in loud, demanding voices. Retail stores displayed over-priced, lumpy-looking wares.

There were plenty of cafés, but nothing in Tel Aviv recalled the aesthetics or style of a European capital. Dizengoff Street, famed abroad for its street life, was an inauspicious avenue lined with fast-food restaurants and a higgledy-piggledy jumble of retail businesses. The renowned fountain at Dizengoff Circle operated only on holidays.

Our lunch on "The Street" was an overpriced "Hungarian" blintz that came swimming in grease and registered eight on the indigestion scale.

Tel Aviv was an unzoned urban sprawl pretending to be a city; but a visit to the Museum of the Diaspora made the trip there truly worth while. My guide book described it as "one of the most sophisticated historical museums in the world". And it was.

The Museum of the Diaspora reconstructed Jewish life throughout the millennia, using the latest in audio-visual technology. A film in a wrap-around, planetarium-style theatre stunningly portrayed the movements of Diaspora communities from the first expulsion to Babylon, in 587 B.C., to the creation of a new centre of Diaspora Jewry in the United States following the Holocaust. More than six million Jews currently lived in the United States, almost twice as many as in Israel itself.

There were mock-ups of famous Diaspora synagogues, including the famous El Transito of medieval Spain. A synagogue in China looked like a pagoda, a synagogue in the Arab world looked like a mosque. (In my own country, Reform temples looked like Protestant churches.) Short films portrayed the destroyed world of the East European village, the world of Greek Jewry, the world of the Moroccan Jews, and the world of the yeshiva student. A famous Hebrew hymn was sung in its many Diaspora renditions, each reflecting the musical tonality and phrasing of the local culture.

In this museum, the suffering of the Jewish people was treated as part of an organic whole, as part of a totality of Jewish history in which tragedy was only one element.

Finally, there was the fulfilment of the ancient dream: the establishment of the State of Israel.

A child of the Diaspora, I had never before perceived Jewish history as primary, or mainstream. It was something I suffered through in Sunday School, a jumble of names and dates that were boringly commemorated at various times of the year. *Real* history was what I studied in real school. We learned British history (when I was a child Canadian history was not emphasized in Canada, but that is another story) and world history—which ignored the experience of Jews, who lived parallel to the mainstream for almost two thousand years, until the eighteenth century when they were accepted as citizens in some Western European countries. Jewish history broke through the visibility barrier mainly at moments of persecution: the Spanish Inquisition, the czarist pogrom, the Nazi Holocaust.

The message of this museum (and it was not a subtle message) was that the Jews had survived, miraculously and against all odds, during two thousand years of dispersal. They had survived with their book, which could be transported from one place on the earth's surface to another whenever it was suddenly necessary to move; and they had survived with memory.

Everyone "remembered" in Israel. And it wasn't always helpful. Many of the old Zionists at Yiftah "remembered" and were apparently unable to accommodate themselves to change. Their children "remembered" when bar mitzvah ceremonies were conducted at a martyrs' monument, mixing potent images of religion and nationalism. At Neve Yerushalayim and in Mea Shearim and Geula they "remembered" an ancient past, but they had fashioned it into a weapon with which to displace the present. The religious-nationalist settlers in the occupied West Bank also "remembered". The soil on which they built their homes was for them not disputed territory where others lived, but *The Land*, God's promissory note to the Jews that they, the settlers, were calling due.

Memory had shaped the collective thinking of Israelis, for their country was born out of the disaster of the Holocaust, during which somewhere between five million and six million European Jews were murdered by the Nazis in an incomparable, systematic slaughter. During the early years of the state, close to half the population were survivors of those dark days. They arrived and found themselves immediately caught up in the battle to secure their new nation, first against the British, then against the Arabs.

One of the first pieces of legislation passed by the fledgeling State of Israel in 1953 was the Law of Remembrance, which brought into being the Holocaust memorial museum, Yad Vashem, and instituted an annual day for remembrance of the dead.

"We began as a society of survivors and we still are," said Dr. Yitzhak Arad, the director of Yad Vashem. "The Holocaust has had a major impact on the way we think."

Dr. Arad was born in Poland in 1926 and spent the war years fighting with an underground resistance unit in the forests. He reached Palestine in 1945 and immediately joined the Haganah. For the next twenty-seven years, the military was his career.

"I had pushed away the Holocaust," he told me in his office at Yad Vashem. "Even when I went to university, it was to study general history and political science, never the history that had affected my own life."

But as the years passed, stifled memories pressed to the surface of his consciousness. He began to do research on the Holocaust, then to lecture occasionally, then to teach, until he realized, one day, that his need to understand and to communicate both the history and his own experience had quite literally taken over his life. In 1972, "after years of pushing it away, I made a switch over," he said simply. "I feel an overwhelming obligation to the people who did not have the luck to survive. It is for them that we continue to build Yad Vashem, to tell the future generations about them."

As "a society of survivors", Israelis live with a deeply entrenched siege mentality. All of Jewish history has combined to produce this psychology, including the events of the post-Holocaust decades.

"Before the 1967 war began, we felt abandoned by the world," said Dr. Arad. "We could see on our television screens the wild mobs in Cairo calling for our death. The feeling of loneliness was very strong, that we were isolated and the world was against our society and we did not have friends. This helped the younger people to understand the feeling of the Holocaust, how the Jews were abandoned by the world to enemies who wanted to exterminate them. The same feeling recurred at the Yom Kippur War. So in Israel we understood from the beginning that we must be able to defend ourselves since we know we cannot count on anyone else. Somewhere deep within us, either conscious or unconscious, is the conviction that we must be strong enough to face another Holocaust if it comes.

"One reaction to the Holocaust is hardness and military strength. Another reaction is humanistic, that we must struggle for a world that is free from hatred and racism since both these things set the scene for disaster. Personally, I think we have to stress both sides. In a world of hatred where power is the main factor, I cannot see how the small nations will survive, so all people must learn to think and act more humanely; but in spite of this, Jews must never be at the mercy of other people or other nations again."

He looked earnest and slightly frazzled, a small, harried man with a worried face and a saving belief in human reason. How else could he make sense of his own life, or his role at Yad Vashem, for that matter? Yad Vashem was a school to educate posterity, to keep a collective memory alive in the best and most constructive manner. Without an abiding faith that future generations could be helped to foresee and avert disaster, the *raison d'être* behind this museum would dissolve.

Running the museum was a huge job. Yad Vashem received up to a million visitors a year. It was also the clearing centre for Holocaust documents, and researchers from all over the world arrived at Arad's doorstep to pore over the museum archives. Politicians and heads of state came on official pilgrimages to honour the dead from whose ashes this new nation of survivors had arisen.

Several days earlier I had talked about the importance of the post-Holocaust siege mentality with the respected Israeli pollster Hanoch Smith.

"Both generations in Israel believe that the Western powers did nothing to save the Jews during the war," he told me. "This is a powerful indictment and it has a strong influence on the way Israelis act and think. The underlying feeling in Israel is that the Arab nations are waiting for the opportunity to wipe Israel out. Therefore Israel must be strong and essentially not trust anyone," he continued, echoing Dr. Arad. "Underpinning this is the ingrained belief that both Christianity and Islam contain the seeds of anti-Semitism and that danger can come from both religions. There is an easing up about Christianity nowadays since the majority of people know that the Christian world is not presently dangerous to the Jew; but most older people continue to feel it is dangerous anyhow.

"The point is that people here *start* with the belief system and it colours what they see. That's what I mean by a siege mentality."

This winter the Holocaust was news again. The trial of John Demjanjuk blared out of radios all over Jerusalem. On city buses the ritual of loud Israeli music punctuated by the hourly news was interrupted. Riders listened in silence to the flat, nasal voice of Demjanjuk's American lawyer, followed by the guttural sounds of a Hebrew translation. The same voices resounded through the pastry shop on Jaffa Street where I stopped to buy a snack, and from the radio of the taxi I hailed to get to my next interview.

Jerusalemites were going about their business as usual—but in uncharacteristic silence, preoccupied by the events in the courtroom.

The radio carried tales of horror recounted in the tremulous voices of elderly people recalling events they were unable to banish from their dreams. The horror filled the strangely quiet spaces of the city. People shook their fists at the voice of the defence lawyer, who capped each question with the word "please", a nicety that seemed to irritate the direct, no-nonsense social conventions of the citizenry. They suspected hypocrisy.

This was the first war crimes trial in Israel in twenty-five years—since Adolf Eichmann sat enclosed in a glass booth and writer Hannah Arendt coined the phrase "the banality of evil" in his honour. Someone known as Ivan the Terrible worked at the Treblinka death camp during 1943 and 1944. This person stationed himself at the entrance to the gas chambers carrying a sword, a whip, an iron bar, or a bayonet. When a group of naked Jews arrived, he stabbed them and tore pieces of flesh off their bodies as he forced them into the chambers. Then he walked to the engine room and turned on the gas.

This Ivan the Terrible selected elderly religious men for special attention. He led them naked to a barbed wire fence and pushed their heads between the wires. Then he whipped them until the victims, writhing in pain, had strangled themselves.

Ivan the Terrible liked to cut off the ears and noses of people just for fun, and to beat them over the head until they died. Once he punished a group of prisoners who had tried to escape by shattering every one of their bones with a iron bar, leaving them to expire in agony.

Ivan the Terrible belonged to that class of brutalized men who emerge—Mr. Hyde–like—at predictable moments in history. Racism and hate propaganda create an environment that unleashes previously repressed violence in vulnerable people. If the price of a tolerant society is care and vigilance, men like Ivan the Terrible are the legacy of falling down on the job.

And so forty years after the event, John Demjanjuk—a bald-pated, bespectacled, cherub-faced, jolly-looking gent who had lived peacefully in the United States until he was extradited to stand trial—raised handcuffed wrists in a show of victory and grinned broadly at photographers as he entered and exited the Jerusalem courtroom. He was not the man they sought, he claimed. This was a case of mistaken identity.

A serious error, if true, and one that disturbed many people. They feared that if Israel had to dismiss the charges, the Holocaust-deniers would claim a victory. Others disagreed, claiming that even more honour would accrue to Israel's highly respected judiciary should it concede on the basis of a fair inquiry that a mistake had indeed been made. "[To acquit Demjanjuk] would be the most outstanding expression of Zion being redeemed through justice," wrote Shevach Weiss, a Labour Knesset member.

But doubts lingered. Should Israel try war criminals rather than leave the job to the countries where they had perpetrated their deeds? Would this trial seriously exacerbate tensions between Jews and Ukrainians, two groups that have kept a gingerly distance from each other based on an unfortunate past proximity in the Ukraine? And finally, should Jews forget what had happened, now that almost half a century had passed?

"I can't believe what I'm hearing," groaned a taxi driver, aged twenty-three. "At the beginning I didn't care. I mean, we have Memorial Day once an year, but I never really knew what it meant. But now.... And to think I'm driving a German car!" He touched the steering wheel with horror.

I entered a little bookstore. Voices from the trial filled the shop.

"I thought all Israelis would know everything about the Holocaust," I said to the young man behind the desk.

"We do, but this is giving us details we didn't know," he replied. "Schools are tape-recording the proceedings to teach it to their students...." He was breathless with the magnitude of the events being described on the radio. We listened to a full, throaty voice testifying in Yiddish.

"That man came all the way from Uruguay to be a witness. He has a good lawyer, that Demjanjuk, but I'll tell you, the chief judge, he's really someone. He's helpful to both sides and he's fair. I think Israelis are very proud."

He smiled appreciatively, and I remembered how fair Hannah Arendt had found the judge in the Eichmann trial. While the prosecutor had attempted to turn the trial into a sensational "trial of Nazism", the judge had quietly insisted that the individual in the dock was charged with specific crimes that had to be proved according to the rules of evidence. How good it was to feel proud of the Israeli judiciary, when opportunistic politicians not only had failed to deal with endemic political problems, but seemed to have produced a nation of despairing cynics.

Just then, the young man's mother entered the shop. She stopped to listen to the voice from the radio. The witness was describing what the word "Yid" meant in John Demjanjuk's mouth.

"I know what it meant and it wasn't a neutral word," she spat disdainfully. "This is why we are living in Israel. We have to know that outside Israel we are 'Yids' and always will be."

Here was the siege mentality again, and right at the root of Zionism. I remembered Yiftah, heard Yoram's voice lecturing me about my responsibilities.

"They may not have the right man," I ventured.

"I don't even *care* if he is Ivan the Terrible, the important thing is that all the details come out," she said, becoming excited. "I believe in the justice of the Israeli courts, but whatever happens, we're still Israel and everyone is against us. If Demjanjuk is not Ivan the Terrible, they will say, 'Look what Israel did!' If he is the man, what will we do with him? Hang him and bury him in *this* country?"

"It doesn't matter what the Gentiles think," interrupted her son. "This trial is important for my generation of Jews so we can understand better." But his mother had good reason for her bitterness. Her father had been the only member of his well-to-do family to leave Poland for Palestine in the 1920s. There had been four other siblings and they had all thought he was crazy to leave. Every one of them was killed by Hitler.

"I feel the Holocaust in my bones," she said in a near-whisper. "I can't even visit Yad Vashem." She looked out the window to hide the glistening in her eyes.

Her son tightened his lips grimly. We fell silent as the radio report went on.

CHAPTER SIXTEEN

Yad Vashem

I have been dancing around Yad Vashem for days now, avoiding a personal confrontation with the museum.

Michelle is as apprehensive as I am. She is aware that the bits and pieces she has learned about the Holocaust will be woven together into a whole that will remain imprinted upon her mind. As for myself, I have been preoccupied by this catastrophe for much of my life, since I first lived in France in the early 1960s and began to understand the magnitude of what had happened. My reaction then was shock. I obsessively read every account I could lay my hands on, spent hours in a Left Bank cinema watching *Judgement at Nuremberg*, and forced myself to visit a concentration camp in the Vosges mountains.

As the years passed, shock metamorphosed into a desire to understand the historical, social, and psychological conditions that led to such a cataclysm. That event and other wars of hatred had been made possible, it seemed, by propaganda and social conditioning that transformed targeted groups into depersonalized abstractions, and desensitized the community towards them. But the horror the Holocaust held for me had never dissipated, and the thought of visiting Yad Vashem left me uneasy at the prospect of facing it head on.

As we walk towards the museum, along a tree-lined lane, I am seized by a familiar grief. Each tree has been planted in the name of a "righteous Gentile", someone who dared to risk his or her life to protect the hunted Jews of Europe. To date, six thousand people have been named and recognized.

A separate plaque has been dedicated to the entire Danish nation, a tribute from the Jewish people. On display is the very rowboat that was used to ferry Jews from Denmark to the safety of neutral Sweden. It looks like a small, rickety toy.

A French priest is honoured. Although France and the French remain ambivalent over the role their nation played in the fate of the Jews, it is also true that every Jewish survivor in that country owed his or her life to brave individuals who were willing to help. Courageous nuns and priests hid children. And after 1942, the deportations slowed down to a trickle because important Church authorities began to resist.

There is a tribute to courageous individuals in Poland: a land with a long history of medieval-style anti-Semitism, where to help Jews would have been a socially unconventional act. The brave Poles honoured here were consequently all the more remarkable. And another to the righteous Gentiles of Germany itself, where to defy the ruling Nazis was to court personal destruction.

It is comforting to see that although no government on earth was prepared to help the Jews specifically as part of its war effort, it is not true that no one cared. These gardens testify to the indomitability of that human caring, to the fact that there remained a nucleus of strong individuals who were impervious to propaganda and willing to take risks. The Jews who emerged from the flames were a remnant, but so were these defiant men and women—a remnant of civilized humanity at a time when it was easier and safer to steel oneself to the suffering of the Jewish minority.

But Israelis refuse to forget that the political world stood by while Jews were being destroyed, then fabricated lies to suggest they did not know what was happening. So it is no accident that the first item one sees on entering the museum of Yad Vashem is a huge blow-up of U.S. aerial reconnaissance photos of the entire Auschwitz complex taken by the American air force in 1942. The transport train is clearly visible on this blow-up and it has just disgorged its human cargo. They are there, the victims, thin black lines of people lined up for the selection process, where it is being decided at this very moment who will live, for a time, as a camp prisoner and who will die on the spot. The black line forks into two, and one section snakes to the right, towards the gas chamber. There it is—the building is clearly visible.

A tour guide describes the photos to a group of American tourists. When he has finished, an agitated man in his sixties approaches.

"We were fighting the war," he says angrily, "*with* the Allies, *against* the Nazis."

"The United States didn't enter the war to help the Jews," retorts the tour guide. "It knew about Auschwitz and never helped the Jews."

The American protests. The Israeli shrugs. "That's the reality of it," he says with finality.

I recall a conversation I had not too long ago with an acquaintance in Toronto who flew bombers for the RAF during the war. One day they bombed a German POW prison at Amiens. The prisoners had killed a guard and all three hundred of them were going to be destroyed if the Allies didn't get there first. The timing had to be precision-perfect, when the prisoners were out on exercise at the other end of the compound.

The mission was successful.

I asked him whether he had known about the concentration camps.

"We knew and we didn't know," he replied. "Of course we knew they were taking the Jews somewhere...."

"Did you know about the Auschwitz camp?" I insisted.
"More or less," he answered. "It wasn't a priority."

No matter how many times one may have seen individual photos of that brutal time, nothing can be adequate preparation for the sustained shock of Yad Vashem. Facts and pictures are presented with stark restraint. The images are unadorned, the commentary is understated. In this spare simplicity, one encounters the entirety of those years.

The history is familiar to me and so it is the faces of the oppressor and his victim that draw my attention. On these walls, the two will live on together, their brief moment of contact eternalized by an anonymous photographer. The walls of Yad Vashem speak of human cruelty—of degradation, humiliation, and torture—before they speak of death. A smiling Nazi cuts off the beard of a religious Jew. The man's eyes half close in suffering; his mouth half opens in a silent scream. On the walls of Yad Vashem, children lie on the streets of the Warsaw Ghetto too weak to cry.

And yet, amazingly, an irrepressible human spirit lived on. Writers documented what was happening, and hid their work in the cracks and crevices of the ghetto. Scholars continued to study, musicians continued to play, and those children who were able actually sang in a choir.

Here are scenes of Babi Yar, a ravine on the outskirts of Kiev where 33,000 Jews were shot in September 1941. Three young women with terror-filled eyes stand together before a pit. Pathetically, they try to hide their nakedness. Behind them are soldiers, their guns already raised, positioned, aimed. In another picture an entire family of naked women—old mother, adult daughters, a tiny granddaughter, and a small baby—huddle together, gripping each other by the arms.

My grandmother's family almost certainly died at Babi Yar. I never knew them. This family of women holding each other during the final, terrifying moments of their lives may be my immediate family. But for an accident of fate, that child cringing at the brink of the abyss would be me.

But this is Israel, phoenix arisen from the ashes, and Yad Vashem ends on a note of hope. The war is over. Survivors seek Palestine, but are turned back by the British. There is more barbed wire, this time in Cyprus.

Yet the State of Israel does come into being. On the wall of Yad Vashem, it is May 15, 1948. Two men on a hill unfurl the new flag. They are dressed, symbolically, in the striped prisoner's garb of Auschwitz.

There is, however, one final room where the lights are low and where all the known names of Nazi victims are recorded. Library stacks line an entire wall. Sections are organized alphabetically; within each section, files containing names are stored in small cubicles.

I want to find out, finally, what happened to the family I never knew, but I am suddenly afraid to learn, afraid to personalize the horror.

"What would you like to do?" I ask my daughter.

She hesitates. "You know you have to decide for yourself," she says.

Okay, but there is another problem, a practical problem. Neither of my parents has ever told me the first names of those who remained in Europe. I doubt if they even know. I have only surnames—and the cities where they lived.

I approach the man behind the desk.

"I'd like to trace my family, but I don't know their first names," I say, hearing how futile and stupid my request sounds. "My mother's name was Lipkin. They came from Kiev."

He looks at me with sympathy mixed with impatience. "Do you know how many Lipkins the Germans killed in Kiev? Hundreds! I could pull out a list of Lipkins and then what would you do? Huh?"

Two ladies standing beside me shake their heads sadly.

"Thank you," I say. "Goodbye."

A vise tightens in my chest, crushing breath. They are twice lost, my unknown relatives. Murdered some four decades ago, they have slipped into oblivion, not to be mourned by their great-granddaughter and great-great-granddaughter who stand here in Jerusalem wanting to weep for them.

I shall weep regardless. I shall adopt the wide-eyed, terror-stricken family of women on the wall in the next room, I shall rock them in my arms and sing softly to them from across the decades. I shall remember them.

Outside the building stretches a broad terrace, and on its outer edge rises a large, bronze sculpture by the Yugoslavian artist Nandor Glid. Stylized human figures are caught on stylized barbed wire. They hang there, sideways, upside down, in various attitudes of agony.

But beyond the sculpture rise the hills of Jerusalem. They are densely populated and their rooftops glint in the optimistic light of the sun.

Life and renewal. Pogrom and Holocaust exorcized. The New Jerusalem.

This, of course, is the ultimate message of Yad Vashem, of Zionism, and of Israel itself.

CHAPTER SEVENTEEN

Menachem

Was it possible to recover from the trauma? The survivors either made it or they didn't. There were plenty of stories of people who took their lives years after the event; of people who never spoke of the horror to their mates, or to children born years later; of people unable to expiate the guilt of having survived when others did not; of people like Dr. Arad who "didn't think about it" for a lifetime, but were eventually compelled to do so by a sort of psychic imperative.

Could I recover? My own grief seemed utterly trivial by contrast. I had lived happily and safely in Canada, had never even heard an anti-Semitic word until the age of twenty-three. Then a deepening knowledge of the Holocaust had devastated me. That knowledge did not convince me that anti-Semites lurked behind every tree, nor did it move me to emigrate to Israel. Instead, it infected me with a horror that lived quietly just under the skin, like a tick embedded in flesh.

What might recovery consist of?

If anything symbolized the post-Holocaust regeneration of the Jews in Israel, it was not rhetoric or ideology, but the technological "miracle" of development. The Negev desert, for example, occupied more than 60 per cent of Israel's land territory. In 1945 the British studied the Arava Valley, where the Negev meets Jordan, and concluded that the land was uninhabitable.

But "uninhabitable" meant nothing to Israel's first prime minister, David Ben-Gurion. He had a far-reaching vision: to populate and develop this desert; and in just one generation it was done. Tomatoes, eggplant, melons, peanuts, strawberries, cucumbers, dates, and peppers grow from green strips that snake along the surface of sand dunes. In 1948 the Negev population was under eighteen thousand; by the mid-1980s, it had surpassed half a million. There are now eleven cities (albeit tiny) and more than two hundred rural settlements.

Ben-Gurion had the dream, but others had to carry it out. The man in charge of the greening of the Negev was still alive and working, I was told. He lived in Beersheva. And he was a survivor of the Holocaust.

The bus took the long road south—the road that did *not* pass through the city of Hebron in the Occupied Territories. No one wanted to travel that route any more, what with daily stories of stonings and the occasional booby-trapped package on the baggage rack.

At a roadside stop, a dozen young soldiers got on, both boys and girls. At home in Canada, these children would be sprawled in a high-school cafeteria, stuffing themselves with chocolate bars and chips with gravy. Here the same pimply-faced adolescents formed a homogeneous youth culture of khaki and guns. At eighteen, they left their families to attend "school"— basic army training—which was seen as the central unifier and educator of Israeli society.

They joked and giggled while their guns clacked together and sometimes jabbed other passengers in the arm or back. No one but me seemed to notice.

Beersheva lies at the northern edge of the Negev. It is an ancient city with its origins at the beginning of history. Abraham and Isaac lived here, and the Book of Joshua relates that Beersheva was incorporated into the lands of the tribe of Judah.

Four thousand years later, Beersheva combines the old and the new. At the bank I saw an old Bedouin woman dressed in traditional costume: a crushed black velvet shawl over her head and shoulders and a long black dress embroidered with yellow flowers. A white cotton veil rose from her throat to just under her nose and a tattoo had been needled into the middle of her forehead. Her concerns, however, seemed entirely modern. Her bank statements swished furiously through the air as she argued loudly with a male teller.

The same juxtaposition of old and new was visible across the road, at the weekly Bedouin market. Camels twitched their nostrils at the sky while their owners, in long caftans, baked pita bread on very modern, portable gas burners.

I hurried to the car rental office. The man I had come to see was waiting.

He was large and comfortable-looking and his broad face had creased into a permanent smile. His office was functional and bare, in typical Israeli style, except for the maps of Beersheva and the engineering plans for Negev development projects that hung on the walls.

Menachem Perlmutter had two related jobs. He was responsible for the engineering infrastructure of all the rural settlements of the Negev as well as being district engineer for the entirety of rural agricultural development. What that meant was that in an extraordinarily hostile environment, he was the person responsible for bringing water to the desert population. It was he who planned and supervised the application of drip irrigation to the many fragile plants that now grew where, for thousands of years, only desert winds had blown. Recently, geothermal water had been discovered about a mile below the Arava Valley floor. The water was hot—about 120°F (49°C)—and salty, but Menachem and his colleagues were learning to cool it and use it for indirect irrigation. Only one inch of natural rain fell annually in the Arava Valley. All the rest was engineering.

Drip irrigation had increased agricultural productivity in Israel by 400 per cent in two decades. Record yields in cotton outdistanced those of California, Arizona, and Egypt. Peanut yields were three to four times higher than in American states like Georgia and West Virginia. New varieties of fruit and vegetables were constantly being developed, including a tomato with a shelf life of four weeks.

Israel had been able to coax enough food from the barren lands to supply its own population with 94 per cent of its needs. Some 46 per cent of agricultural production was exported: the highest rate anywhere. Without exaggeration, Israel's scientific ingenuity had amazed the entire world, including experts at the United Nations who had forecast that a country so poor in land and water would need a generation merely to double its food production.

"The world has heard too much about the military side of Israel and not enough about our peaceful accomplishments," said Menachem. "Fifty-two countries in the Third World now benefit from our growing knowledge about the desert and irrigation, and we have no diplomatic relations with many of them. We are working in quieter ways to develop local agriculture and food production which will help end famines on many continents.

"Not a long time ago I met a delegation that was here from Zambia, Kenya, Sri Lanka, and other places with food problems, and the leader said to me, 'You have to understand that hunger in the Third World is a greater threat to peace than the bomb.' But we have demonstrated how to transform the wasteland into fruitful areas that can produce food. I feel so deeply that in the Negev the spirit, the scientific talent, and the dedication of the Jewish people have been translated into a miraculous achievement."

Menachem seemed to like words like "miracle", "a light unto the nations", and other religious metaphors for the "redemption" (regeneration) of Israel.

In 1952, the year Menachem Perlmutter arrived in the Negev, there were only seven thousand people living in and around Beersheva, most of them Bedouin. David Ben-Gurion had not yet moved to his desert kibbutz, Sede Boqer. The region endured in its historical empty, arid state.

Much of what had been accomplished since 1952 was due to Menachem's efforts, though he modestly denied such a role. The joy he expressed as he spoke of his work seemed to transform his shabby office room.

"I know what it is to feel hunger," he said quietly. "I have a number on my left arm. I am like someone who survived the flames of a furnace. Sometimes I think I was like the dry bones the prophet Ezekiel spoke of. But then I also think that Israel was made for people like me. We have been reinjected with life through what we have done here, by building a new country and by rebuilding the family. I came here alone as a stranger after fifty-one of the fifty-three members of my family were destroyed, and last Passover I had around my table twenty-six people to whom I am related.

"The greatest thing about Israel is that people like me, destroyed people, we were able to rebuild the family and become useful members of society. So I always think it is my greatest personal achievement to have created a family—and such an honour and a privilege to be able to live a normal life."

He meant it about the honour and the privilege. His blue eyes quite shone with happiness. To build something substantial from the "uninhabitable" wasteland of the Negev was no different from rebuilding body and soul from the ashes of Auschwitz. He didn't distinguish between the two.

Menachem Perlmutter was born in 1928 in the city of Košice, in eastern Slovakia. Slovakia was a poor, barely industrialized province of Czechoslovakia, and most of its 135,000 Jews were small-scale artisans and retailers eking out a subsistence living. Menachem's father, by contrast, was an accountant, a professional man. The family's middle-class status was something Menachem understood even as a child because he and his brother had bicycles, which were considered amazing possessions.

Slovakia had a nationalist movement and a pro-German leadership that were both sympathetic to the Third Reich. Menachem's father, like many of the elite, also loved Germany, but for quite different reasons. He had served as an officer in an Austrian brigade of the Austro-Hungarian Empire; and like many such people, he believed in the superiority of German language and culture. The elite spoke German and read Goethe, Heine, and Schiller. No one with any pretensions to education would deny the centrality of German—and the elder Perlmutter definitely had such pretensions.

The first decade of Menachem's life was a happy and privileged time, but tinged with such ironies. The Slovakian pro-Nazis and the *nostalgiques* of German culture (including the Jews) lived side by side, each wrapped in admiration for different aspects of the *Vaterland*.

On March 14, 1939, when Menachem was ten years old, the Slovakian provincial legislature in Bratislava took Hitler's advice and seceded from Czechoslovakia to become a satellite of Nazi Germany, thus preparing the way for Hitler's invasion of the rest of the country the following day. By June of 1939, all Slovakian Jews had been placed under German jurisdiction, including a series of decrees restricting their professions and occupations.

In September 1941, the Slovak government produced its own anti-Jewish legislation, which included the creation of ghettos. Deportations to Auschwitz-Birkenau began in March 1942, and by the time the war ended 83 per cent of Slovakian Jews had perished.

Menachem was aware of "changes" in the early years of the war, but he was a child and did not think beyond the day. Some of his teachers had become openly anti-Semitic. One—the literature teacher—called the three Jewish students in his class by the same last name. " 'All Schlesingers come here,' he used to say. Then he would ask us, 'How much gefilte fish did you eat yesterday?' and everyone would laugh. It was embarrassing, but my position in the class was very strong because I was a good athlete. I used to play basketball and soccer and volleyball. Some of the boys would call me a dirty Jew, but I could live with it.

"But one day, it was around nine o'clock in the morning, an SS officer came to the school and he said to the teacher that all the Jewish kids in the room had to stand up. The three of us stood up. My heart was beating so hard. Then he said, 'You have to leave immediately and not ever come back here.' That was my first personal meeting with a Nazi."

Menachem's memories were filtered through the eyes of the child he was then. First "they" began to build a wall around the district where the Jews lived. Then, in April 1944, the family and all the Jews of Košice and the neighbouring areas were forced to leave their homes and all their possessions. "They" barred the doors behind them. Everyone was moved to a place called the brick factory where there were no houses at all, but open, windowless barracks that had been used to dry the bricks.

"After ten days they took us to a small railway station, then they brought in the trains and pushed about one hundred and fifty people into each wagon. The family was all together until we arrived at Auschwitz. Then we were separated."

Menachem's story of the slow destruction of his family— from middle-class, German-loving professionals to victims on the selection ramp at Auschwitz where, at age sixteen, he was separated for ever from his parents—was familiar and unutterably tragic. But what made his experience unique was that Menachem and his brother, Ladislau, three years older, were among a tiny handful of people who actually escaped.

Furthermore, the survivor of that horror had somehow managed to enter middle age with smile lines etched into a loving face.

He attributed it to the closeness of his early family life, and his youth. "I was so innocent, believe me. I had no idea of what anything meant and I felt secure because I was near my parents," he said.

But recently the nightmares had become worse. "I think it is because now I am, myself, the grandfather of small children and now I understand things better. I believe I survived because I did not understand where I was. To me, Germans were good people—the very best. This was my education and this had been the attitude in my family, so it was very hard for me to understand what was happening and this probably protected me. After three days in the train in such terrible conditions, we came to a place where we saw chimneys with fire. I remember somebody asked an SS man, *Was ist das?*, what is this, and he said, 'Very soon your parents will go out that chimney.' I thought this was a joke. After, when I saw people throwing themselves onto the electric fence with babies and children, I did not understand why they did it. *They* understood where they were, but I did not."

At the critical moment of the selection when, with a wave of the hand, it was decided who would walk the road to the gas chamber and who would walk the road to the camp, Menachem was saved by his brother.

First they were separated from their mother. Then they were separated from their father. Both parents took the first road.

The guards then collected a group of young people who looked strong enough for slave labour. "They said, 'Everyone over eighteen to the right. Everyone under eighteen to the left.' I was sixteen and my brother was nineteen. He pulled me with him to the right and when they asked me how old I was I said nineteen, just like my brother. The sergeant came up to me and said, 'Nineteen? We shall see.' I didn't know what would happen, but they left me alone.

"To this day I write that I was born in 1925 and not 1928 because I never want to forget that it is thanks to this that I lived."

Menachem's older brother, who now lives in Caracas, Venezuela, continued to sustain Menachem's life. Throughout their ordeal, they embraced and hugged and comforted each other. At night in the barracks they pressed together for warmth. "I know that I survived because of his love and because we had had so much love from our parents. I had beautiful parents, I was their little one. It gives you protection," said Menachem softly.

They survived in the holding camp for eight months.

At 4:00 a.m. on January 18, 1945, four thousand prisoners were called out to the central field of the camp. The Allies had made rapid gains and the Russians had started their push towards the west. "We were told that a decision had been made to move us to Germany," recalled Menachem, "and that we would go on foot. Then the SS said, 'People who cannot walk, come forward. You will go in cars.' Of course they were all shot. I think they knew it and they decided it was better to finish off their lives.

"We started with about three thousand people and we walked three days and three nights without food. Anyone who fell down was shot in the head. So many dropped.... I remember when they counted us the last time, I heard them say there were something like nine hundred left."

The circumstances surrounding his escape remain blurred by trauma. "All I remember next is that after the count a guard looked at us—there were six of us standing together—and he told us to bring him something, quick. Later my brother said he thought it was coffee, but I don't remember. The guard started to speak to another SS man. There was an open field. My brother said, '*Run, run,*' and we started to run, all six, and there was shooting and I looked back and there were only three of us, my brother, me, and someone else, he was running with us, then there was another shot, we kept running, and when we looked around we were by ourselves.

"My brother tells me that I lost consciousness and that he carried me on his shoulders."

Menachem paused and looked at me, but I could not speak. The nobility of this brother transcended the terror of two suffering boys desperate to live. It conjured up mythic loyalties of blood and devotion: of the frail and aged Anchises rescued from the flames of Troy on the back of his son, Aeneas.

He continued. "I came to and we walked. We were very cold, we had only our prisoners' clothes and it was January. We did not know where we were. I don't know how long we walked, but we came to a place where there were two houses. One had a fire in the chimney. We walked in, there was no one there, and I only remember that there was a whole loaf of bread on the table and that we started to eat it uncontrollably. We locked the door, then we lay on the bed and we slept, I don't know for how long, maybe an hour, maybe a day. It was warm. There were blankets.

"Suddenly there was a knock on the door. Someone said in German, 'Open the door.' I remember nothing after this, but my brother told me just last year that he said not to open the door. They shot the door open. A German came in—I think he was a pilot from the air force or something because the uniform was different. He fired in our direction and my brother fell down. I thought he had killed him and I started to scream, but my brother had just tripped and fallen down.

"He could have killed us, but he didn't. He took us and beat us and he didn't let me take my shoe, the one wooden shoe I had left. He took us to some sort of police station, I think. It was in a village and the houses were already bombed because the front line was very near. There were a lot of Hitler Youth people at the station. Again I do not remember what happened next, but my brother told me that one young man came to him and said, 'Don't be afraid.' He said that. It was a human touch.

"There were several prisoners there because the convoys going to Auschwitz passed by the town and sometimes people escaped. There were also other people from concentration camps.

The Germans at the police station were shooting prisoners three at a time. They always took them to the wall in threes, and when it was our turn they came with a shovel because they made you dig your own grave first. I fell unconscious again and my brother told me later that he saw it was the end and he had a feeling it was better. But he told them I was unconscious and a German officer said, 'Okay, that's enough for today.'

"That officer came to our cell afterwards with a girl called Grecia—I remember her name—and he asked the girl where she was going. She said she was taking some sick people to the hospital. The officer said to take us. I don't know why he saved us.

"There were Polish nuns at the hospital, and a German doctor came to check us. The nuns washed us and hid us in a place in the hospital that had already been evacuated. They said, 'Don't go away,' and the old one brought us food.

"We were there four or five days, maybe more. There was shooting all the time, then we heard people outside speaking Russian, so we went out to see where we were. We saw a lot of dead German soldiers. They were frozen; it was about 15 or 20 degrees below, centigrade. We started to take their shoes and sweaters and coats. My brother put me in an empty house while he went to look for food because I was so weak, then he couldn't remember where I was and he looked around all day, crying, until he found me in the evening.

"Lucky for us, the Russians were not very well organized and they were looking for food as well. I remember all these soldiers sitting around a big pot, eating potatoes. We said we were hungry and they invited us to eat, and they gave us bread too, without asking who we were. They just shared."

Menachem and Ladislau heard rumours that Slovakia had been liberated, so they set out for home, on foot. With their fair skins and blue eyes they were often taken for Germans; again and again they were arrested by the Russians. Once, a group of Russian Jewish soldiers tested them by speaking

Yiddish, a language they did not know. "What kind of Jews are you if you don't speak Yiddish?" the soldiers asked. But in Czechoslovakia, speaking or not speaking Yiddish was class-related. The assimilated upper classes like the Perlmutter family emphatically did *not* speak Yiddish.

One soldier persisted. "You don't even look like Jews. You're blond," he charged. "Okay, what does a Jew say when he eats a piece of bread?"

Menachem managed to recite the correct prayer, and the soldier arranged to get them as far as Cracow.

At the end of January 1945 they crossed the Polish border at Cracow only to see a large, makeshift sign. "We want a free Poland without Jews," it declared. Only 300,000 of Poland's 3,000,000 Jews had survived. Those who made their way home found this welcome.

In a bombed-out house in Cracow, a small group of Jews attempted to help camp survivors as they stumbled in. Menachem and his brother were offered blankets and Russian officers brought bread and potatoes. Men and women lay on the floor together, sick and vomiting, crying, and shouting out in their sleep.

"Somehow my brother got us papers saying we were Czech citizens trying to go home—there were a lot of Russian stamps on these papers—and we started to walk again. Sometimes we hitched a ride on a train.

"After a month we reached the Carpathian Mountains, where there were Polish nationalists who had fought the Germans and were now fighting the Russians. They stopped the trains in the forest and shot any Russians aboard, and if they found Jews they shot them too. We didn't look like Jews so we survived.

"Finally, at the end of February, we reached our town of Košice. Only twelve Jews had returned."

Every day Menachem went to the train station to wait for his mother or his father, an aunt, uncle, or cousin.... No one ever came.

The reaction began to set in. First a sort of euphoria at the rediscovery of ordinary life. The United Nations and the Jewish Joint Distribution Committee sent rations and a few items of clothing. There was a lot of food—more than he could eat—and Menachem traded it on the black market. A piece of cheese for a pair of shoes or a pullover. It was the clothing more than anything else that made him feel human again.

"When you go in rags, everyone looks at you and you feel very bad," he told me. "Now I could buy a bar of soap. It made me feel like a person again."

Menachem's brother was "taken away" to the army (where he was treated well) and Menachem was assigned a bed in a hospital. It was there that he first experienced after-shock.

"All the time I was at Auschwitz, and afterwards, I concentrated on survival. I pushed away anything that could hurt me. In moments of unbearable stress, I fainted. When you are in terrible circumstances, your mind narrows. For twenty-four hours you think, 'I saw a piece of bread over there, how can I get it?' You think, 'How shall I get from point A to point B without being beaten a hundred times?' That was all.

"But some of the refugees at the hospital were committing suicide. Every night they jumped out of windows and hanged themselves. They were older than I was, about twenty-eight or twenty-nine, and they had had wives and husbands and children. They knew by then what had happened to them, so they preferred to die.

"I had to leave there because I was afraid I also would commit suicide. For the first time I started to think, where are my parents, my cousins, my friends? Then, slowly—what has happened to me? This was the most terrible time as I began to think. I was wetting my bed all the time and I thought, what is happening to me? Who will help me? Finally the question came, why should I live?"

He decided there might be hope for him in Palestine, but his brother returned briefly and insisted that he had to complete his schooling first.

So Menachem studied history, physics, and mathematics and forgot about Palestine. It was 1946 and he was eighteen. He graduated and moved to the Sudetenland, where he got a job. He started to play basketball again and he made friends with a group of young Czech boys and girls his own age. He even had a girlfriend named Vlasta with whom he made love. The best part of the relationship was that Vlasta worked in a bakery and always brought him fresh rolls. The fear of hunger never diminished.

"Every Sunday morning I went with my friends to a park where everyone was dancing polkas. We would buy a beer and sip it all day. We would walk in the woods and make love with our girlfriends.

"But somewhere in the back of my mind I always had the feeling that all these good things that were happening to me were to pay me back for my sufferings. To be honest, I felt I was owed something. I liked to laugh and dance and I never, ever, talked about what had happened. I thought my friends did not know I was Jewish.

"One Sunday we all went up the mountain. It was beautifully warm and sunny and we could hear the music from the dancing nearby. A gypsy girl of sixteen or seventeen was selling roses on the road. She was wearing a dirty shirt and she did not have a brassiere on.

"The boys started to tease her. I said, 'Don't,' and they said, 'She's just a gypsy,' and they started to touch her. In my mind I remembered what I had seen happen to Jewish girls in Auschwitz. I became enraged and I said, 'She's a human being,' and I hit one of them. Then all three came at me and one of them said, 'Jews, gypsies, you're all the same.' I hit him again; then, of course, they beat me up. They stood there laughing and calling me a dirty Jew.

"The gypsy girl was trying to hold me up and she took a piece of dirty cloth to wipe off the blood. She asked me why I helped her when she was only a gypsy. So I told her.

"She said her mother had taught her to tell fortunes and she asked to see my left hand, the one closest to the heart. Then she told me that I was at a crossroads, that I would go far away from Czechoslovakia and I would be a builder.

"The next day at work I had bruises all over me and two of the boys who had beaten me up started to make fun. A week later I left that job. I said, that's it. I'm a Jew and there is only one place for a Jew and that is Palestine.

"Now I am fifty-nine years old and I think that God reveals himself from time to time, because what happened there brought me to Zion and to Zionism."

Menachem left Czechoslovakia and in April 1947 he finally boarded a ship leaving illegally for Palestine from Sète, in the south of France. There were 2,700 Jewish refugees on board. When they reached Tel Aviv two weeks later, they were arrested by the British and shipped off to a camp in Cyprus.

In July 1948, Menachem finally reached the newly declared State of Israel. He fought in the army on the Egyptian front and studied to be a land surveyor. Then, in 1952, he heard that the Beersheva Settlement Development was looking for a chief surveyor. There weren't too many applicants—no one wanted to live in Beersheva in 1952—so they accepted him on seven months' probation. He has been there ever since.

For forty years, Menachem never spoke about his wartime experiences. Not to his wife, not to his children, not even to his brother, who had lived through it with him and with whom he kept in regular contact.

In 1984 the brothers met in Florida, as they had met many times before. This time, as they drove along the highway, Ladislau remarked that the landscape looked familiar, like Europe.

"So we started to talk about the past for the first time. It's not as though we said, we shall never speak of this. We just never did."

Menachem had already started to have debilitating nightmares, and pains. Not long before, he had gone to the doctor because he had pain in his legs. They had done an X-ray. The doctor had wanted to know if he had ever been in a car accident, or if he had been wounded. Menachem had said no.

When he met his brother in Florida, he questioned him.

"Don't you remember?" asked Ladislau. "When we were taken to work every day, you were beaten constantly with a rifle butt."

"I had forgotten the beating because the physical pain is nothing compared to the emotional pain," Menachem said to me. "When I had nightmares, I always told myself that I had to overcome everything and be strong. But it got worse and I spoke to a professor of psychology at the university. He said that my problem was that I never spoke about it. He said I had to speak about what happened to me. So after forty years I spoke to students of psychology at the university, and I told them for the first time what I had never told my wife or my children. And I spoke without stopping for one and a half hours.

"I have never been to Yad Vashem and I don't read what is happening in Jerusalem about the Demjanjuk trial. All this is a good thing for the new generation, but not for me. When Eichmann was here, people committed suicide because they couldn't stand the memories. So I keep myself busy. But it's not easy."

Menachem and his brother speak on the telephone at least once a month. Menachem writes every Saturday and Ladislau writes every Sunday. They see each other at least twice a year.

And Ladislau continues to keep a loving eye on him. "When we were separated from our father, he said to my brother, 'Now you are responsible for Menachem.' I am a grandfather now, but he still treats me like a kid." Through this brother, both mother and father lived on, watching over him with love.

Menachem was reborn—and food grew out of the dry, ancient sands of the Negev.

CHAPTER EIGHTEEN

Son of the City

If I had danced around Yad Vashem before gathering courage to go there, I had also been dancing around the world of East Jerusalem and the West Bank, where the Palestinians lived. It felt like years since the night I had arrived in Israel and Naim, the hotel waiter, had promised to guide me into the Occupied Territories. I would contact him, although by now the "heaven that sent me to him" had certainly proved a disappointment.

He was gracious and friendly and didn't mention heaven once.

It was a Friday morning, about eleven o'clock, as we set out on foot for East Jerusalem and the Old City. Naim was thirty-seven years old, small and compact, with dark, curly hair and an open, unguarded face. He chattered comfortably in English and proffered much advice about bargaining, should I wish to shop. "Whatever price they offer, you say no," he advised. "It's a game. And keep an eye out for pickpockets, but don't worry about anything. You're safe with me because I am a son of the city."

For a while we walked in silence. "I see you are married," he said finally, glancing at my left hand.

"That's right."

Undissuaded, he pursued the subject of love. After his Canadian wife left him, he wrote her many times and gave her ultimatum after ultimatum, he said. Finally he took out an ad in an East Jerusalem paper, telling the world that they were divorced.

Since then he hadn't found anyone else, possibly because he was attracted only to foreign women: Finnish women, English women, French women, German women—all foreign, possibly rich, and certainly carrying with them the experience of horizons beyond his ken. Naim had left Jerusalem only once in his life, to spend a few days in Amman, Jordan. He had hated Jordan. It was dirty, he said, not like Israel. And not "free".

"Here I can say, 'Fuck Peres' if I want to and nothing will happen to me, but if I said, 'Fuck Hussein' in Jordan I'd be thrown in prison and no one would ever hear from me again."

We were passing the Monument of Peace that faces Mount Zion and the walls of the Old City. In both Hebrew and Arabic, the words of the prophet Isaiah are engraved into the stone: *And they shall beat their swords into plowshares, and their spears into pruninghooks: nation shall not lift up sword against nation, neither shall they learn war any more.*

The city seemed to be filled with such messages of peace, including its very name—"Jerusalem, City of Peace", which was written on the street maps. But reality, as usual, took a different tack. In recent weeks there had been stabbings by Arab terrormongers and counter-rampages by radical Jews. Tension in the city of peace was palpable and raw.

The fabled Jaffa Gate loomed before us. From this spot Jaffa Road runs to the city of Jaffa, the Mediterranean port of Jerusalem since the beginning of history. In the shadows of the sixteenth-century stone arch, thin, long-faced vendors hawked honeyed sweetmeats and tourist trinkets. Eastern music wailed from a dozen radios in a cluster of stores and cafés, merging with the prayer call of the muezzin. A delicious aroma of Turkish coffee and grilled shishkabob wafted through the air, making my mouth water. Guides and taxis waited patiently, ready to pounce on the overwhelmed tourist. Men in caftans and keffiyehs crouched along the sidewalks, watching.

We made our way through the winding byways of the souk in search of a friend, someone Naim thought I might want to meet. An old woman stretched out a wrinkled hand to beg, her head reaching forward imploringly, her face hidden behind a black veil. Other women in long, embroidered dresses lined the narrow street, seated behind rows of fresh and dried herbs. Men sipped tea and played backgammon inside smoky shops. On the street, tourists haggled mercilessly with vendors over the price of Bedouin rings and necklaces. Often they were accompanied by guides just like Naim.

Naim admitted to me that he did not like to take tourists shopping. Once a group of Belgians became angry with him because they found similar items for less money a few stalls away. This upset him, he said. He was also embarrassed when his friends sold their goods for too low a price.

He disappeared inside an arched doorway and beckoned me to follow. Inside were two men in their early twenties. Ahmed was a music teacher. His young pupil sat beside him on a bench, struggling with the notes of an Arab organ. From a small table, the teacher sold odds and ends like Chiclets, toilet paper, and soft drinks. His friend Radwan kept him company.

Aside from the bench, the table, and a few chairs, the room was bare. Green paint peeled off the walls around dog-eared American posters, *circa* 1940, depicting wholesome, pink-cheeked men and women smoking Player's cigarettes.

Naim exchanged a few words with the others in Arabic. They examined me closely, then gestured for me to follow them up the stairs to a second-floor office. It seemed that Naim would remain downstairs.

This was a bit worrisome, since my self-appointed protector had been warning me not to go anywhere with the men I interviewed. ("Just stay in the café. All they want is love....") I suggested we stay downstairs. They all looked miffed, including Naim.

Ahmed shooed his pupil away, then disappeared into a back room to make mint tea. Radwan cocked his head to the side and looked at me with curiosity.

"You are a teacher? In Canada?"

"That's right." Years ago I had taught high school English.

Radwan had been a radio producer for children's programs, but there was no money in that work. Now he bought and sold baklava in the market. "It's better to work for yourself. Then no one can send you away," he said with the certainty of one who had examined the alternatives.

His words struck me with a sharp remembrance; they were the words of my own father, the language of the immigrant even in the second generation. They were the fruit of a deeply ingrained insecurity: if *they* don't like you, *they* will get rid of you, deprive you of your living. Better to be independent, whatever the cost.

Radwan wanted to deliver a message. He longed for peace, he said, and he thought others did too....

"There can be no peace, only war," interrupted Ahmed sharply, his face enveloped in an incongruously pleasant smile. "The Israelis took what was ours and we will take it back. It's very simple. If someone steals your radio" (he pointed triumphantly to a battered receiver on the shelf) "you don't act nicely and forgive him, do you? No. You get your radio back. It's very simple."

Ahmed thought Yasser Arafat, chairman of the Palestine Liberation Organization (PLO), was a traitor. Arafat, it seemed, was willing to negotiate some form of peace. Ahmed spat out the word "peace" like a mouthful of rotten tomato. "But I'm not a *terrorist*," he said, staring at me. It seemed to be only the word he rejected, a calumny fabricated by the Western media to deprive him of his right to direct action. "I am the proudest of men and my cause is noble. If people die, it simply must be.

"I used to dream of being a soldier when I was little," he continued, his perfect white teeth gleaming behind the smile. He paused a moment, then corrected himself, seeking the most accurate expression of his childhood wish.

"No, it was more than being a soldier. I wanted to be a general...and I still do. Maybe I'll be a general in my own country."

"Are you a soldier yet?"

"No." Ahmed was not planning to admit to "military action" of any sort.

He was three years old in 1967, when the battle for East Jerusalem and the Old City took place, and he vividly remembered the sounds of shooting; these were the earliest memories of his life. Israeli soldiers had surrounded his house and told his parents to turn out the lights. His mother had started to go outside, Ahmed did not know why. A soldier had shouted at her.

"I didn't know why he shouted. I was terribly afraid."

"Perhaps your mother was putting herself in danger by going out."

He shrugged doubtfully. That an Israeli soldier might behave humanely did not fit his preconceptions.

His own dream of being a soldier—powerful, brave, and in control—began when he was four or five years old. He had lived with it ever since, a fantasy compensation for the impotence of living under occupation.

Ahmed said his political work consisted of preparing Palestinian youth for the coming revolution. "Disseminating information", he called it. Ahmed and his friends talked to high school students, cajoling those who might be wavering in their commitment to the cause. They provided material help and comfort to families whose homes had been destroyed by the Israeli army in retaliation for a real or presumed connection with the PLO.

Ahmed was undoubtedly good at this work because he saw the world in stark terms of good and bad, right and wrong. There were no shades.

"I see the Palestinian struggle from only one side, my own side. The Jews and the Israelis are our enemies," he told me with disarming candour. "You know, if I were an Israeli I would see it only from the other side."

"Your enemies are Jews?"

"Yes."

"Jews everywhere?"

He hesitated, then began choosing his words more carefully. "Zionists—Zionists are our enemies."

Word of my visit had apparently spread throughout the village atmosphere of East Jerusalem. Naim materialized, looking a little rueful—possibly because the heaven that had sent me to him seemed to be letting him down once again. His courtesy intact, he placed a bottle of warm orange pop in front of me. Ahmed stared at one of the posters on the wall. I followed his gaze. A resolutely cheerful girl with Colgate teeth smiled on for ever, over the peeling paint and the talk of armies, frustration, and rage. Ahmed poured himself a glass of Coca-Cola and drank it at a gulp.

Then Radwan spoke up, his mouth pulled tight with anxiety. "I was not a political person until I was a teenager. I didn't even read a newspaper," he said. "Then one day some Israeli soldiers stopped me when I was coming home from school. They arrested me and they beat me.

"I was just a child, and I was innocent. I was more hurt inside than outside. I understood what the occupation meant for the first time. I was not free."

A third voice pierced the air, coming from the direction of the door. "The dogs are living better than us." The new voice snarled with rage. The man entered the shop and sat down. He seemed to be trembling.

We sat in silence. I asked his name. He remained silent. I asked if he wanted to talk to me. Again, he did not answer. I stood up to leave.

"Go ahead, leave. The streets are safe for *you* but dangerous for *us*. After dark we are stopped and checked and beaten. *You'll* be just fine." His voice crackled with barely controlled rage.

"The soldiers search us, manhandle us, ask for identity cards, ask what we are doing here. We live here! Where else are we supposed to be? I have been in jail four times, for forty-eight hours each, without charges. It is rule by fear. Ninety-nine per cent of the young people have been in prison. You're a terrorist or something, you're guilty, because you're a Palestinian."

"They think we're not human, like chimpanzees," piped up Radwan, picking up courage.

The man ignored him. "These very streets are a prison. I want to study Oriental music in an Arab country and I cannot. I have no future. *We* have no future. Only 5 per cent of the Israelis sympathize with us. The rest don't even want to acknowledge we exist."

His forehead creased in deep ridges, he accused me with his eyes. His fist clenched and unclenched on the table before him, the white bone of his knuckles showing through the taut skin. "I'm waiting for an imam, someone who is strong enough to rule by Islamic law," he offered.

"Like Khomeini?"

"No." The disdain was total. "Moslems are not allowed to fight one another, like Iran and Iraq." But he could not or would not articulate more about this beloved holy man who would save the Palestinians.

"It is impossible," he said flatly. "Everything is impossible. There will never be any peace with Israel, not now, not ever. Nothing will change. There is no hope."

He stopped speaking as abruptly as he had begun. The rest of us remained silent, stunned by the rawness of this despair.

"How old are you?" I guessed he was thirty-five.

"I'm twenty-three," he replied.

One day soon, I thought, I will learn that he has murdered Jews in a suicide mission. The others will venerate his memory and praise his devotion. Perhaps they will remember this afternoon's desperate encounter.

"You won't put their names in the paper?" Naim asked worriedly.

It occurred to me that Naim might be in trouble should his friends learn he had misled them about my identity. Why did he choose to trust me?

"I do not have to trust *you*," he said, smiling. "You have to trust *me*. You are a foreigner and you do not know the games. I can help you because I am a son of the city."

We entered the market street, walking past men in long desert robes, selling strips of apricot paste and spices and Turkish coffee pots on copper trays.

Naim certainly did have friends everywhere. He shook hands left and right and introduced me as his friend from Canada. "Tea? Tea?" offered a smiling, toothless man with a wizened face. He waved us over. "Mint tea, please? You are welcome."

So we drank sugared, mint-leaf tea in a small, bare café. Naim leaned forward. "So you want to know what's going on? Well, I don't like politics or religion. They both cause trouble. I have Arab friends and I have Jewish friends, especially Jews who are used to living with Arabs. That Rabbi Kahane guy isn't important. He's crazy, like Hitler, and no one pays any attention to him in the Knesset. He wants to get rid of all the Arabs. I don't understand the way he thinks or the way Hitler could have thought. I don't understand killing one person, and when I try to think that Hitler murdered six million Jews I cannot understand at all. When I have an insect in my house, you know what I do? I pick it up and put it outside. I just want to be happy every day. Now I'm thirty-seven. Maybe I'll die when I'm forty or fifty. So I just want to be happy."

He drew a picture of an ant on the paper placemat and looked depressed.

Naim said he thought of himself as a realist of sorts. "There will never be a separate Palestine," he confided softly. "It would be too dangerous for Israel. We have more children. And then when we were strong there would be another war. Israel will never allow it."

Since Naim believed the battle was already lost, he tried to avoid talking politics with his friends. The reason was obvious. He did not play the game—the PLO game—and in a community where more than 90 per cent of the population supported the PLO (without acknowledging membership, which is illegal), having distinctly different views might well create problems.

Naim put his faith in King Hussein of Jordan. He dreamed of a cosmopolitan state of Jews and Palestinians, under the control of Israel. Not an occupying control, like the present situation, he said, but something resembling Berlin, which is overseen by the Allied countries. Under such a plan, Palestinians would be "independent".

Naim was describing an idea first proposed by Menachem Begin: a state of "autonomy" in which Israelis would remain a legitimate collective group on the West Bank, and Palestinians would have a lesser status. Naturally, the autonomy idea was never stated quite that baldly—usually it was emphasized that there would be some form of local government. Real power, however, would remain in the hands of the Israelis.

Begin was no longer politically active, but the autonomy idea was still being promoted by right-wing ultra-nationalists, some of whom had chosen to live in settlements on the West Bank.

Naim was thus endorsing an idea that would establish him in a permanent second-class position. I looked at him with fresh curiosity. He seemed tired, middle-aged. Now I saw the thin strands of white that had invaded his dark hair, and the creases that snaked across his forehead. His friends were young, but he was not. For eighteen years he had been working as a waiter in

West Jerusalem and he liked what he saw there: the power, the freedom, the money. Naim wanted that world and he wanted that world to want him. I was reminded of Frantz Fanon's classic, bitter polemic on colonization, *The Wretched of the Earth*:

> The native town is a crouching village, a town on its knees, a town wallowing in the mire. It is a town of niggers and dirty Arabs. The look that the native turns on the settler's town is a look of lust, a look of envy; it expresses his dreams of possession…to sit at the settler's table, to sleep in the settler's bed, with his wife if possible. The colonized man is an envious man. And this the settler knows very well....

Naim longed to be co-opted, accepted, a feeder at the trough of plenty he saw all around him. Three times a day, six days a week, Naim served at tables in the hotel restaurant, where he saw tourists with more money and freedom than he could dream of. At night he walked back to his Old City apartment, through the Jaffa Gate, into a world where he lived under the gun. Perhaps he thought that, under the political solution he desired, he would be less of an outsider.

As part of his pursuit, Naim was attracted only to "white" women: those who represented the outside world, freedom and power. So he had married a Canadian. When she left him, he was more vulnerable than ever.

But still he pursued "her". A few months earlier, a couple of Swedish girls staying in the hotel had allowed him to show them the sights of the Old City. Naim had not wanted to be paid for this; he was not a servant but a friend, he told them again and again. When they insisted on paying, and refused to see him again, he was wounded.

He was, of course, playing the same lost game with me.

"I want to see you every day," he said as we walked away from the café.

"That is impossible," I replied. I turned towards him to say goodbye. He looked like an old man. I thought he was going to cry.

It was late Friday afternoon and the last slanting rays of the sun glanced golden off the stone walls of Old Jerusalem. Bearded, black-coated Jews with their wives and children marched purposefully to the Western Wall.

I followed down the winding street, past a procession of Franciscan priests and their faithful carrying a wooden cross along the Stations of the Cross where once Jesus walked. The lead priest looked grim. The hustle and noise of the souk were not exactly conducive to spiritual concentration, I reflected, yet this street must have looked much the same in the time of Jesus, as he made his way through the market among his fellow Jews.

The alley bent to the right and, suddenly, there was the Wall below. On June 7, 1967, when the Israeli forces captured the Old City, they met here at the Wall. Officers and soldiers, young and old, touched the stones that day and wept in a moment that effectively changed the direction of Israeli history. Religious fundamentalists believed the recovery of ancient Jerusalem was a miracle indicating that the Messiah must be close at hand. And on the secular side of things, of course, the occupation of the captured territories began.

Above the Wall, on the Mount of the Temple, rose two large mosques: the Dome of the Rock, with its shining golden cupola, and the El Aksa Mosque, with a smaller silver dome.

Soldiers checked my bag, a grim reminder that this place holy to both Judaism and Islam was also one of the world's most unpredictable and dangerous spots. Below, a throng gathered. The Wall was divided, women on one side, men on the other. It was not originally intended to be so, but in 1967 the Chief Rabbis had declared this place to be a synagogue—and so the sexes had to be separated.

I made my way down to the Wall past North American and European tourists who had come to watch and perhaps to pray, noting observations in a small notebook.

"Put that away," commanded a stern American voice from behind a full black beard on a face that was not yet twenty. "This is the Wall! This is the sabbath!"

A woman standing nearby began to signal wildly, pointing first to her eyes, then to her head, while talking in non-stop German.

"Parlez-vous français?" I asked her, hoping to find a common language to decipher this clearly important communication.

"Oui, je parle français," growled the young man, who was apparently obnoxious in at least two languages, and possibly others I had not yet discovered. *"Ici, c'est Le Mur."*

The German woman's eyes were positively flashing. Her index finger was whizzing from eye to forehead and back again.

I worked it out: I should memorize what I saw and write it down later. This was, of course, excellent advice. I smiled appreciatively.

She was, however, not deterred. She pointed at the men swaying back and forth before the stones of the Temple Wall, she pointed at the line of singing and dancing Hasidim welcoming the sabbath, she smiled, she laughed, she talked, she gesticulated.

I edged away. She clutched my arm. "Goodbye," I said gently.

"Adieu," growled the young man.

The women's side of the Western Wall was a forlorn place indeed. Here at the heart of Judaism, at the newly recovered shrine of an ancient people, the essential male-centredness of the religion was revealed with wordless clarity. A few women and their daughters gathered around, reading prayers and touching the holy stones, but most of them were pressed against the barrier that separated them from the world of men on the other side. There they watched the real world of the Jews. The men danced, the men sang, and clusters of boys with curled forelocks chased each other under the watchful eyes of their fathers. The men swayed, the men chanted, the men moved in and out of a cave-like room where ceremonies inaccessible to me were taking place. Singing filled the air. A column of fifty or sixty students came dancing, four abreast, down the steps from their yeshiva on the hill, to join the others in welcoming the sabbath. They gathered before the Wall, in the men's section, in Orthodox sects: the Hasidim of Vilna, the Hasidim from a village in Hungary. An old, revered rabbi with a kind face was carried into the enclosure by his adoring, dancing disciples.

This was Orthodoxy as it had existed in the villages and towns of Eastern Europe for a thousand years, the Orthodoxy that my parents and most of their generation dropped like a hot potato in their scramble to integrate into the Canadian mainstream. It was an Orthodoxy utterly foreign to me as an individual, though as close as a heartbeat to my people. I was both attracted by the genuineness of the emotion and repelled by its medieval forms. Most of all I was reminded of a comment by the American writer Cynthia Ozick: that when she sits upstairs in the women's section of her synagogue, praying to her God, and she hears the rabbi below talking of the Jews, she knows he is not speaking of her.

"Sure is a class system," twanged a mid-western female voice at my ear, as if reading my thoughts.

She was smiling at me, a slim, fortyish bottle-blonde from Chicago. She and her friend, a plump, friendly-looking woman, were here with their husbands on a three-week tour organized by Hadassah. The men were over in the men's section "getting the feel of things," said the blonde.

"Are you Orthodox?" she asked.

"No, I'm not."

"Nor I. I'm a Zionist and I've done a lot of work for Israel, and to be honest with you I've given a lot of money." She waited for a response. I nodded encouragingly.

"Some of these Orthodox people don't even believe in the State of Israel." She was warming to a favourite subject, nursing a deep resentment.

"The Messiah hasn't come yet," I offered.

"I don't get it. For people who don't believe in the state, they have too much power. I'll tell you, I was brought up in an observant home, but as far as these people are concerned I'm not even a Jew. I'm a, I'm a...*shiksa*, for God's sake. They're practically taking over."

"Don't worry, it'll never come to that," said the plump lady. "People like us would just kiss the whole thing goodbye and take our money with us. They need us, so they won't go too far."

"They'd better not," muttered the first woman. "Because I'm a Zionist, but I would just pull right out."

Earlier the same day the blonde woman's nephew, who lived in Israel, had rented a car to drive them all into the West Bank, or Samaria, as it is now increasingly called even by the liberals. They went to Nablus, the town where the moderate mayor had his legs blown off a few years ago by angry Jewish settlers. The two women and their husbands knew nothing of this. The trip into the West Bank was "beautiful", they said, except for all the Arabs who lived there.

"My nephew told us the most incredible story. An Arab in Nablus found out his wife was cheating on him, so you know what he did?"

"No."

"He cooked her."

"He what?"

"He just put her in the oven and cooked her."

This was so patently absurd that I began to laugh. The women laughed too, but they assured me the story was absolutely true.

"You'd think he could have at least killed her first," said the plump one, clucking reprovingly.

The twentieth century was drawing to a close, but the thought forms of the Middle Ages persisted. An offended Arab husband cooked his wife in an oven. Jews used the blood of Christian children to bake their Passover matzohs. Christian women had sexual intercourse with the devil, turned into witches, and flew into the bedrooms of saintly priests to torture them with sexual fantasies and nocturnal emissions. In our own time, Jews in Germany were endowed with a quasi-magical ability to "take over the world".

All ways and means of dehumanizing "the other".

A ridiculous tale believed by two American women from Chicago hung ominously in the air of volatile Old Jerusalem.

I made my way back through the darkening souk to the modern, westernized world of New Jerusalem. Over dinner I learned that while my Chicago friends and I chatted at the Temple Wall, two ultra-nationalist Jewish teenagers were stabbed by PLO infiltrators—*fedayeen*—just a hundred yards away.

CHAPTER NINETEEN

The Face in the Mirror

In my dream last night I was overwhelmed by anguish. Someone in authority wanted to arrest me. He spoke harshly and wrote my name on a list. I appealed, to whom I did not know. My appeal was ignored.

I awoke in a sweat, dressed, and stepped through the iron bars of my apartment complex. Across the lower roadway behind the ramparts of Old Jerusalem, the Church of the Dormition gleamed in the clear morning light. "City of Peace"—a wish unconsummated for two thousand years.

I thought of Rafi Horowitz, the media relations official I met when I first arrived. "We are at war," he said. Endless war.

The "Palestinian question". It sounded uncomfortably like what used to be called the "Jewish question" in pre-war Europe.

The "Arab–Israeli conflict". Learned seminars were held. Scholars debated its origin, development, and likely future. Usually advertised as impartial attempts to advance the cause of peace, the seminars were too often marred by ideological fervour. Just before making this trip I had attended such an event on the campus of the University of Toronto. The speaker was Edward

Said, a member of the Palestine National Council and the author of *The Question of Palestine.*

There was a standing-room-only crowd at that meeting and a scent of trouble in the air. Many of the students edging into the hall were Palestinians. The young, militant Jews with their knitted skullcaps were also there. They passed out leaflets reading, "Edward Said, GO HOME."

"I would if I could," replied Said with an ironic laugh. "That's what I came to talk about."

Said may have been a member of the policy-making body of the PLO, but that afternoon he looked every inch the North American college professor. His leader, Yasser Arafat—steel-nerved and blessed, it seemed, with nine lives; his head swathed in a keffiyeh, his face unshaven, commander of random terror strikes—Arafat was nowhere in sight. In Toronto, on this crisp autumn day, the PLO wore a tweed sports jacket and a white shirt with colour-coordinated tie, and conjured up images of common rooms, sherry, and the Arts and Leisure section of *The New York Times.*

Said's lecture was calm and reasoned, as befitted the academic setting. There were 2 1/2 million Palestinians in exile, he said, and they would not capitulate. In the Occupied Territories, Palestinians were treated badly. The world thought of them as terrorists, but they were not terrorists, only desperate resistance fighters. Although Said did not reject the violent solution, he took the high road. What the Palestinians wanted, he said, was not the destruction of Israel, but the partition of Palestine.

The only answer to the Palestinian crisis was a conscious decision to negotiate about justice and injustice, for both Palestinians and Israelis, he said. Even his enemies could not argue with that. He had managed to make the PLO sound like a United Church Sunday School club.

Then he laid his carefully argued script down on the lectern.

A Jewish girl stood and asked a question. She was trying to understand, and she thought she did understand, the Palestinian position as Professor Said had presented it. But what about the Israelis, the Jews. Didn't they have rights too? And if they did, what *were* those rights, in Professor Said's opinion?

A rumble undulated through the room.

Professor Said ignored this student who had summoned up the courage to ask a lengthy question in a predominantly hostile climate.

"Next question?"

A knitted skullcap bobbed into the air. "Answer her now!" he shouted. "The PLO is just a terrorist organization...."

Six goons materialized around him, moving in menacingly. One grabbed his arm. The student sat down, subdued. Professor Said said something dismissive. The audience laughed.

"Do you condemn or do you condone the recent murder of civilians at the Wailing Wall?" came a question from the back of the hall. The professor neither condemned nor condoned. He explained about justified resistance.

The student insisted. The professor turned red. "My entire family was expelled by the Israelis in 1948," he shot back. Made homeless, turned into refugees.

The room fell silent. Now we were no longer talking abstractly of national destinies. Behind the tweed jacket, the genteel aura of the common room, and the prepared professorial lecture was a man burning with anger.

A short while later, at a prestigious international conference organized by Canadian Professors for Peace in the Middle East, the same passions surfaced. All was well as scholar after scholar advanced convincing legal and political arguments. A sense of controlled fairness prevailed. A professor from McGill University spoke of the inherent conflict of belief systems operating in Israel with each side claiming aboriginal rights. He said that any attempt to deny the legitimacy of a Palestinian identity was "misguided" and "morally wrong", and spoke of a solution which must eventually contain "the principles of least injustice". A professor from Rutgers University spoke of the desperate need for compromise, and the double-sided, growing danger of political and religious intransigence in Israel and the Arab world.

But raw emotion flared like a kerosene flame after a presentation on human rights in the West Bank, despite the fact that the speaker, a lecturer at Harvard Law School and deputy director of the Lawyers' Committee for Human Rights, was as careful and balanced in her presentation as the occasion and good sense warranted.

Israel, she confirmed, had made its own Supreme Court available to hear charges of abuse on the part of its own occupying army. Furthermore, the military-legal system administered in the Territories used the same rules of evidence as applied in criminal cases within Israel itself. But having said that, she admitted that there were serious loopholes in the human rights protections Israel had put into place, and that these permitted abuses to occur. House demolitions—the destroying of the homes of people suspected of terrorist acts—were prohibited by the Fourth Geneva Convention, she said, but Israel routinely applied this penalty.

The problem was the summary nature of the punishment: formal proof of terrorist activity was not necessary under military law. And the collective impact: sometimes more than twenty people were rendered homeless; the average was seven.

She went on. Deportations from the Territories were also prohibited under the Geneva Convention, but Israel continued to mete out this punishment as a deterrent. And finally, there was the practice of administrative detention, which allowed up to six months' incarceration—with the possibility of renewal—without charge or trial. The potential for abuse here was simply too great, she suggested.

Most of the international lawyers, political scientists, and historians gathered in the conference room that day knew that Amnesty International had come to similar conclusions about conditions in the Occupied Territories, so there were no surprises here. Still, her words seemed to strike a double chord of embarrassment and anger. Embarrassment that after forty years of endless war and skin-of-the-teeth survival, Israel, the Jewish homeland built from the ashes of the Holocaust, stood charged with human rights violations. And anger as a defensive rebuttal, as a precursor of an alternate view of the "facts"—those basic elements so hotly contested in any discussion of the Middle East.

And so the public accusation that followed. A respected international lawyer in the assembly stood, red-faced with rage, his voice controlled and cold. The Harvard professor and her organization were liars and Arab propagandists, he said.

A collective gasp rose in the room.

An esteemed professor of international law from the province of Alberta joined the attack. It was "a little improper to apply our standards of criticism when we are unaware of the prevailing situation," he said, as though it were somehow not permissible to comment upon conditions in the world beyond one's own community (yet, were we to heed such advice, his own profession might not exist!)

A professor of government and international relations added that he disapproved of human rights organizations reaching negative conclusions about "friends" because such conclusions could be used by "enemies" to delegitimize that country. Then he immediately contradicted himself, insisting that universal standards of human rights must be applied everywhere. "The support of Israel comes not just from the Jews," he chided. "The maintenance of a universal commitment to Israel demands that these high standards be respected."

"Removing layers in the Middle East conflict is more like peeling an onion than an artichoke," mused an Israeli professor on sabbatical at New York University. "Because at the end we are left in tears."

Hadn't Ahmed the music teacher put it succinctly? He viewed the issues in black and white. "If I were an Israeli, I'd support the other side," he had said matter-of-factly. For Ahmed compromise was anathema, objectivity a betrayal, the search for "truth" a naive pursuit. What mattered was group loyalty.

The apartment on the other side of my wall was being gutted and rebuilt. Arab workers passed back and forth carrying equipment. Sometimes they sat before my barred door sipping coffee. There were no "good mornings", although we already knew each other by sight.

I planned to relax this morning, to take an emotional breather. The day before, I had visited Radwan Abu Ayyash, head of the Arab Journalists' Association in the Occupied Territories, and he had agreed to pull together an itinerary of places to go in the West Bank interior. We had sat in his shabby, airless East Jerusalem office furnished from rug to couch to curtains in varying shades of green.

Ayyash had spoken about politics, including a strictly enforced censorship of Palestinian journalism. It was typical of Israel, I thought, that I had already read an article on this subject in the resolutely free Israeli press. I had also read a reliable study called *Palestinian Press in the West Bank*[1], which demonstrated that, by their own definition, West Bank newspapers were part of a "mobilized press" and not to be read according to the norms of objectivity that were prevalent (though not always adequately observed) in the Western press.

The Palestinians would accept U.N. resolutions 242 and 348— recognizing the existence of Israel and her need for secure borders—in return for an independent Palestinian state in the West Bank, the Gaza strip, *and* East Jerusalem, said Mr. Ayyash. He spoke of self-determination, of an international conference to solve the conflict, and of his perception of Palestinian weakness. "We would need one hundred years to acquire the superstructure to deal with the reality of Israel."

Apparently, both Jews and Arabs saw themselves as under siege.

---

[1] By Dov Shinar and Danny Rubenstein. The study was part of the West Bank Data Base Project; see Chapter Twenty-five.

He talked on and drank sweet tea and chain-smoked cigarettes under his framed picture of Yasser Arafat with the Pope. He wanted to write about his life, which had begun some thirty-five years ago in a refugee camp, he said, but he lacked the necessary objectivity to do so. His parents still spoke of going "home" to Jaffa, from which they had been expelled in 1948....

Then something strange occurred: his voice became thin and hesitant. He flushed, stopped speaking, and stared morosely at the floor. Did he think that I was not listening, that his carefully chosen words were lost, or that they were inadequate carriers of a message he was unable to impart? We sat in silence, wordless and embarrassed because despair had broken through the frail skin of professionalism.

After a moment he rallied, became official again, and promised to make arrangements. I muttered my thanks and slipped out the door.

I then made my way to the offices of *Al Fajr*, one of East Jerusalem's leading newspapers. The masthead of the paper was itself a grim token of this part of the world: "*Al Fajr* Arabic newspaper was founded in 1972 by Yusef Nasr. Nasr edited the paper until his kidnapping in 1974. He has not been found since."

A narrow, ill-lit staircase led to a set of offices located on the top floor. The depressing poverty of these rooms stood in striking contrast to some of the rich, streamlined, computer-equipped newspaper offices of my own country. Black monster typewriters from another era sat on paper-strewn desks. On the walls the ubiquitous peeling paint of East Jerusalem etched multi-coloured designs of decay.

I was to meet Hanna Siniora, the editor of *Al Fajr* and a political moderate who is considered by Israel a potential Palestinian delegate to an international conference on the Middle East, should such an event ever take place. The sticking point was, of course, the PLO. Membership in the organization was illegal, so no "visible" Palestinian was formally a member. But reliable polls suggested that more than 90 per cent of the population in East Jerusalem and the West Bank sympathized with the PLO and thought of Yasser Arafat as their leader.

Israel, of course, refused to countenance the presence of the PLO at an international table. The PLO had never amended its covenant, which called for the destruction of Israel and for the "armed struggle", a fancy name for terror that made back-stabbers in East Jerusalem and thug-hijackers on airplanes sound like soldiers on a battlefield. And Arafat, for all his attempts at statesmanship, still continued to approve of selected terrorist acts while noisily repudiating those of his break-away enemies such as Abu Nidal.

The person behind the desk was not Hanna Siniora but Daoud Kuttab, the managing editor of the English-language edition of the paper. Siniora had been held up at a meeting, he said. He assured me that an interview with him would yield precisely the same information.

I clicked on my tape recorder. Kuttab began to explain, as Ayyash had explained. He talked of the Arab position on the proposed international conference. The Arabs, including the Palestinians, wanted a forum where negotiations would take place on the spot. Israel, or rather Foreign Minister Shimon Peres, wanted a conference as a stepping-stone to individual negotiations with separate Arab countries, along the lines of the Camp David Accord. (Israeli Prime Minister Yitzak Shamir wanted no conference at all.) The Arabs were proposing a trade-off as outlined in the 1982 Fez plan: recognition of Israel's right to exist in return for a withdrawal from the West Bank and Gaza.

Kuttab spoke of problems of language and perception. What did "territorial compromise" mean? For the Palestinians, he said, a "bottom-line compromise" was to accept a Palestinian state in the whole of the Occupied Territories. This was "partition" as projected by the United Nations in 1947, but was already unequal in favour of Israel, he said. The Israelis, on the other hand, were certain that the Territories were theirs—had belonged to them since 1967. So any compromise *they* were likely to make would automatically fall short of Palestinian demands.

These were negotiating stances, but they seemed carved in stone long before even the idea of a conference had been agreed to. Disunity among the Palestinians was endemic. And most Israelis I had talked to were cynical in the extreme about the possibility of peace, or even an authentic peace process. Nothing would happen, they argued, until the "unity government" of Labour and Likud finally got a divorce and called an election. Nothing would happen, they claimed, until there was some electoral reform in Israel that removed undue power from tiny fringe parties that represented only a handful of electors, yet could dictate terms in exchange for their coalition support.

Language and perception. At the press office in Jerusalem, every foreign journalist was handed a backgrounder kit containing glossy pamphlets on the PLO and terrorism. Statistics, speeches, the PLO covenant, a statement about the "indivisibility" of Palestinian terror (in case any one of us might be tempted to think that Arafat, for example, was not directly responsible for terrorist acts inflicted on the world by his Palestinian enemies); a briefing on "the pervasive violence of the Arab world", and a defence of the Israeli position as seen through the telescope of Jewish history.

> The Land of Israel is the historic homeland of the Jewish people where, over nearly 4,000 years, it became a nation and developed its distinctive language, law and culture. Down through the centuries, although the Land was often occupied by foreign powers, no other nation ever attained independence in it, nor regarded it as the core of its national or spiritual existence.

Finally there was a refutation of the Arab bargaining position. "There is certainly no other state, big or small, young or old, that would consider mere recognition of its 'right to exist' a favour, or a negotiable concession...."

In the offices of *Al Fajr*, Daoud Kuttab presented me with the Palestinian version of the press kit, in the public relations battle for the international media.

"You talk about violence," he said in reply to my question. "We're very much against violence committed by Palestinian extremists, but we're also against the violence committed by Israel. In the West Bank and Gaza, soldiers use live ammunition to put down demonstrations. People get beaten and tortured. In Lebanon, the camps are bombed and innocent people are killed. So Palestinians are not innocent, but they are not the only guilty ones. It's dirty, it's tragic, but it's war.

"Many people outside believe that all the Israelis are yearning for peace and that it is the Palestinians who are not responding. This is a misrepresentation.

"I am sorry if I am saying something you do not want to hear...."

"I beg your pardon?"

I looked at him, startled. Was skepticism written so plainly on my face? I was, of course, skeptical of press kits, regardless of their origin. There was always a dimension missing in the re-tailing of an official "point of view", a selectiveness concerning which facts would be promoted and which would be rationalized or suppressed.

I was also aware that this tragedy did not date from today, or even twenty years ago. In 1948, the Palestinians rejected the possibility of having their own state and opted for the armed struggle instead. That choice led to acts of terror that led to other acts of terror, all of which fed into the siege mentality that characterized the Israelis and made compromise less and less possible with each passing year.

I also knew more about the PLO than my interviewee might have guessed. In the course of researching my book *Unhealed Wounds: France and the Klaus Barbie Affair*, I had stumbled upon interlocking connections between PLO and Nazi elements in Western Europe. It was widely known that in 1939 Haj

Amin el-Husseini, the notorious Grand Mufti of Jerusalem, took refuge from the British by escaping to Nazi Germany with his followers, where he founded his own SS division under the admiring supervision of SS chief Heinrich Himmler. Himmler sent a prescient little note to the Mufti during their association. "The struggle against Judaism is at the very heart of the natural alliance between National Socialism and those Arab Moslems who burn with a desire for freedom," he wrote.[2] This seemingly bizarre relationship continued in the 1950s when nostalgic, out-of-work Nazis were invited to Egypt by President Gamal Abdal Nasser to reorganize the Egyptian secret service and the military. That initial contact led to a joint effort on behalf of the Algerian FLN in its protracted and ultimately successful anti-colonial war against France in the late 1950s and early 1960s, and to the training of the first Palestinian terrorists who attacked Israel from the Gaza Strip. During the 1960s and 1970s, the connection evolved into an era of Euro-terrorism, and a merger of ultra-leftist and neo-Nazi cells throughout Europe.

In 1969, Yasser Arafat sent a PLO representative to a meeting of the neo-Nazi *Neue Europäische Ordnung* (New European Order) in Barcelona to request money for the dissemination of anti-Semitic and anti-Zionist literature, as well as new personnel for sabotage operations, and subsequent to this meeting Palestinian leaders advertised in the Munich *Nationalzeitung* for "war correspondents" with "tank experience". By the 1980s it had emerged that young neo-Nazis from Germany's Hoffmann group, for example, were training with Palestinian fedayeen in an Al Fatah camp in Lebanon. One of them tied it all together neatly. "The PLO are fighting for the rights of their people as we are fighting for the German people. The Palestinians and ourselves

---

[2] Centre de documentation juive, Paris, DXX111-1309, 1310, 1313, quoted in L. Poliakov, *De Moscou à Beyrouthe*

have the same enemy: international Zionism, the Jews...."[3] The most recent manifestation of the relationship surfaced during the legal defence of Nazi war criminal Klaus Barbie, in France.

Kuttab was at pains to deny this projection of hatred. "We have nothing against Jewish people. We have Jewish friends. Our problem is with the Zionist movement in the State of Israel, which is trying to take our homeland. In the same way as it is important for the Jewish people to have a haven, so it is important for the Palestinians to have a haven."

I didn't think that old or new Nazi-Palestinian convergences meant that Palestinians, as such, were Nazis, approved of Nazis, or acted as Nazis (although "Nazi" had certainly become a favourite, facile epithet of some Palestinians and some Israelis when describing the other camp). What I did think was that the distinction between "Zionist" and "Jew" was less clear-cut than Palestinian intellectuals such as Kuttab were at pains to suggest. This was a part of the story the Palestinian press kit emphatically did not include. As it did not include the fact that 78 per cent of Palestinians questioned in a poll conducted by Kuttab's own newspaper in 1986 supported the use of violence.

I knew all this, but I also knew that here in the dusty, winding streets of East Jerusalem, I was being deeply affected by the despair that surrounded me—and that despair was also dangerous. This was a reality that went beyond the newspaper story, beyond the learnèd conferences, beyond the predictable debates. Human beings were suffering here. How many Israelis had ever talked seriously with a Palestinian man or woman, I wondered. Few seemed to venture into East Jerusalem, or beyond.

Was I being naive? Was I a dupe to feel the pain of people whose avowed leader, Yasser Arafat, encouraged the "armed struggle" and the stab in the civilian back? Did not simple

---

[3] *Unhealed Wounds*, chapter 9

loyalty to my people and a horror of violence demand a steely reserve now that I was, so to speak, on the scene? Should I not confine myself to a considered appreciation of *realpolitik*? Things tough on the West Bank? No need to look further than the PLO, the Syrians, the Jordanians, was the standard reply of Prime Minister Yitzak Shamir. No further than the terrifying youths who undulated around dark corners with weapons concealed under their clothes.

True, but only partially true. Self-servingly true. Distortedly true. The press kit truth.

The xenophobic thinking that nourished that narrow vision shrivelled compassion—relegated it to the waste bin of irrelevant emotion. Press kits and propaganda were designed to minimize empathy; let ordinary human beings feel compassion and they might refuse to carry out hostilities.

But one thing seemed clear enough to me. In this tiny, claustrophobic dot on the earth's surface, where enemy-neighbours could, if they looked, see the face of their own nationalism distorted in each other's mirror, there would be no peace without compassion.

Twenty years had passed since the triumphant victory of 1967, but how many could remember the circumstances of that war, and how many were clear about what had happened in the interim?

By early 1967, the mood in the young State of Israel had turned black. The economy of the country was chaotic, immigration was down, emigration was up, and the handful of men who governed the country were petulant, querulous, and as old as the ideas they proffered as solutions. Would the Jewish state even survive? Both inside and outside Israel, Jews had hoped that the return to the ancient soil would, among other things, give a measure of meaning to the terror of the Hitler years. The destruction of the new state would be seen as an unparalleled tragedy, perhaps the end of the dreams and hopes and the very will to survive that had sustained the Jewish people throughout their millennia of exile.

On May 15, 1967, Egypt mobilized its army. On May 17, President Nasser ordered the United Nations to remove its troops from the Sinai, where they had been providing a buffer patrol between his country and Israel—and to the shock of the Israelis, U.N. Secretary General U Thant complied. On May 23 the Strait of Tiran, entrance to the Gulf of Eilat, was closed to shipping traffic serving Israel. By May 25, a hundred thousand Egyptian soldiers and a thousand tanks had gathered along the Egyptian–Israeli border. Finally, on May 26, Nasser declared his intentions: the total destruction of the State of Israel.

In this "holy war", Nasser was enthusiastically supported by other Arab states. On May 30, King Hussein of Jordan formally committed his troops to Egypt. Syria began to mobilize; Iraq moved troops into Jordan; Algeria and Kuwait moved troops into Egypt; and Saudi Arabia offered money.

As the perfumed month of June burst upon much of the world, Israel found itself alone and surrounded.

Israelis huddled around their radios, listening in growing dismay to enemy voices originating from only a few miles away. They would be "pushed into the sea", "annihilated", and the land of Palestine would be retaken.

The strain was unbearable. Mobilization of the citizen army was ordered on May 23 and was in full effect May 25. And in the early hours of June 5, Israel's air force attacked Cairo's air fields.

"O Almighty God, what a miracle it was that war came along to save me from death," wrote Israeli author Aharon Megged in *The White City*, his fictionalized account of that war. For despair turned into triumph. In six short days, Jerusalem—which had been cried over and dreamed about for so long—once again belonged to the Jews.

When the Six Day War was over, East Jerusalem and the historic Old City were under Israeli occupation, as were the Gaza

Strip and the entire west bank of the Jordan River. And a whole new era began, a new play upon the antique stage of the Middle East.

Hundreds of thousands of Arab refugees were living in the newly occupied territories, in United Nations camps, and they had been there since the creation of the Jewish state in 1948. The question of what to do about them was a major logistical problem, as was the question of all the other Arabs suddenly under Israeli control. To most Israelis, an Arab was a Palestinian who carried out terrorist attacks, or a Bedouin you met on a hike through the Negev, or one of the "Israeli Arabs" of complex and somewhat dubious status who lived in Nazareth or on the hills overlooking Haifa. In the mind-set that had emerged from decades of war and fear, an Arab was the hostile "other" bent on destroying the Jewish state and, with it, the last hope of the Jews.

In spite of these fears, the initial occupation of East Jerusalem was courteous, if somewhat confused. Defence minister Moshe Dayan is said to have appointed combat officers who were, he hoped, free of anti-Arab prejudice. And in his book *The West Bank Story*, Israeli Arab journalist Rafik Halabi claimed that "the policies championed by [Jerusalem mayor] Teddy Kollek...won admiration and support among Arabs."

But how long could it last? The city's Palestinian population began to fight back—with political rejectionism and "armed resistance", which consisted of acts of sabotage and random violence. With each one of these acts, with the spread of "Euro-terrorism" directed at Diaspora Jews, and with the continued passage of years without serious prospects for peace, the spiral of hatred and repression escalated, until, by the late 1980s, the occupation—once so courteous—found itself condemned by Amnesty International for human rights abuses.

Danny Rubenstein, veteran reporter for *Davar*, knew the Occupied Territories well. We met in a Jerusalem restaurant that served Eastern European Jewish food. We laughed to discover that our families had originated from neighbouring towns in

Galicia. Common Jewish origins were a reality of Israel. Neither of us spoke the language of Galicia and we had matured under utterly different circumstances on opposite sides of the world. We were perfect strangers, but we might have been blood cousins from the destroyed world of Polish Jewry.

Rubenstein wrote tough, critical articles about the West Bank occupation, which was acceptable because his paper was the official organ of the Labour party and was read only by people who agreed with him. "My paper is considered serious, which means it is boring," he said with a laugh. "Most of its readers are old intellectuals. The intelligentsia of this country is 100 per cent liberal and left wing. However, if someone were to take my column and put it on television, for example, I would probably be killed in the streets."

"Pardon?"

"A little while ago I was on prime time television in a debate on Jerusalem. My opponent was somebody from the right wing and he was talking about co-existence with the Palestinians, the autonomy stuff. I said, sure, co-existence between the horse and his rider. In the story of Moses and the children of Israel, the Egyptian horse and his rider drowned together in the Red Sea. Well, the next day in the street people were very angry. They were furious at the idea that our fate was tied to the Palestinians, that we might go down together. They all know their Bible. They shouted and shook their fists. I rolled up the windows of my car. I was actually frightened."

"Do you really think you'll all go down together?"

"Actually, we'd go first. They are much, much stronger than us, the Palestinians."

"Everyone says they are weak, including the Palestinians themselves."

"That's because everyone wants to pretend he's a victim. In the long run there is no doubt. There are 150 million Arabs surrounding this area. We are a small island and we are bound to die if peace does not come, if we do not come to terms."

When I write about events in my own country I am not called upon to countenance the possibility of its destruction, or my own destruction, or that of my family, and remain fair and open-minded while doing so. I am not charged with the responsibility of describing a painful, intractable dispute that leaves me feeling uncertain and angry. It is easy to be a journalist in my country. Danny Rubenstein, on the other hand, is deeply pessimistic about Israel's future, and pessimistic about the possibility of peace after twenty years of increasingly entrenched positions on both sides—especially with a new generation of Israelis and Palestinians who never knew the pre-1967 world.

"What keeps you going?" I asked.

He stared into his plate. "If I were motivated only by logic I might give up, but I can't stand it and I can't stand doing nothing. The fact that the Palestinians are under occupation puts me in a situation where I don't feel free. I know what's going on in the West Bank and in the refugee camps and it's almost as though these things are happening in my own house. I need to change this. I try to change this.

"You ask me a personal question. Yeah, I try to promote any kind of conciliation, any kind of negotiation. Direct meetings, indirect meetings, an international conference, I don't really care. I have to talk about it. I have to do something. People are afraid now. When I tell my friends that I'm going to a town like Ramallah they look at me as though I've said I'm going to take a walk in Central Park at midnight. There's almost no contact any more. And that is truly dangerous."

In silence we busied ourselves with the familiar dishes of our Galician grandparents. In another time and in another place they too spoke despairingly of the fate of the Jews.

CHAPTER TWENTY

A Day on the West Bank

In the shared taxicab no one spoke a word as we hurtled north on a sixty-kilometre drive to Nablus, the largest town on the West Bank. Six men in caftans and striped keffiyehs sat motionless on the torn leather seats. Six pairs of eyes looked away abruptly each time mine met theirs in the rearview mirror.

Outside, the boulder-strewn, olive-clad hills of ancient Samaria sped by. The silent men did not look at the familiar landscape. The driver turned on the car radio. Eastern music blared forth, its "Spanish" cadences reminding me of the pervasive Arab influence on that country over the centuries.

Nablus—the ancient Hebrew city of Shechem—lay between Mount Gerizim and Mount Ebal, both of biblical repute. Jacob pitched his tent here and dug his famous well. Joshua came here with the tribes of Israel. During the Roman occupation of the first century A.D., the town was renamed Flavia Neapolis—New City—and Nablus was simply a corruption of that name. Jesus met the Good Samaritan here, and there was still a community of Samaritans living in the town.

Now, two thousand years later, the Israelis were occupying this site—and in recent weeks the following events had occurred:

A large number of sheep belonging to residents of the nearby village of Jaftlek were confiscated by the authorities, who claimed they were grazing inside a military zone. The farmers were required to pay heavy fines to get their animals back.

The authorities declared the confiscation of 12,000 *dunum*s of land from the adjacent village of Kufr Qaddoum, claiming that the land (which was planted with olive and almond trees) was state property. Land owners were given forty-five days to appeal.

One thousand olive trees were uprooted on confiscated land.

Mohammed Hanoun, twenty-four, was sentenced to six years' imprisonment for membership in Al Fatah and possession of a gun.

On this January day, commerce was thriving at the city's central market. Children clustered around vendors who were selling sweets that oozed honey onto large, round trays; vegetable merchants shouted their wares and pointed to stalls of zucchini, eggplant, tomatoes, and avocado; wizened old men grilled lamb on open grates; and on the main street, taxis pulled in and out screeching their tires.

I was to meet someone called Zohair, but no one was waiting at the agreed-upon corner. I lingered somewhat apprehensively by the taxi stand, noticing that there was scarcely a woman in sight.

Suddenly a voice sounded at my ear. "You are welcome," panted a young man with a broad smile stretched across his face.

We quickly determined that "you are welcome" was Zohair's only English phrase, and since my Arabic had just recently expanded to include hello, goodbye, and thank you, prospects for meaningful communication did not look good.

Speechless by necessity, we crossed the square to a local bus that was headed for An Najah University, which had just re-opened after being closed for two and a half weeks by the military authorities. The Israelis thought the West Bank universities had become PLO incubators, stewpots for rebellious activity. Students had taken to demonstrating for Palestinian nationalism loudly and publicly. In return, the military had upped the ante: tear gas and live ammunition, arrests, two students killed at Bir Zeit University at Ramallah.

I began to read An Najah's public relations brochures. Zohair noticed, leaned over to check, and smiled approvingly.

The basic facts were simple enough. An Najah School was created in 1918 and became a university in 1977, as one of several West Bank universities established under Israeli legislation. (During the Jordanian administration of the area from 1948 until 1967, no university institutions had been permitted.) In 1981, An Najah was accepted as a member of the International Union of Universities. By 1985, 3,000 students, almost half of them women, were registered in Arts, Science, Engineering, Education, and Economics and Business Administration. In a faculty of 367, 150 held Ph.D. degrees. But the message of An Najah (one of the brochures was actually called *An Najah Message*) was essentially political:

> When An Najah School was born in 1918, Palestine was witnessing a political shift: the British had just replaced the Ottoman Empire, and as Palestinians we had realized from the start that the existence of our culture, customs and political identity was at stake, and that their preservation was a responsibility we had to bear....
>
> In 1948...the majority of the Palestinian people were transformed into refugees outside their homeland, or in what was left of Palestine. But we clung to the consciousness that continuity, patience and hard work on the part of our generation were the only answer to the tragedy that had overtaken us....
>
> In 1967, what was left of Palestine was occupied, but our will to struggle was not touched.... An Najah was from its inception built to be

the symbol of the Palestinian people's determination to strengthen its steadfastness in its own homeland and for its intellectual and national enlightenment. It follows that the preservation of this institution is a holy duty for each and every one of us....

A "holy duty". This mix of religion and nationalism struck me as ominous, just like the bar mitzvah ceremony at the Martyrs' Monument near Kibbutz Yiftah.

The authors had also reprinted a highly dramatic address to the fourth graduation class, January 10, 1985, which referred indirectly to the consequences of violence:

Ladies and gentlemen: You will find around you those who have allowed despair to enter their lives. Many of those bear within them the seeds of the destruction of their society.... So do not let despair enter into your hearts. Strive to be the light of our dark nights.

Witness with us that even though this building was prevented from being completed, we were able to use space designed for storage and transform it into a place in which to conduct our fourth graduation ceremonies. This day will enter into the history of the struggle-fraught journey of An Najah. Tell your children, have them tell their own, that our determination was stronger than all challenges. Our generation has borne the pain and hopes, and will continue to do so, and will pass them on to the next generation, until our national rights are materialized.

This is your destiny, Najah; this is your destiny, my people; this is your destiny, my nation.

An Najah looked more like a small college than a university. One building contained classrooms, administrative offices, a cafeteria, a small canteen for a quick falafel snack, a central courtyard for strolling, and a mosque. Five times a day, the three thousand students were called to prayer, and 70 per cent of them attended. An explosive combination of Islam and radical Marxism was gaining ground, here as elsewhere.

The majority of these students came from Palestinian refugee camps and the rural areas of the West Bank. They were, to put it mildly, not the economic elite of Palestinian society.

Zohair waved goodbye and a young woman named Anahid approached. She had been designated as my "inside guide", she said.

Anahid was small, vivacious, and humorous. She dressed in Western clothing and spoke a slangy, colloquial American English. She had been to school in Detroit, she said.

She led me past young women in a variety of dress. Most wore long skirts and long sleeves and covered their heads. Some wore the grey, shapeless dress and headgear of Iran's Islamic revolution. One girl hid herself behind a veil of purdah; only her dark eyes peered at me curiously from a narrow slit in grey cloth. Another was equally startling at the opposite end of the spectrum, in black high-heeled shoes, lacy net stockings, and shoulderpads that would have passed for the latest style in Paris.

The sexes strolled separately. Girls talked to boys only in groups.

"You can't talk to a boy alone," said Anahid with a quick laugh. "You would get a bad reputation and then you might not be able to get married."

Anahid's parents had given her permission to talk to any boy she wanted to get to know, but she had to be careful not to attract attention. Their attitude was progressive—and potentially dangerous. Current practice still favoured the arranged marriage. The parents made the connection and the prospective couple shared about five minutes of conversation before they were joined for life.

Anahid was twenty-seven and she had been offered a chance to return to the United States to do graduate work; but she needed to marry first. If she hadn't married by thirty, her prospects within her own society would diminish. So she had her eye on a fellow student, and he had been watching her too. Later in the day they would exchange a few words, supposedly by chance, in the upstairs hall, she whispered conspiratorially.

"Don't tell anybody. I might get a bad reputation," she warned.

Just days earlier, soldiers had surrounded this campus and arrested several students. Guns had been fired, stones thrown. Almost every student leader here had been in prison. Arrest was a badge of honour—almost a prerequisite for student council membership. Yet in the most trying of circumstances, I reflected, the eternal dance went on. A bright, hopeful girl in a violent place. I was reminded how astonished I had been by this universality some two decades ago, as a Canadian student in France. It had come as a warming surprise to realize that my new friends were absorbed by familiar desires.

In a large, bare office down the hall, Dr. Abdul Latif Agel, the university director for public relations, poured two demitasse cups of thick, cardamom-spiced Turkish coffee. Agel was a professor of social psychology with a Ph.D. from the University of California, of which he was extremely proud. His title seemed particularly important. Radwan Abu Ayyash had referred several times to Dr. Agel with a distinct emphasis on the "Dr." In an occupied society, one emphasized dignity and status.

Dr. Agel's voice was cultivated. His dark eyes were strikingly sad. He was particularly upset because An Najah had recently been closed again, for the umpteenth time in its history, because the authorities thought the students were preparing a pro-PLO demonstration.

"It is part of the freedom of students to express themselves politically—they do it all over the world," said Dr. Agel in an agitated voice. "Now the Israelis are punishing the universities, the very institutions of our daily life, as though they were punishing PLO supporters. They are asking us, the administrators, to control the political thoughts of our students and their expression. This is not our job as academics. I do not have the will to interfere in this way...."

Despair was present in this room as in every room in these territories, a dark presence insinuating itself between me and my interlocutor, cracking voices and informing anger.

The distraught voice crackled, stopped and started again, punctuated with barely audible sighs. "I am a peaceful man. I don't want Israelis to be killed or Palestinians to be killed, but we do not control this world [of factionalism within the PLO]. When it comes to that minority in the Palestinian leadership, we condemn it. But in the West we are all considered terrorists, which is a very cruel generalization. The Arabs don't accept us either. We are isolated.

"I will speculate, though. I do believe that if the Palestinians continue to live as deprived as they are now, and if they begin to think that they are losing everything and they have no hope, the younger, more radical generation will initiate a new round of terrible violence. This is humanly true. If there is unbearable provocation—which, by the way, is how many Palestinians perceive the arrival of fanatical Jewish settlers on the West Bank—if there is no escape valve and no give in the rope, if desperation and despair become endemic and there is nothing to lose but a life that is intolerable, human beings will explode."

Yet I seemed to be getting a mixed message from this institution. Dr. Agel spoke of peace and moderation, and he was without any doubt a peaceful, moderate man. But the public relations literature put out by his own department spoke not of academe, but of collective politics. The struggle for a national homeland was integral to the origins and on-going purpose of An Najah University, it said, its very *raison d'être*. Dr. Agel claimed academic remove, but his material did not. At An Najah, a complex of academic and political issues had merged indivisibly.

Anahid was at the door, waiting, she said, to introduce me to my guide to the Balata refugee camp just down the road. Balata had been in the news recently. Demonstrations there had resulted in the shooting death of a boy of fourteen by the Israeli army some weeks earlier. The military government was particularly concerned about Balata, which they considered to be another PLO stewpot.

Mohammed was waiting in the student council office down the hall. He was nineteen years old, small and delicate-looking, with an open face. And he was studying English literature, which he was anxious to try out on me. Tomorrow was his exam.

I apologized for taking him away from his studies.

"I have been studying for twenty-one days," he said proudly in a slightly self-conscious English. He opened his notebook to the section on Anglo-Saxon literature and began to tell me excitedly about Beowulf, of all things.

Beowulf? I had skipped that course during my own university days because I thought the language was too difficult. Mohammed's face tensed with the effort of reading his notes aloud. I watched him, astonished. He was born in a refugee camp; his daily life and that of his parents were of a difficulty that I could in all honesty barely comprehend, coming from a privileged life in a privileged country. The repeated closures of his school might effectively end his academic career. Yet Mohammed, like Anahid, seemed to have remained innocent in his core—a lover of Beowulf.

Around us in the council office, other less innocent students murmured conspiratorially while examining an Arabic newspaper that spoke, no doubt, of their recent experience. They glanced at me suspiciously.

"What are they talking about?" I asked Mohammed quietly.

"Politics," came the all-inclusive answer.

Mohammed and I take a taxi to the Balata camp, and Mohammed insists on paying although he is the refugee and I am the rich visitor.

I feel uneasy at the prospect of visiting a refugee camp. I have heard much about these places. Breeding grounds for terror. Citadels of hatred and despair. Wounds in the flesh of the world.

Muddy hell-holes where an entire generation has been steeped in an all-pervasive ideology of the homeland.

We pass the prison fortress of Jnaid. Mohammed has three cousins in there, he says with some pride. They were convicted of membership in the PLO and of throwing bombs.

There is scarcely a family on the West Bank that does not have someone in prison, and the subsequent suffering endured by women and children is a source of concern. Children's homes abound to care for girls and boys whose mothers cannot cope, or whose fathers and brothers are either in prison or dead. The latter are "martyrs" in the common parlance; the exalted language of religion and death has entered the vernacular.

There is only one main entrance to the Balata camp, home to fifteen thousand people. The others have been blocked off by the military. The yellow clay ground is wet today and little rivulets of muddy water zigzag through furrows and around stones.

Squat, concrete row houses originally erected by UNRWA line the main street. There are several small businesses: a barber shop, a drygoods store, and a grocery shop displaying a handful of vegetables and a few tins. A former sports centre stands locked and deserted, closed five years ago by the military government on the grounds that it served as a centre for anti-Israeli activity.

It is wintry this January day, but two underdressed little girls play in the mud, wearing open sandals. A small boy passes carrying a kerosene can; there is no internal source of heating in these hovels.

Mohammed and I are soon surrounded by a crowd of the curious, including about five or six young men—the radical heart of the camp, I would guess, and probably the object of some Israeli concern. A few women step out of their doorways to observe me with narrowed, unfriendly eyes. Do they disdain the foreign visitor, or merely mistrust the appearance of a woman surrounded by men? Children whisper and giggle and point. They are everywhere, peering out of doorways, running down the roads. The young men shoo them away. The camp's four schools have been overloaded by the growing population of children, and classes are held in shifts. This is the demographic reality of the Occupied Territories. It is estimated that by the year 2002 there will be 2 million Arabs in the West Bank and Gaza, as compared to 1.34 million in 1985.

A muezzin calls the faithful to prayer from the camp mosque; the wailing sounds pierce the surrounding ugliness. Three-quarters of the camp's occupants will stop what they are doing to pray.

This camp attracted international attention not long ago when four people were injured and two "fell as martyrs", as they say. They were all children by anyone's standards. They threw stones and pop bottles and were met by a return volley of bullets. But this recent tragedy is related to me with total neutrality, in the context of the ongoing "struggle".

The programming of the young is thorough and begins, literally, at birth. A stunted-looking boy of twelve is named Tha'ir—the word means "revolution". Tha'ir knows what village in Palestine his family came from, he knows why he no longer lives there ("because of the Zionists"), and he is sure that one day he will go back.

A man of twenty-five, looking forty, tends the drygoods store. He has very little stock.

"Why don't you open your shop outside the camp?" I ask through Mohammed, my interpreter.

"I know the people here. I know they cannot afford the prices in the town, so I must help provide for them. But more important, it is forbidden to leave the camp until the revolution."

"Forbidden by whom?" I ask.

"It is a holy thing to remain here," explains Mohammed.

When the shopkeeper was twelve years old, the army came to the school, arrested him, and jailed him for twenty days. He claims he and four other boys were pulled out at random, no questions asked, no explanations offered. Whatever the facts, that experience thirteen years ago honed his rage and shaped a lifelong commitment to a cause. His radicalism has never faltered.

The crowd of adolescents accompanying me on my rounds is growing larger; they are tough-looking, with strong bodies and wily faces. It is surely these young people who represent the future of the West Bank if a negotiated settlement cannot be found. This hard young generation born under the Israeli occupation, the generation with nothing to lose, is less likely to be amenable to compromise than their elders.

Hatem, the leader of the group, is twenty-five and the camp barber. Inside his shop with its storefront facing the main street of the camp, about fifteen young men press around smoking cigarettes.

They invite me in. The room is almost bare. A barber's chair and a mirror face each other along one wall. A few folding bridge chairs line the back wall like soldiers standing stiffly at attention.

They offer me a chair and gather round.

They tell me that children are beaten and slapped by soldiers and pursued into their homes, that tear gas is lobbed into the camp on a daily basis, that people don't leave their houses after dark, although there is no official curfew. Tension is running high and the Israeli soldiers on patrol are very nervous. Fingers tremble on triggers. None of this is news. The Israeli papers have openly described conditions here.

I nod. I am sympathetic. They decide to trust me.

"How many of you have taken part in military actions?" I ask, using their own glamorized expression to describe just about any activity on behalf of Al Fatah, including terror.

They glance at each other, smirk, and raise their hands as though I were a schoolmarm and they were in class.

Hatem was arrested for "security reasons" when he was eighteen, and sentenced to nine years in prison. He was convicted of membership in the PLO and violent activity. Hatem does not deny either charge, although he will not identify the kind of violence he engaged in. He served seven years of his term and came out, a few months ago, looking thirty-five and brutal.

His friend Faisal served six months for attempting to take revenge on a Palestinian "collaborator". Hakim was arrested for throwing stones.

"We will continue fighting until we get rid of Israel," they recite in a well-rehearsed chorus. "Death to Israel. We will fight to our own death. We will hope for ever."

Only the music is missing. I think of television newsreels of the Iranian revolution, a thousand fists raised as one, a thousand voices proclaiming their willingness to die. I think of Leni Riefenstahl's *The Triumph of the Will*, the Nuremberg rally, a thousand voices raised in the same collective commitment to a revolution and a cause. There are only fifteen men in this room, but they are blood brothers to the rest.

But now a smooth-skinned boy of fourteen with a child's face presses through the crush of his elders, wanting to be seen.

"Would you die?" I ask him quietly.

"Oh yes, oh yes." He nods enthusiastically, as though I had asked if he would try out for the soccer team.

A serious, intelligent-looking young man draws up his chair. He is earnest. Brown doe-eyes implore me to listen. "Our daily life is what you see here. We have no hope so we must believe that there is a way out. Maybe death is our way," he says. His English is excellent. He enjoys school. He would like to be a teacher one day, he says, if he can.

They are intransigent. The only acceptable Israelis, they say, are those who were here before the Balfour Declaration of 1917. In the state they envision, these few Jews and a few Christians will live under the aegis of the PLO.

But these men-boys are followers, not leaders; they are the foot-soldiers who will be sent into the fray. In the final analysis, they will accept whatever a victorious PLO decrees. Should the PLO wish to wipe out Israel, they will carry out its bidding.

Should the PLO wish to recognize Israel and accept a separate Palestinian state on the West Bank, they will accept that too.

Who is the leader you respect most?

The answer comes swiftly, amid smiles. "Abu, Abu, Abu."

Do they mean Abu Nidal? He is probably the world's most-feared Palestinian terrorist. But one of them explains that "Abu" is their familiar name for Arafat.

"What about George Habbash? Or Abu Nidal?"

They hate Nidal as they adore Arafat. Arafat also hates Nidal. Indeed, hatred is the cardinal emotion here. Hatred of the Israelis, hatred of Arafat's enemies, hatred of those who "collaborate" with Israel, hatred of King Hussein of Jordan, who is currently at odds with Arafat.

"The Israelis want to kick us out of this land," hisses a thin boy in English. He is visiting from Ramallah. He has just been released from prison for participating in the riots at Bir Zeit University several weeks ago.

His hands shake as he raises a cigarette to his lips. "We must find the bad Zionists who do these things and kill them. I am permitted to do *anything* to attack my enemy." He pauses, watches me for a reaction. "If you imprison a cat it will become a lion."

I catch my breath. "Is it Israelis you hate, or Jews wherever they are?"

The question provokes a long, animated discussion in Arabic.

"It's the Zionists we hate, not Jews in general," says Hatem, the leader. "The Zionists led the Jews to Palestine. They said it was an empty country, but we were here. They forced us to leave our land."

"Do you all think that?" I ask, looking around for some expression of the discussion that preceded this answer.

There is a momentary silence. "We all think the same," says Hatem firmly. The others nod wordlessly.

Suddenly they rush to the window of the barber shop and look down the road. The Israeli military patrol is here. A crack of gunshot breaks the air.

I jump up from my chair to look. A few metres away, several soldiers are pointing guns. They are wearing riot helmets with plastic masks. There is scurrying in a narrow path just opposite me. A little girl of four or five rushes for cover. A teenager emerges, hurls a stone, then runs to hide.

Someone grabs my arm and pushes me back to my chair. We sit in stillness. No one breathes.

One of the soldiers stops in front of the shop window. He stands with his back to us, one foot before the other in a position of readiness, pointing a gun down the lane opposite us, where the child and the stone-thrower scurried to safety a moment ago. He is the same age as the young Al Fatah men who are protecting me in a confusing, topsy-turvy reversal of ethnic allegiance.

The soldiers move on down the road. A youth runs into the shop, a cloth in front of his nose. Tear gas.

My heart is pounding. I am afraid to move. Eventually the soldiers leave—as abruptly as they arrived.

For several minutes I cannot speak.

"This is our daily life," says Mohammed, the lover of Beowulf.

Outside my apartment that night, there is the strangled sound of someone going berserk in the street. His voice is garbled, but I think the language is Arabic.

Why is he here? What is happening to him? Is my door properly locked?

Earlier in the day, I cowered with Palestinians before an armed Israeli patrol. Tonight I am vulnerable, as a Jew, to a Palestinian at the end of his tether.

CHAPTER TWENTY-ONE

The Politics of the Messiah

There were three distinct worlds on the West Bank: the Palestinians; the Israeli military infrastructure that maintained the
occupation of the territories; and the messianic nationalist Jews
and other supporters of "Greater Israel", who had settled there
to demonstrate that Judea and Samaria, as they called the region,
belonged to the Jewish state by right.

In this Lilliputian universe, a modern Gulliver could step from
one community to the other in a single stride.

The settlers' world had been implanted alongside (and sometimes inside) the Arab communities, but the Palestinians ignored
it except as an irritant, a provocation, a symbol of the encroach-
ing Israeli occupation. Similarly, the Jews ignored the Arabs
except as a proletariat who constructed the settlements and did
other manual labour, except as a potential threat to property and
perhaps to life itself.

The "invisibility" factor was perfectly symbolized by the new
Trans-Samaria highway, which linked the Jewish settlements by
bypassing Arab towns and villages on its route. When the road
was finally completed, it would be possible to drive the length

and breadth of the territory without ever encountering Palestinian society.

"This is an act of God!" panted David Bedein. I had walked into the Jerusalem office of the committee that spoke and lobbied for the Jewish settlers of the Occupied Territories. "We were just discussing how to create more PR for the settlement movement when you appeared! Could you help us place articles in Canada? They are already written." He smiled an engaging, friendly smile.

I smiled back. "I'm not in public relations."

He looked embarrassed.

His colleague got up to leave. "Tell 'S' that I've read a few issues of *Al Awdah*, the mag put out by Ayyash, and as far as I'm concerned it is not only anti-Israel, but anti-Semitic. And Siniora, I've got some stuff on him, too," he said.

"Sure," replied David, glancing in my direction.

Who *were* these Jewish settlers who lived in the population centres of the West Bank? Admittedly there was no guarantee of safety anywhere in Israel; but to choose to move house and family into one of the world's hottest political cauldrons seemed a barely rational act.

In an ironic twist, the right-wing settlers of the West Bank had apparently managed to appropriate the myths of secular, left-wing Zionism. In fact, the extreme right now considered itself the true heir to the Zionist dream. *They* had settled the new borders. *They* protected Jerusalem and Tel Aviv from surprise attack by their very presence amid the enemy. Their settlements were a buffer, they said, the way the socialist kibbutzim used to be. While the Labour Party and the combined institutions of the left had become flabby and ineffectual, while the kibbutzim sat on the richest land and their members lolled around swimming pools, *they* were carrying on the difficult, pioneering traditions of Israel.

Merely to mention the verb "to build" in this country—or "pioneer" or "settlement" or "border defence"—was enough to evoke an instant catch in the breath or skip of the heart. So the old-new appropriated language of the Judea and Samaria settlement movement appealed to a war-exhausted population whose energies were traditionally fueled by idealism.

The extreme right might have successfully revived the ideological fanaticism of the original exalted ones—the young Zionists who emigrated to Palestine from Russia in the early years of the century—but the content of their ideology was entirely different. For one thing, the settlers were not "building" in quite the same way. Their modern two-storey villas provided a quality of life that was undreamed of in the early kibbutzim and unattainable even in modern Israel. Nor did they farm the land; almost 40 per cent of those who were employed commuted to Tel Aviv and Jerusalem. The others worked in the settlement bureaucracy, or within the important religious infrastructure.

The religious component was also new. Unlike the ultra-Orthodox in Mea Shearim and Geula, who barely tolerated the existence of the state and largely repudiated Zionism, the religious nationalists of the settlement movement had assigned God an active role in contemporary Middle Eastern politics. Not unlike the imams of Iran, the fundamentalists among them believed that everything one needed to know about the modern world could be found in Holy Writ.

Their rallying call was Judea and Samaria, the heartland of the ancient Jewish kingdoms. God had promised His people that they would return to the Land of Israel, and they had. Judea and Samaria *were* the Land of Israel, and a thousand times more important than Tel Aviv would ever be. The territories must never be negotiated away for anything as politically naive as "peace"; or for any other reason, including the decisions of a democratically elected government. Since the Arabs could not be trusted, to give up territory would be tantamount to murdering the Jewish people, not to mention an unpardonable affront to God which would not remain unpunished.

The movement began with the Chief Rabbi under the British Mandate, Rabbi Abraham Isaac Kook. Unlike most of his colleagues, Rabbi Kook was in favour of close ties between the atheistic kibbutzniks and the Orthodox. He argued that Jewish settlement in Palestine was the first stage in the prophesied redemption. Secular Zionism was not merely spiritual degeneration, as the other Orthodox rabbis thought, but "descent for the purpose of ascent". It actually laid the framework for a religious rebirth. So the establishment of the State of Israel, and the history of Zionism itself, were interpreted by Kook and his followers as part of an irreversible messianic trend.

The early political Zionists who had modelled their beliefs on nineteenth-century European liberation movements, and who had moved to Palestine precisely to escape the stifling Orthodoxy of their ancestors, must surely have felt uneasy at this transformation. But no one complained too loudly, for Rabbi Kook headed off conflict by making Zionism respectable in religious circles.

Kook's son, Rabbi Zvi Yehuda Kook, also discerned a mystical, messianic sub-text to ordinary political events, but just days before the outbreak of the Six Day War he upset his devotees by appearing to take a more political tack. He told his audience that without its holy cities of Hebron and Nablus and Jericho (all of which happened to be in territory controlled by Jordan) Israel was a mutilated body.

When the Six Day War broke out and Israel gained the West Bank, Rabbi Kook's followers saw the victory as concrete evidence of God's active presence in history. Was any further proof needed? Rabbi Kook was clearly a latter-day prophet.

In 1973, the six-year euphoria abated. Israel was attacked again, on the eve of Yom Kippur, and for the first twelve hours things looked bad indeed. The war was won—but at great cost.

Immediately following the Yom Kippur War, a group of young Orthodox men gathered in the religious kibbutz of Kefar Etzion. They were part of the Rabbi Kook–inspired Gush Emunim—The Bloc of the Faithful—and they challenged the religious camp in Israel to move more forcibly into politics. What they wanted was clear and simple: the annexation of the West Bank, Gaza, the Golan Heights, and parts of the Sinai.

For the zealots of Gush Emunim, the connection between redemption and radical politics was obvious. They believed that the Land of Israel was holy not just symbolically, but literally. Every rock, stick, and olive tree was sanctified by God and included in the holy promissory note. God had decreed that every pebble belonged to the Jews. Only when they claimed the Land in its entirety would the Messiah come—and by settling in Judea and Samaria, they were helping to hasten that day.

In 1977, when Menachem Begin was elected in a social revolution that ended the rule of the left and gave voice to the non-European, non-socialist, non-secular population who had lived outside the national power structure for thirty years, the Gush Emunim movement became mainstream. Begin was delighted to have a group of young "pioneers" who espoused a right-wing, revisionist Zionism and were prepared to settle in controversial areas. Once they were ensconced on the land, territorial trade-offs in return for peace would become difficult, if not impossible.

Almost immediately, the new "Redemption Zionism" won recognition from the World Zionist Organization as a "pioneering movement" and was thus seen as equal to older Zionist institutions such as the kibbutzim. This financial and ideological support sent a signal to Jews, Arabs, and everyone else that the idea of an expanded "Greater Israel" beyond the Green Line had acquired mainstream respectability, even outside Israel.

Between 1983 and 1986, the number of settlers on the West Bank increased by 118 per cent, housing units increased by

45 per cent, and public investment by 56 per cent.[1] Indeed, in this winter of 1987 the World Zionist Organization was leading tourists on guided visits of the settlements—presumably along the Trans-Samaria highway.

Back in 1968, a small group of Gush Emunim fundamentalists had moved to the city of Hebron, in the heart of the West Bank. Hebron held special significance for religious Jews, who considered it the second most holy city, after Jerusalem. Hebron was the site of the Tomb of the Patriarchs, the Cave of Machpelah, which Abraham purchased for four hundred silver shekels in order to bury his wife Sarah. Isaac and Jacob were also buried there, along with their wives, Rebecca and Leah. David founded his kingdom in Hebron and ruled there for seven years before he conquered Jerusalem. Pockets of Jews had inhabited the city almost continuously through the millennia until 1929, when more than sixty people were murdered in an Arab pogrom. That event had been seared into the collective memory.

But Hebron was also holy to the Muslims, for Abraham was also the father of Ishmael, and they too venerated the Tomb of the Patriarchs. They had converted it into a mosque and excluded Jewish worshippers.

The Gush Emunim group (which included several dozen people) was led by Rabbi Moshe Levinger, a disciple of Rabbi Zvi Yehuda Kook. In defiance of the military government and the local Arab population, the settlers squatted in the town's central hotel for six months, until they were forcibly transferred to an Israeli military camp.

For four years Levinger refused to leave this camp, until he was finally granted authorization to build a Jewish settlement, Kiryat Arba, on the eastern outskirts of Hebron.

---

[1] West Bank Data Base Project, 1987

Kiryat Arba was first settled in 1971, but development remained limited by lack of land until 1977. Then, with Begin's co-operation, the legal power of the Israeli authorities was brought to bear. The military government appropriated a barren area around Hebron "for security reasons", and Kiryat Arba expanded.

But the High Court of Justice rejected this method of land acquisition, forcing the authorities to find another way. They did: all unregistered, uncultivated areas around Arab communities were now called "state land", regardless of their previous status.

In 1979 Levinger, his American-born wife, Miriam, their children, and seven other families moved from Kiryat Arba into the heart of Hebron, where they were granted permanent residence under military protection. The Arabs reacted with outrage, claiming that Jewish settlement would change the Islamic character of Hebron and create further conflict. In the summer of 1983, a Jewish settler was stabbed to death in broad daylight in the Hebron market. That same summer, three Arab students were murdered by the local Jewish underground.

The director of Israel's Shin Bet intelligence service was reported to have called the Gush settlements "psychological hothouses for the growth of Jewish terror." An underground emerged, which attempted to assassinate Arab mayors, attacked a Moslem college in Hebron, tried to blow up Arab buses, and plotted to blow up the Dome of the Rock mosque in Jerusalem.

By early 1987, the 65,000 Jews living in the West Bank were estimated to possess no fewer than 10,000 firearms of all types,[2] and civil strife with the Palestinians was increasing. Before 1982 there were about 500 "disturbances" per year; by 1987 there were more than 3,000.

---

[2] West Bank Data Base Project

"I'd like to talk to you about the Gush Emunim movement," I said to Miriam Levinger over the telephone. Although her husband, the rabbi, received most of the press, several people had suggested that she was the real spokesperson for the movement.

"It's all in the Bible. Do you know the Bible? It's all there." She sounded tired. Shouldn't everyone know the Bible by heart? Why would I want to interview her when I could get the story in half the time?

Nevertheless, she agreed to see me.

I placed another call to a woman in Kiryat Arba. She was also American-born, like so many of the Gush settlers.

"I've been burned too many times. Why don't you interview Rabbi Kahane instead?" she suggested. "The leftist pollsters say his popularity has dropped, but I can tell you that three hundred people came to hear him in Ephrat and he was very well received. They were people who were against him when they lived in the United States, but when you're here, let me tell you, it's not Manhattan. You have to *think* about things."

I placed a third call to Eliakim Haetzni, a lawyer and secular Kiryat Arba militant who was constantly in the news. Lately he had charged that the exploration of peace options with Jordan "threatened to turn Jewish West Bank settlers into cockroaches in a bottle".[3] Clearly a man who did not mince words.

Haetzni would be happy to see me.

So I braced myself for another trip into the territories, into the parallel world of the Jews.

Last time, I had travelled here in an Arab sherut surrounded by silent, expressionless men. This trip—in an Israeli bus—entailed different risks. Stonings of Israeli vehicles had increased recently. And this morning's newspaper reported new disturbances at An Najah and the Balata refugee camp. The university had

[3] *The Jerusalem Post*, January 27, 1987.

been closed once again, this time for a month, and a curfew imposed on the camp. Eleven Balata residents had been wounded with rubber and live shot, including a teenage girl who was hit when she left her house to collect a younger brother.

Since almost no one ventured into the West Bank these days except those who lived there, had business there, or were doing their military service, my fellow passengers were an interesting lot.

A woman soldier of nineteen or twenty had done her best to feminize her uniform. She wore three earrings in her left ear, a jaunty ponytail, and a leather shoulder-bag, and she simultaneously chewed gum and smoked a long, thin cigarillo. A rifle hung casually over her shoulder like an airline tote bag.

An American youth listened to his Walkman with rapt concentration, utterly oblivious of his surroundings.

The middle-aged woman beside me conversed loudly with her friends in the row behind and dropped a steady stream of crumbs from her chopped egg sandwich onto my shoulder.

A wild-looking fat man with long, unkempt hair sang rousing songs of the early Palmach in a booming baritone. He stamped his foot on the floor in rhythmical accompaniment. No one seemed to notice.

A passenger engaged the driver in animated conversation from halfway back in the bus. The driver turned constantly to address his friend face to face while at the same time waving at every vehicle that passed, whether Arab or Israeli. To my consternation, watching the road did not appear to be one of his current interests.

A soldier walked up and down the aisle checking the baggage racks. Didn't they do this *before* the bus left the terminal? It occurred to me that I was almost certainly the only person on board who was not armed.

Outside, some of the world's most ancient and emotionally laden landscape rolled by. To the left was Rachel's Tomb; to the right, the new Jewish settlement of Elazar, named after the brother of the hero Judah Maccabee who was crushed to death while killing an elephant brought into battle by the occupying Greeks. The town of Bethlehem displayed a small sign directing visitors to the Church of the Nativity, but there were no tourists in sight. Christians were as wary as Jews about entering the West Bank these days.

A second billboard announced—to my mystification—that "Jesus" was at the King David cinema.

A road sign in several languages warned travellers that they were passing through the area at their own risk, and that they should not drive after dark.

Along the roadside, the Dheisheh refugee camp spread its prison-like squalor. A young Palestinian woman stood squarely on the pavement and stared at us as we passed. I met her hard eyes and looked away. She communicated hatred: unmistakable, implacable hatred. Yesterday I had come accompanied by her friends. Today I was the enemy.

Stones and boulders dotted the land like splintered meteorites. A thick mist rose from the valleys and wafted about the hilltops, hiding and then revealing the settlements below. How appropriately symbolic, I thought to myself, since the underlying reality of this place seemed to reside in the dreams, the fantasies, and finally the rage that enveloped its warring inhabitants.

I got off at the central marketplace of Hebron. Two Arab women who had been on the bus approached me as I stood apprehensively at the edge of the market, wondering where to go. "Aren't you afraid?" they asked in English, with direct curiosity.

"Should I be?" I replied, taken aback and feeling suddenly fearful. They laughed and patted me, then disappeared into the crowd.

Unlike the Arab bazaar of Jerusalem, the Hebron market did not cater to tourists. A crush of people milled about, the men in keffiyehs, the women in long, embroidered dresses and covered heads. Carts overflowed with avocados, oranges, lettuce, and eggplant. Vendors cooked shishkabob on portable grills while others displayed stacks of baklava and other Eastern sweets dripping with honey and pistachio nuts.

The market snaked off to the left through a narrow, covered alleyway, and an intoxicating smell of cardamom, cinnamon, saffron, and a thousand other spices filled the air. Whole goats and lambs hung from hooks, to the evident delight of a horde of flies.

I watched—and I was watched. Was I a new settler in the heart of this city? A tourist? The latter was an unlikely possibility these days.

Where should I go? Mrs. Levinger had said she lived beside the market, at the end of the road, but I had no idea which road she meant. Was it this large, congested square? And which direction should I try?

Two Israeli soldiers moved off together at the other end of the market. I began to run after them, dodging people, carts, and goats as I followed them into the labyrinth of the souk. They were walking quickly.

"Excuse me, excuse me," I called out. I was afraid of bumping into someone who was feeling jumpy about my presence. I smiled broadly as I weaved around old men and children, but I was attracting a lot of unwelcome attention.

Gasping and out of breath, I caught up with the soldiers. "Mrs. Levinger?" I panted.

They did not speak English but they pointed in the direction I had just come from. *"Toda, toda,"* I said, turning back disconsolately to the open section of the market. "Thank you, thank you."

But now I saw it: a tiny entrance area to the settlers' enclave guarded by two soldiers who had an air of readiness in spite of their deceptively casual, unmilitary bearing. They asked me questions, checked my ID, then indicated a small gate just behind them which opened into a narrow pathway.

To the right stood the ancient synagogue of Rabbi Avraham Avino. The path led a few feet farther into a small courtyard, where several old wooden doors stood ajar. It was lunchtime and cooking odours filled the air.

I entered the door to the Levinger apartment, walked up a few stairs, and knocked (if that's the word) on a sheet of opaque plastic.

"Hello?" I called out optimistically.

An American voice invited me to enter. I walked through a narrow, whitewashed corridor into a large, open kitchen. Miriam Levinger was seated at a long table in the centre of the room, peeling large numbers of potatoes. She was about fifty, with an open face and a girlish smile. Her hands were reddened from a lifetime of scrubbing. Wisps of greying hair escaped from beneath the scarf that covered her head. The old apron she had tied around her waist had seen better days, but then, Miriam Levinger was not interested in designer aprons.

She invited me to sit down at the kitchen table as she moved deftly from potatoes to carrots and garlic buds. Her children ranged in age from twenty-seven to six, she said. She had given birth constantly throughout her fertile years and her youngest child was the same age as her oldest grandchild.

We were immediately engaged in a universal female ritual, Mrs. Levinger and I: two women talking at the kitchen table over peeled vegetables. There was something about this familiar, shared experience that helped break down barriers of time, place, and belief.

But the illusion of commonality did not last long.

Miriam Levinger was utterly untroubled by the conflict engendered by her choice of residence. Life, for her, was supremely simple—which may have accounted for her unlined face and serene expression as she peeled carrots in her kitchen at the heart of an Arab souk.

Her arguments had been honed on countless other occasions and they rolled off her tongue with practised confidence. They seemed to have been shaped according to a tried-and-true technique: appropriate the language of your foe and use it against him.

For example, Mrs. Levinger wanted to talk about pluralism and democracy, the prized principles of liberals. Mrs. Levinger was anything but a liberal, by definition, but she was not averse to using their ideas combatively.

"People always say, 'How can you live here? It's so provocative,'" she volunteered, anticipating (quite rightly) that the questions she was likely to hear from me were the usual ones. "Well, the people who ask me that question believe in pluralism, but even from *their* point of view I should have the right to live in Hebron, shouldn't I? Why would I be excluded? It is *democratic* for me to live here."

"What rights do the Palestinians have?"

"They came seven hundred years after the destruction of the Second Temple, but before that there were more than four thousand years of Jewish history. There was Abraham, Isaac, Jacob and so on. The Arabs came afterwards, so I am afraid I cannot accept their claim to this land.

"The Arabs can stay, but not if they start to kill us. In any case, the Bible says the enemies of the Jews will eventually leave, although this does not necessarily mean they'll all go right away."

Jews and Arabs could live together temporarily—until the Arabs left. This was "pluralism".

Her notion of democracy seemed to be even more selective. "The State of Israel is the government of the Jews, and I appreciate the fact that this is a country where Jews are at home and not at the mercy of rulers who can become hostile. I'm sure the Jews of Russia or Iran would like to see a Jewish soldier." But for her this soldier had to be a Jew first and a servant of the state second. As a Jew he was defined by the Bible and not by the secular state.

Democracy was a useful tool as long as elected leaders acted according to God's directives. If and when they stopped doing that, democracy would naturally take a back seat to God.

Her husband was even more direct. "Jewish national renaissance is more important than democracy," he told two French journalists. "You can no more democratically suppress Zionism, the Law of Return, and colonization than you can forbid people to breathe or speak."[4]

Between 1977 and 1984, when the government of Menachem Begin had the "right" priorities and Jewish settlement in the West Bank was a major item on the political agenda, democracy was seen as a good thing. However, the unity government of Peres and Shamir was definitely on shakier ground, with its half-hidden, half-open negotiations with King Hussein of Jordan over the possibility of returning parts of The Land. God did not *want* The Land returned to the Arabs.

In Mrs. Levinger's vocabulary, the word "Arab" was strangely non-specific. Arabs were merely the most recent "enemies of the Jews" in a never-ending history of anti-Semitism. This depersonalizing of the "enemy-other" seemed to be a necessary first stage of any war. The enemy became "the Gook", "the Hun", "the Jap", "the Jew", or "the Arab". Young soldiers needed to forget they were dealing with people, needed to practise running bayonets through anonymous straw figures with hideous "enemy" faces. That was what "basic training" was all about, in every country—teaching hatred. I thought of the conditioned hostility of the young men in the Balata refugee camp, and the gullibility of the American women at the Wailing Wall who believed Arab men cooked their wives.

Mrs. Levinger's religious beliefs combined effortlessly with the Israeli siege mentality (Jews are for ever isolated, alone and

---

[4] Raphael Mergui and Philippe Simonnot; quoted in *Meir Kahane: Le Rabin Qui Fait Peur aux Juifs*

unprotected) *and* the essential message of Zionism (only in Israel can a Jew be protected from a future Holocaust). The predictable result was the generic Arab, seen as the most recent incarnation of the Romans, the Spanish Inquisitor, and the Nazis.

She scrubbed vegetables at the sink and I thought again about the deceptive banality of this kitchen and the housewife who ran it. Her window looked out into the *Jewish* compound. The souk, only a few metres away, was as invisible as the entirety of Palestinian society from the Trans-Samaria highway.

The Levingers' eleven children had grown up here, so it was not surprising that the husband of one of their daughters was a member of the Jewish terrorist underground and had been sentenced to life imprisonment for murder.

"There are incidents, yes," said Miriam Levinger, turning from the sink to look at me. "You may call them terrorism, but we call them self-defence. We don't think about the immediate future, we think about the very long term, about the future of the Jewish people. We came here because God told us to come and we stay because that is what He ordained. We are the vanguard."

She insisted on walking me back through the market and out to the road, and waiting until the bus arrived. We did not speak of danger, but I was safer with her at my side. Everyone in the market knew who she was, and who her husband was, and that they were protected by the IDF.

"Those who want to remain Jews come here," she said matter-of-factly. "We are safer here than in the Diaspora."

Had I heard right? I looked back at the Hebron market. What kind of fantasy would describe this as the safest place in the world for Jews? Was she "safer" here than in London, Manhattan, Paris, or Miami? What did "safer" mean in her lexicon?

It occurred to me that for Miriam Levinger, the "Jewish vanguard" was as vague as the "Arab-enemy". She and her family were merely part of an inexorable, divinely proclaimed process that would culminate in the coming of the Messiah. Destiny would prevail, even if individuals did not.

I glanced back at the soldiers who guarded the entrance to her compound. Like it or not, the taxpayers of Israel and the Diaspora Jews who contributed to Israel were also actively preparing for the coming of the Messiah, for the Levingers' physical safety did not depend on God's will, but on the officers who guarded them night and day at public expense. If the Levingers and the other West Bank settlers were "safe" while they squatted in the heart of Arab Hebron, it was because they were backed by the military power of the modern state.

In an otherwise fantasy world, *that* was reality.

CHAPTER TWENTY-TWO

Kiryat Arba

Kiryat Arba was a sprawling development of about four thousand people, and quite luxurious by Israeli standards. Two-storey villas stood white against the sky, their roofs decorated with solar heating panels. There were green lawns, playgrounds, shopping areas, a community centre, and a hotel.

At first glance, Kiryat Arba looked like a 1950s-style suburb, a retreat from the city core for young families wanting to raise their children with fresh air and living space.

This was partly true; but a poster on the wall of the community centre conveyed a more accurate message about this place. It was an aerial photo of Masada, the mountain where besieged Jewish Zealots committed mass suicide rather than surrender to the Romans. Across the picture was printed in large, black letters: *MASADA LIVES.*

In the settlement movement, the past propelled the present.

Eliakim Haetzni lived in one of these villas. The wide picture windows of his spacious living room displayed a wondrous view of the Judean Hills—as well as the ubiquitous barbed-wire fence at the foot of his garden.

Inside, the house was painted white and decorated with paintings of biblical themes. A large oil of David with his harp covered one wall; a pastoral scene from ancient Palestine and other paintings of indeterminate subject looked down from different parts of the room.

A coiled plastic cobra rose from the top of the television set, ready to strike.

"What's that?" I asked.

Mr. Haetzni smiled a wry smile. "That represents the media," he replied.

Eliakim Haetzni came to Israel from Germany in 1938, just in the nick of time. His family was "more or less Orthodox", he said, and the socialist, kibbutz experience was not their style. They were refugees, not idealists.

Haetzni was indifferent to his parents' religious practices, but he did become interested in Zionism. *Real* Zionism. Not the washed-out, dried-up, bankrupt Zionism of the left-wing kibbutzniks, but the neo-Zionism of the new pioneers, of the settlement movement.

Haetzni wasn't religious; in fact, he thought fundamentalist Judaism "takes us back to the Middle Ages". But Judea and Samaria remained the heart of the Land of Israel, he explained. "These are the places Jews dreamed of returning to. And the whole sense of Zionism was The Return."

Eliakim Haetzni was sixty years old and looked physically strong. He also had a loud voice. "I'm not yelling at *you*," he shouted, five minutes into our discussion, jabbing a finger in the direction of my chest. "I am yelling at all the people who will *read* you and whose questions you are asking!"

The bulk of his anger was aimed at a large, amorphous entity called "The Left", a coalition of old-style Zionists, the kibbutzniks, the media, the Labour Alignment, sell-out peacemakers, liberals, and everyone else who did not see the world as he did.

"The leftist camp which originally built the State of Israel got tired and all their ideological arteries got plugged. But the people who are afflicted with this disease do not feel it. They hold onto the wheel until rigor mortis sets in and they are very jealous if someone else wants to take their crown away. It's like Saul and David."

Metaphors did not seem to be his forte, but the point was clear. We both glanced over at David playing his harp. He smiled approvingly.

"Before 1967 there had been no new settlements in the Galilee for fifteen years. The kibbutzniks got very selfish and the egotism of the individual became the egotism of the collective. That produced all the scandals of today. They play the stock market, there is hashish on the kibbutzim now, and they have land they cannot cultivate themselves so they bring in foreign volunteers. The volunteers bring in the opposite of everything the kibbutz stands for, and then take the kibbutzims' best children away with them."

These were, of course, the very concerns I had heard voiced on Kibbutz Yiftah by some of the kibbutzniks themselves. The latter suffered from the second-day-of-the-revolution syndrome. Mr. Haetzni and his fellow settlers were in the first flush of their right-wing revolution.

"So this is a disease," he continued. "The leaders are not pioneers or trail blazers, they are self-satisfied men." Inexplicably, he began to laugh uproariously.

Suddenly he interrupted himself. "Are you Christian?" he asked.

"I'm Jewish."

"Oh...."

I waited, but there was no follow-up. He returned just as abruptly to the subject at hand.

"If these leftists had achieved their aim and all the Jews in the world lived here, if we had no more wars and the Arabs did not plan and scheme and dream out of the very essence of

Islam to destroy the Jewish state at every border, if Islam was not getting more and more rabid and extremist, which it is, if all these problems were solved, then we could say Israel had finished its revolutionary stage and we could settle down and be like everyone else, like France, for example. But it is not so. We need to fight against the militancy of Islam and to do that we need people who are not tired of fighting. The leftists are tired, but we are still in the process of regaining Israel and the job has not been completed yet.

"We are keeping the whole Zionist dream alive. We protect the entire state, and the minute we go, the whole thing will blow up. There is a settlement that overlooks Ben-Gurion airport, and as long as there are Jews in that settlement, the airport is safe. As long as we are here, Judea and Samaria will not come under Arab rule.

"Not to understand this is to be sick in the mind."

His index finger stabbed holes in the air. His voice boomed off the wall.

"*They* [the leftists] are doing what the Jews in Europe did. Their leaders told them to mount the trains that took them to the gas chambers. When the victims got to Auschwitz they saw a sign, 'Work makes you free.' There was a band playing, and at the gas chamber there was a sign that said, 'Showers'. Now the word 'Peace' is written on the gas chambers. But the same gas is coming out."

I was not prepared for the cynicism of this argument.

"What's wrong with peace, Mr. Haetzni?"

"For peace, you need two sides. Chamberlain thought that if he believed Hitler, there would be peace. So what do our new *ghetto* leaders say about their talks with King Hussein? They say that what he says to the Arabs is for internal consumption. In the early 1930s, my father said Hitler's speeches were for internal consumption."

"I suppose your experience in Germany has helped shape your thinking," I suggested. This struck me as perfectly logical and natural.

"What?" he shouted. "This is not personal! This is the experience of all Jews! *We are all survivors of the Holocaust! Our genetic code is stamped for thousands of years with the stamp of the Holocaust!*"

We seemed to have come to an impasse.

After a moment he remembered that although I was "the media", I was also a visitor in his home. He disappeared into the kitchen to prepare coffee.

I absently looked at his bookshelves.

His collection was thin but revealing. The emphasis was on war and conflict—and the acquisition of power. There were several volumes on the life of Napoleon; Gibbon's *The Rise and Fall of the Roman Empire*; Machiavelli's *The Prince*; the complete set of Churchill's memoirs; the autobiography of Charles de Gaulle; *Power* and *Spartacus*, both by Howard Fast; and Herzl's *The Jewish State*. In the category of "know thy enemy", the Koran sat on a shelf along with a book on the Ottoman sultan Suleiman the Magnificent, who occupied and rebuilt the city of Jerusalem in the sixteenth century.

Mr. Haetzni returned to the living room looking composed and friendly. Now he spoke of the Palestinians among whom he lived.

His description of his neighbours fit perfectly into a colonial mould. Most Arabs were "quiet", "law-abiding", and "co-operative" with the military government and civilian administration, he said. They were also "ready to accept Israeli rule".

"There is no popular uprising, except in the media. The PLO is 99 per cent public relations."

But there was a catch. Underneath their submissive skins, Arabs were devious and primitive. They informed on their fellows ("for every terrorist, there are ten who tell"); they committed atrocities ("a boy stabbed his sister because the family thought she was not a virgin").

"We take our Arab neighbours as we find them." He sighed benevolently.

So much for the lumpenproletariat. It was the intellectuals whom Eliakim Haetzni truly feared, and he never missed an opportunity to claim that they were front men for the PLO. The fact that some of them had begun to promote non-violence and civil disobedience in the style of Martin Luther King did not deter him. Non-violence only hampered Haetzni's plans; his goal was to get the intellectuals deported from the region.

At the time of our meeting, he had just brought charges against a Jerusalem notable named Faisal Husseini. "The law forbids any expression of support for the PLO and Faisal Husseini said he was the legitimate representative of the Palestinian people. Siniora, too. I would like to see both of them deported."

"You've studied history so you know you can't suppress ideas," I pointed out. "Isn't the return of the Jews to Palestine a perfect example of that? Someone else will emerge to replace the leaders you're having arrested."

"So he also will be deported. If they are living under Jewish rule, they have to abide by that rule, because this is our part of Palestine."

If Aladdin had come along with his magic carpet and transported Mr. Haetzni and myself and everyone else in the West Bank to say, Algeria, in the 1950s, we would not have felt entirely out of place. The French did not hold that God had promised them Algeria, nor did they need to worry about the safety of their families back in France—at least, not until the warfare began—but they did approach the local population with the standard colonial baggage of paternalism, contempt, condescension, and exploitation. Before the Algerians were radicalized by angry militants in their midst, the peasant population had appeared similarly co-operative and submissive to their over-lords. Quite a few Algerian notables had curried favour with the French, for which they were immediately rewarded with medals, money, and other incentives.

Their pandering changed nothing. In spite of a bloody colonial war which, in turn, produced a civil war in France between those who would hold onto Algeria at any cost and those who favoured independence, the outcome was inevitable.

Civil war was something Mr. Haetzni had already contemplated. He would not obey a political decision to trade land for peace, he said, and his reasons went to the heart of the ambiguity inherent in the Israeli state. Was Israel the state of the Jews, who, like any other democratic population, were constrained to live under the laws and edicts of their elected government? Or was Israel a *Jewish* state, whose laws and edicts had to satisfy a set of criteria determined by non-elected, non-democratic sources such as the ultra-Orthodox?

Haetzni opted for the second definition, although he rejected the religious component. He liked the politics of the Gush—the emphasis on Jewish power and territory—and if he had to associate with fundamentalists to achieve his aims, that was a small price to pay. "A government that voted to give away territory would have deserted the Land of Israel," he said. It would be traitorous. There would be rebellion in the army.

"There would also be war between us and the Arabs because they are just waiting for us to be weak. That is very clear in Islam. But we have guns to shoot with and I am sure that many thousands would come to our aid.

"No Israeli prime minister would remain in office for one hour after such a decision. This is democracy? Hitler was duly elected, too. No, we would not leave. We are not wedded to the Israeli government. We are wedded to the Land of Israel."

Having compared Shimon Peres to the Jewish leaders in Nazi-occupied Europe, and denigrated his election by comparing it to

Adolf Hitler's, Haetzni went on to tar Peres with the brush of Fascism.

"We do not accept that the Land of Israel be *judenrein* [free of Jews], or that this government practise Nazism," he said. "Peres is worse than Marshal Philippe Pétain [the leader of Vichy France], who lost his legitimacy when he signed an armistice pact with the Germans."

As for Yitzak Shamir, he was dismissed summarily. "Shamir is old and weak. He is manipulated, he has no authority and no leadership. Every minister in his government has a fiefdom."

Haetzni paused for breath. We both did. I was breathless at the hodge-podge of ideas contained in this new "press kit". Haetzni had pasted together an ideological system based on a selective reading of the books on his library shelves, starting with the same false analogies to the Holocaust that the world used to hear from Menachem Begin and ending with the Arab-Israeli peace process as the last ride to Auschwitz and with—as he put it—the word "peace" written on the door of the gas chamber.

Had this man not been quoted every other day in the press, and been so doggedly successful in his attacks, one might have been tempted to dismiss him as a maverick. It was true that he was an extremist among the extreme, "a good hater", as the *Jerusalem Post* put it. It was also true that there were many people living in West Bank settlements who were not ideologues, but were living there in order to enjoy the material comforts of a villa. But like Rabbi Levinger and his wife, Eliakim Haetzni was the spearhead of a movement that had succeeded in infiltrating its ideas into a much larger public. As such, he could not safely be dismissed—nor could Gush Emunim.

Driving back towards Jerusalem, he pointed out the Jewish settlements on the ridges overlooking the road. Each had its own history, its own reason for existence.

"A Jew was stabbed in Bethlehem. The day after, we put up that settlement with our own hands."

We drove past the Dheisheh camp. "That camp is on Jewish land," he muttered.

He slowed down here and there to indicate points of interest. Young Palestinians eyed us—the Israeli plates on the car made us a conspicuous target. Although he had been living at Kiryat Arba since 1971, Haetzni had never been stoned. His son had, though. "It's just a matter of luck," he advised me cheerfully.

"There's a Jewish quarry," he said, pointing to the side of the road.

"Is there much Arab industry on the West Bank?"

"Some." He was silent for a moment, then spoke accusingly. "I notice you are very interested in Arabs. Everyone is interested in the poor Arabs. No one is interested in the Jews. It's a pathological attitude of Gentiles, a pathological anti-Semitism. That's why the whole world is concerned about this area that is smaller than greater Los Angeles. Does anyone care about Iraq? Or Afghanistan? No. Just the Jews."

His face had turned dark with rage. Anyone with different views was either a blind fool, an anti-Semite, or both.

With some trepidation I raised the subject of Jewish terrorism in the settlements. Some of the men involved had been from Kiryat Arba.

I needn't have worried. Mr. Haetzni was proud of Jewish terrorism.

"You must meet Zambish," he suggested enthusiastically. "He was convicted for the wounding and maiming of the [West Bank] mayors. He's a wonderful boy—at the origin of every fight we've had in Hebron."

I dutifully copied down Zambish's telephone number.

"You know, the army hates the Arabs and the leftists as much as we do. When we go to jail, it's a party. We're among our own. When the leftists are in jail, the army gives them a hard time."

He laughed loudly and slapped the steering wheel with pleasure.

When I reached home, I called Zambish. We arranged to meet, back in the heart of Hebron.

I slept badly. Fear was creeping over me like a slow, inexorable tide. I had been to the West Bank four times that week and something told me I was pushing my luck. Jerusalem acquaintances were looking dubious about these trips.

"But there are always soldiers on the buses," I protested to a new friend.

"The Palestinians can shoot from a distance," she replied. "And the stonings...."

I was constantly being asked by both Arabs and Jews if I was afraid. Finally, I was afraid.

Was this the price of living in this country?

It was 6:00 a.m. and I needed to decide quickly if I was to catch the bus on time. Buses go in there every day, I argued with myself. People *live* in there.

Of course. I would go. None the less, I found myself checking my passport to make sure my husband's name and phone number were listed. "In case of accident or death," the Canadian government explained reassuringly.

Nonsense. I was not superstitious. I did not care one whit that my calendar revealed the date as Friday the 13th.

Was I afraid to meet Zambish? I began to feel angry. Perhaps I did not *want* to talk to a "Jewish terrorist". As the daughter of a people that has suffered from "terror" throughout the centuries, perhaps I was profoundly offended by this man who acted, he said, in the name of the Jews. What Jews? Not me.

I do not distinguish "Jewish terrorists" from any other kind of terrorists. They belong to the same spiritual family as Abu Nidal, the Islamic Hizballah, the czarist pogromists, the Red Brigades, the IRA, and the solitary knife-wielders of East Jerusalem. All enraged haters, all death-dealers cast from the same well-worn mould.

I was still debating with myself as I left the apartment. Ten minutes until the bus arrived.

Two soldiers crossed the road directly in front of me. I let them pass. No! I changed my mind and called out loudly.

"Excuse me, excuse me!" I smiled apologetically. I explained. "I am a writer, I have been to Hebron twice this week, I am scheduled to return this morning but, ah..., the truth is I have grown a bit fearful...."

I was embarrassed. Behind my back they would laugh at me.

"Where are you going?" asked the first man. "To the Hebron Casbah?"

"Yes. To the Jewish settlers."

"We've just come from there." He looked dubious. "Can you do your interview by telephone?"

"Then you think it's not safe?"

"Not really. Don't go unless you have to."

"Thank you." I turned around, relieved beyond description. The number 60 bus to Hebron rolled by.

I returned home and sat down with a leisurely cup of coffee and the newspaper.

It was time to take a day off.

CHAPTER TWENTY-THREE

Questions and Answers

"I've asked the question several times in recent years—just how *do* people feel about the Gush Emunim movement?" reflected pollster Hanoch Smith in his Jerusalem office. "The results are always about the same. Approximately 25 per cent of the population feels some warmth, some identification. The biggest shift in this direction has come from the traditional, ultra-Orthodox camp. Many have moved away from their anti-Zionist position. They're not exactly pro-Zionist, but the new attitude is that as far as their values and beliefs are concerned, it is no worse to have a settlement on the other side of the Green Line than on this side of the Green Line. So large numbers have begun to support the Gush Emunim movement and become deeply involved in the West Bank.

"Most Gush Emunim support, religious and secular, comes from the Likud side of the political divide, which means the Sephardic community to a large degree. The Sephardim are not the leaders, or even actively involved—the leaders of the Gush are essentially an elite of European origin—but they like the anti-Arab point of view and they have strong feelings about the Land of Israel. Let's put it this way. The Sephardim support the West Bank settlements in principle, but they are largely poor people so their spending priorities are different. They prefer to have public money invested in their neighbourhoods and in the development towns where they are the majority."

"What kind of support does Rabbi Kahane get in your polls?"

"In August 1985, direct support among eighteen-year-olds and older reached 9 per cent. In elections he gets 2 or 2 1/2 per cent. But the essential thing is that Kahanism has won. The basic idea he preaches, which is that the Arabs should go somewhere else, has become entrenched.

"I ask the question as neutrally as possible, such as: 'Agree or disagree: I support whoever actively tries to get the Arabs to leave.' I don't say 'chase them out' or use other emotional language. The last time I asked this question—late 1986 or early 1987—38 per cent of people said they agreed. That's the highest I've seen."

"Where does Kahane's support come from?" I asked.

"Some American immigrants, but mainly from the young people in the Sephardic community, people who are educational failures and are having trouble getting decent jobs," said Smith.

"You're talking about the same dissatisfied population that has historically supported populist, Fascist movements," I suggested.

"I didn't say that, but I'm giving you the pattern and I'm not correcting you," replied Smith.

In 1977, the Begin revolution split Israel into "two political cultures", as West Bank expert Meron Benvenisti put it. As always, there were significant exceptions and cross-overs, but there was enough evidence to categorize each group in a general way.

On one side could be found the conglomeration of interests Eliakim Haetzni called "The Left". The first thirty years of Israel leaned in this direction. These were the European secular founders, the Labour Zionists, the kibbutzniks, the trade unionists, the Communists, the socialists, the liberal democrats, and the rest. These people urged negotiations to trade land for peace; some of them formed the Peace Now movement to protest the war in Lebanon; others opposed the growing strength of the ultra-Orthodox with increasing violence of their own.

Some attempted to encourage moderate Palestinian spokesmen. Others brought Arab and Jewish schoolchildren together hoping to dispel mutual stereotypes and increase respect for civil rights. Still others tried to set up a dialogue between the Orthodox and the Reform to head off a social confrontation of unknown dimensions. Almost all read Danny Rubenstein's newspaper, *Davar*. And almost all supported the Labour Alignment.

Opposing them were the ultra-Orthodox and other messianists; the religious-Zionist settlement movement on the West Bank; the secular "Greater Israel" supporters who considered all territory conquered in 1967 to be an intrinsic part of Israel, although they wouldn't necessarily move there; extreme nationalists of the Kahane persuasion; hard-line proponents of the view that "there was no one to talk to on the Palestinian side" and therefore any talk of negotiation was tantamount to Jewish suicide. Almost all supported the Likud bloc.

By the late 1980s the split was fairly even, as indicated by the need for a "unity government". But demographically, the long-term trend looked different. The Sephardim and the Orthodox tended to produce much larger families.

If tolerance for pluralism was any indicator of liberal democracy, Hanoch Smith's polls already registered in the danger zone. Forty per cent of people questioned had recently answered no to the question: "Should Reform and Conservative Jews have the same recognition as the Orthodox?" Here as elsewhere, said Smith, his respondents split along the increasingly familiar and dangerous faultline.

And so twin conflagrations threatened the future: the first, an internal "war" between Jews and Palestinians; the second, an internal "war" between religious and secular Jews. Both battles had to do with power: a struggle between Jews and Arabs for control over territory, and a struggle between competing ideologies for dominance.

In the latter struggle, the religious ideology was gaining. The Orthodox could point to an entrenched system of belief that shaped and gave meaning to a specifically Jewish life, while the secular were forced to fall back on more difficult, less definable issues of equality, social justice, pluralism, and individual responsibility—most of which were anathema to their opponents.

But the secular also claimed Jewish precedents. The prophets of the Old Testament had stressed justice, and moral reasoning held a primary place in Judaism. But above all else were "the duties of the heart", as an eleventh-century moralist described them: the merciful and just heart was the mark of the true Jew. Judaism was unique in the obligation it placed upon people to stand by the truth as they perceived it, even against God, if need be.

The secular called upon Spinoza, the seventeenth-century philosopher who based his metaphysics and ethics on reason alone (Spinoza had also come into conflict with the Orthodox community of his day), and they held conferences under his portrait and addressed impassioned speeches to each other. But their abstract ideas were less appealing to ordinary people than religion and religious nationalism—for doubt is always less appealing than certainty.

The ultra-Orthodox retorted that neither God nor the enemy would brook such wishy-washy dithering. God demanded obedience and the enemy was always held in check by strength.

Secular Israel was definitely on the defensive. A controversial play called *The Last Secularist* was being performed. The plot was simple: The religious have taken over. There is only one secular Jew left and they are looking for him....

For several years, activists in the pluralist camp had been trying to build bridges over these twin chasms of Israeli society. Interns for Peace, for example, was a small group of Jews and Arabs that tried to bring together residents of Jewish and Arab towns in the Galilee to combat stereotyping. They arranged school exchanges, social events, joint meetings, and the like, but they had to combat much opposition and fear. In his book *Arab and Jew*, David Shipler quoted a young American-Jewish activist who found that Jews in Israel did not distinguish between Israeli Arabs and Arabs on the West Bank. "They think I'm living with eight thousand PLO terrorists," he said. He found that they stereotyped Israeli Arabs as violent, craven, primitive, and exotic, while the Israeli Arabs in turn stereotyped their Jewish countrymen as alien and arrogant.

Another organization called Gesher had been founded by Daniel Tropper in 1970. He was an American-born rabbi, a moderate and a liberal, and his main interest was to reconcile the increasingly polarized camps of Orthodox and secular.

Rabbi Tropper worked out of a tiny office just off the main thoroughfare of Jaffa Street. Machine noise in the next room was excruciatingly loud, but after almost two decades in Israel he had become accustomed to working under difficult conditions. He had also grown accustomed to being constantly interrupted by people who burst in without knocking. (I glared at the fourth intruder, who only looked perplexed.)

Since 1970, Gesher had brought groups of religious and secular high school students together for four days at a time in a retreat setting. No one was forced to do anything at all. The secular girls wore pants; the religious girls wore dresses. The religious students prayed in the morning; the secular did not.

At first it had been easy to get the kids to come, but nowadays each camp was much more suspicious of the other. Some parents objected to having their children mix at all.

In 1986, Gesher created a group called Hagut to fight anti-democratic trends among the ultra-Orthodox. Their founding document carried the names of twenty prominent religious men (no women; presumably "woman", "religious", and "prominent" would be seen as a contradiction in terms). The language of these men left few doubts as to their collective state of mind:

> We reject the continued indiscriminate pressures on the part of the religious community, as well as the progressive erosion of Israel's Jewish character on the part of the secular community.... We call a halt to all new [religious] legislation supported by non-religious members of the Knesset because of political or coalitional agreements.... We unequivocally reject the current practice of engaging in indiscriminate public battles over any and all religious issues, with no distinction being made between primary and secondary issues....

"Most organizations like to set a clearly defined goal with visible results, but we're trying to make small changes in an entire society. You have to be really patient for that."

He paused several long seconds.

"It is very, very difficult to live in this country. I have a son entering the army in three months, and in Israel that means there is a very good chance that he will be fighting in a war. It's a free country. Why should people stay here and face everything we must face when they can leave freely?

"A lot of people do decide to leave, and there is every *logical* reason to do so. What we have to explain is why people stay.

"Ideology provides the reason, and that is why it plays such a big role here."

I checked statistics. In 1985 and 1986, 22,518 immigrants arrived in Israel and 30,800 Israelis left. Even more serious, there was a major brain drain. A 1980 study of 1,000 Israeli professionals living in the United States and Canada revealed that a full 25 per cent had been educated to the doctoral level.

Was Tropper right? Would only the committed believers remain? And how would that affect the future?

Oz Ve Shalom was a religious-Zionist peace group whose name derived from the Book of Psalms: "The Lord will grant His people strength, the Lord will bless His people with peace"(29:11).

The "peace" part was clear enough, but Rabbi Paul Laderman, the movement's education co-ordinator, wanted me to understand the bit about strength. "This is not a classical pacifist organization, because in this part of the world you can't be a pacifist on the model of Gandhi. But from a position of strength, you can talk about peace," he said as we talked and drank coffee in the living room of my apartment.

Oz Ve Shalom was organized in the mid-1970s as a response to the rise of Gush Emunim. While the Gush looked back to the Bible for spiritual truths, Oz Ve Shalom represented a liberal, Western, post-Enlightenment ideology, and sought to reconcile this approach with religion. Their concerns reflected their point of view. At a 1986 seminar held in New York (and not, significantly, in Tel Aviv), they discussed compromise on the West Bank—which they called the West Bank, not Judea and Samaria; peace as a Jewish value; Meir Kahane as a "false prophet"; the dangers of messianism and politics, and the like. They claimed a galaxy of intellectual luminaries as members, men such as Aviezer Ravitsky, Uriel Simon, and Rabbi Aharon Lichtenstein, to name just a few.

Then, in the wake of the Lebanese war, a second, parallel group called Netivot Shalom emerged.

"They were religious soldiers," said Laderman. "They came out of their tanks and they said, there's something wrong here, this war is a mistake, it's immoral and evil. Their organization was based on another verse that says, 'The ways of the Torah are the ways of pleasantness and all its paths are paths of peace.' " But the very existence of "religious" peace groups only served to underline the religious-secular hostilities.

"What about Peace Now?" I asked.

"Peace Now has run out of steam," said Laderman dismissively. "In any case, we approach peace from a religious perspective. People feel that Peace Now desecrated what is sacred to the Jewish people. They demonstrated on the sabbath with a sense of 'We don't give a damn.'

"We're an alternative. We use the Bible, the Talmud, and religious law as a basis for finding peace. We go to the texts to find out whether territorial compromise is possible under Jewish law and values, whether it is permissible for non-Jews to live in the Land of Israel, whether a non-Jew can hold public office in a Jewish state. We are researching and trying to come up with religiously authentic positions which express an openness to the non-Jew. We want to play ball with Meir Kahane in his own ballpark, with chapter and verse, and the same thing with the Gush and the Hasidic rabbis. We say in answer to the latter that the Zionist movement is not heretical or an apostasy, and that within the Jewish historical, legal tradition there is room for a more dovish position that accepts territorial compromise and welcomes the non-Jew. I think we are the only people in the religious community who talk about a pluralistic society."

"Why choose to operate on their terrain?" I asked. "Do they listen?"

"Okay, they say we're not authentic. They've got the jump on us by a few years and, like all extremist ideologies, they attract a lot of money. But we're hoping that within the next couple of years we will be able to come by enough funding to make a big splash."

Like most of the "bridge-builders", Paul Laderman was an American—with a vengeance. He was utterly convinced, for example, that the American Way of Life was essentially Jewish—an idea that might have come as a surprise to America's founding fathers.

Laderman's father was an Orthodox rabbi in Denver, Colorado, and every fourth of July the family would sit on the porch of their house and read passages from the Declaration of Independence and the American Constitution.

"We read it as a religious document," said Laderman, "the way we read from the religious text at Passover. My parents' generation was trying to work through the process of Americanization. When I was very little I asked my father, 'What am I, an American first, or a Jew first?' and he said without batting an eyelid, 'You're a Jew first.' I said, 'You're wrong, I'm an American first.' All my life the dialectic of this thing was central and it wasn't until the end of the Vietnam War, when I was director of the Hillel Foundation at the University of California, that I was able to free myself of these hang-ups."

Along with the Christian clergy at the university, Laderman invited 5,500 U.S. marines who were being shipped out to the war to desert and take refuge in their institutions. Only nineteen heeded the call. Thirty-six hours later the men were flown back to their ship; they would stand trial, but they would receive a general discharge and be allowed to return home.

"It was out of that horrendous experience that I realized just how profoundly American I was, even in my protest," said Laderman. "Then I could move to Israel. Then I was ready."

"What's the connection?" I asked. I was genuinely perplexed.

"I could come here knowing that the American system works," he explained. "I am so deeply American that wherever I go and whatever I do, it is with me. As I said, the American Declaration of Independence is my favourite Jewish document. All human beings are created in the image of God and have a right to life, liberty, and the pursuit of happiness. Now, that's not from any Jewish text, of course, but I have the feeling that it comes right out of our biblical tradition. Therefore, if a Jew wants to deprive Arabs of their birthright in the name of Judaism, that, to me, is a perversion of Jewish and American values. I cannot tolerate that the country in which I live, the country that I call Jewish, should in any way, shape, or form take on the political reality of South Africa with its second-class citizens."

"What about the millions of Israelis who don't come from countries that reflect your ideas? What do you have to say to them?"

He retreated into silence. Were the Sephardim even a part of his equation? Or was all this no more than an idealistic fantasy?

"Well," he said finally, "I have a lot of faith in the American historical experience and I would like to see tolerance and pluralism as contributions that America will make to Israel—because they are also Jewish values."

I knew what Laderman meant; although his formulation of America as a "Jewish" culture was startling, American and Israeli ideology did overlap. Figurative or literal messianism was central to both the "American Dream" and the "Promised Land" of Israel. In a Manichaean universe of "darkness" (Communism) and "light" (Americanism), Americans were the self-appointed bearers of light—a modern counterpart to the ancient Jews who were enjoined to be a "light unto the nations".

There were other similarities. Both countries had incorporated the pioneering ethos into their mythologies. And where else in the world could private citizens pack guns with such impunity?

In the Golan Heights, ex-hippies turned neo-Zionists lived according to an updated version of the dream that shone briefly in sixties America but lived on in Israel, where ideas of communality, sharing, and anti-materialism were central to Zionist thought (if no longer to reality). On the other hand, emotional refugees from an uncertain world without absolutes escaped to the comforting rigours of ultra-Orthodoxy, a universe that defined itself in total *opposition* to America.

For or against, America and its values were integral to Israel.

I recalled a young Bedouin I had met in Beersheva who explained to me that the American cowboys he watched on television westerns were really Bedouin.

"Pardon?"

"The cowboys are Bedouin," he repeated. "They live like us, except they eat cows instead of sheep. They do everything themselves. They have an area to graze animals. And they live in the desert."

I nodded in astonished agreement.

But this identification with America reached its zenith with Rabbi Laderman. His belief system was essentially an import, which is not to say that I didn't sympathize with his hopes. But try as I might, I could not believe that my Moroccan taxi driver with his ancient heritage of rabbis who saved their people from hostile potentates with magic and mysticism and dreams would be remotely interested or impressed. He and almost half the population of Israel wanted Arabs out, and Reform and Conservative Jews in a secondary role at best.

Enough. It was Friday. I was tired of problems and passion-driven beliefs. I would relax a little, take a holiday in downtown Jerusalem. I wanted to sip cappuccino and eat strudel in a café, read the paper quietly. Nothing more.

I set off for downtown under a warm sun that promised heat later in the day. The almond trees flowered white on the hill beside Herod's Tomb. For the first time in days, I noticed the birds and the flowerbeds.

I joined the surging Friday afternoon crowds on Ben Yehuda Street. It was Tu B'shvat, the holiday of the planting of trees, of agriculture, of the fertility of the earth. Vendors sold plants. Posters celebrated the work of the Jewish National Fund, the main tree-planting agency of the country. What could be more important to Israel? I thought about Menachem Perlmutter and the Israel he represented. A man of love.

But political tensions were never far away in this beleaguered land. As I moved through the crowds I passed four middle-aged men with pinched faces holding signs written in Hebrew and English.

"For Peace and Security, Close All Arab Universities and Move Refugee Camps to Arab Lands."

"Israeli TV Serves the Interests of the PLO and Other Enemies."

A young man argued with them. A small crowd gathered, but the eternal debate languished on this holiday afternoon and the pinch-faced ones were soon abandoned to their vigil.

A few feet farther on, a group of fifteen or twenty black-cloaked Orthodox men clustered around a table and bench trying on phylacteries and skullcaps. A couple of recruiters pulled male strollers over to sample the religious wares. Some refused rudely; others agreed to see what was going on.

The Orthodox rolled up the young men's sleeves and tied black phylactery boxes around their arms. Then they presented them with a mimeographed page of prayers. A young soldier struggled with the words while his girlfriend looked on, bemused.

At the other end of the bench where this sacred activity was taking place was the only necking couple I had yet seen in Jerusalem.

I positioned myself at an outdoor café—a front-row seat at the theatre. An earnest high-school band massacred Schubert under the baton of their proud music teacher. Bystanders beamed indulgently.

A circus of two performed farther down the street. He rode a unicycle and juggled two torches, she scraped out an accompaniment on a violin.

Young soldiers strolled by in groups. A grey-headed, uniformed reservist on call-up duty passed. A triumvirate of elderly women, linked arm in arm, chattered loudly in Yiddish.

I read the paper. The news was bad, as usual. The daily horror story from Lebanon was spread over the front page; on the domestic front, the Labour-Likud coalition was under strain. Foreign Minister Shimon Peres was calling for an international conference to get the peace process moving, but Prime Minister Yitzak Shamir rejected this categorically. There was the compulsory daily scandal; today it concerned something called "The Great Judaica Rip-Off"—fake antiquities on the market.

After two months in Israel, the strangeness of some of the stories—and ads—still amazed me. In one long news story, it was revealed that a Hasidic rabbi of the Lubavitcher sect in Brooklyn was accused of promoting himself as the Messiah. "If there is a better candidate for Messiah, let them put him forward," retorted one of his defenders. Elsewhere I learned that rabbis in Jerusalem were debating whether to restore kosher status to a social hall where a French couple had allegedly fornicated in front of an audience. A feature story explained that in the Geula neighbourhood, children traded cards with pictures of Hasidic rabbis instead of baseball players.

In the advertising department, I read the following:

Newly printed...the Flashflood, by Dudaim Basadeh—Mandrakes in the Field—For merit in Lurianic Lore

Concise, carefully phrased Kabballah traditions as taught in the modern city of Jerusalem—now rendered in terse, lilting English.

Sluices away our overgrown disbelief.

Farther down, the Jerusalem Institute of Biblical Polemics announced that four of its students had received diplomas "after completing our intensive course on refuting missionary teachings". Counselling services were henceforth available from said graduates.

One promising item did catch my eye. An Arab-Israeli journalist by the name of Atallah Mansour had been awarded a prize for promoting inter-community understanding. This was a man I wanted to meet—right away.

It was getting late and the air felt wintry again. On my way home, I stopped to browse in a little bookstore. The owner was folding newspapers and preparing to close for the sabbath.

"You can't make a living out of books," he complained.

I commiserated.

"And the newspapers...." He looked disgusted.

"What's wrong with them?"

"Listen," he said, looking me straight in the eye. "This is a sick, sick country. News, news, news, all the time. You can't live that way. We need to get away from the news. Think about the weather, instead. I hear it's going to be warm and sunny this weekend."

He turned away.

The sabbath dropped on Jerusalem like a heavy blanket. At the bus stop, people pressed to board what might be the last vehicle. The number of cars on the road thinned quickly. Soon, in Mea Shearim and Geula, the whistle would sound, telling housewives to light the sabbath candles.

It was surprising how quickly the holiday crowds evaporated. By the time I reached home, my solitary footsteps echoed in an empty street.

CHAPTER TWENTY-FOUR

The Award Winner

Atallah Mansour, the journalist who had won the award for promoting peaceful relations between the Jewish and Arab communities, turned out to be a weekly columnist on Arab affairs for the Israeli daily *Haaretz*; he lived in Nazareth, a predominantly Arab city. "But I'll be in East Jerusalem tomorrow," he said over the telephone. "I'll meet you there."

So there I was in East Jerusalem again, climbing a cold, concrete stairwell in a dilapidated office building. A party was taking place on the third floor. About fifty men and two women were jammed into a room drinking something out of styrofoam cups. The occasion, someone said, was the opening of the Jerusalem edition of a small Nazareth newspaper.

Atallah Mansour was dressed in a beige corduroy suit with professor patches on the elbows, an appropriate outfit for someone who had just returned from a stint as journalist-in-residence at Duke University in the U.S.A. He was a big, burly man in his early fifties with an apparently jovial manner. So much the better for a man who has just won a peace award, I thought.

We looked for a place to talk. There were only bare, dank corners in bare, concrete hallways.

He disappeared into the party for a few minutes and returned with a colleague, a senior editor on the East Jerusalem *Al Quds* daily. They motioned for me to follow. Down the stairs, into a car. In a minute we had arrived at the *Al Quds* building, where we were ushered into a quiet room. Mr. Mansour sat on a chair facing me and prepared himself to be interviewed.

"What did you win the award for? What are you trying to do with your column?" I asked enthusiastically.

"I'm not *trying* to do anything," came the answer. "I just inform people."

"I see."

"Last week I wrote about an Arab and a Jewish team that played soccer together. The Arab team played well and the Israeli press were all gasping. They said, 'What is *happening* with these people? The goaltender finished his studies and is going to university in Germany! And they are so kind! They give flowers to the players!' So I wrote my column saying these Arabs did not live in the centre of the earth, but in a township only ten minutes from the centre of Tel Aviv, and that they and thousands of other Arabs are walking around—only you, the Israelis, do not see them. They are invisible. In another piece I wrote about the use of Arabic in Israel, and how, when the Jews use it, they make many, many mistakes. My son took his driving test and he asked for the instructions in Hebrew because the Arabic was so faulty. So I wrote, if you want to use Arabic, please do, but show some respect for the language and for people who must use the Arab-language forms. Another time I wrote about how a Jewish teachers' union went on strike to show solidarity with Arab teachers who were not receiving their salary from a local Arab council. That was the first time in the history of Israel that that kind of solidarity had happened. So I inform—and I criticize, if necessary."

He was sweating profusely and coughing as he lit one cigarette from the butt of another.

Atallah Mansour was fifteen in 1948 when the State of Israel came into being. His schooling was interrupted, so he lived on a kibbutz for a year, to learn Hebrew. Later, he worked as a youth leader with Arab children. But he had some difficulty understanding just what his status was as an Arab inside Israel.

In 1953, David Ben-Gurion resigned as prime minister and retired to Kibbutz Sede Boqer in the Negev. He held a rally for young people, outside Tel Aviv, and called on them to follow him.

Atallah Mansour wrote Ben-Gurion a letter. "I wrote, 'When you say "all Israelis", do you mean Jews, or all the people who live in Israel, including Arabs?' "

Ben-Gurion invited the Arab youth to Sede Boqer, and Atallah stayed there for a day and a night. "We talked about many things and I had the impression that he knew very little about what was happening inside the Arab community in Israel. We were living under military rule and we had to ask for a permit to travel from one village to another. I was telling him about the harsh conditions of our life, and I believed that he understood, and agreed that Israel should be a place for all the people who live here.

"But this has not been solved. No problems have been solved in this country in the last thirty years. There is no vision. People say, forget it, tomorrow will take care of itself. So we live from day to day."

I thought about my landlady, Miriam, who had said something similar from her very different perspective.

"There is no mixing between Arabs and Jews in Israel, except at the university level. God forbid there should be mixed marriages. Just imagine an Orthodox Jewish child walking with an Arab! People have filthy minds." His bitterness seemed uncontrollable.

"Doesn't prejudice work two ways?" I did not want to listen to another "press kit" of half-truths.

"Yes, but we start from different places. Arabs think they have been injured by the establishment of Israel, so they may resent mixing with Jews because they think of the Jews as enemies. But from the Jewish side, it's more on racial lines. They are the chosen people, the better educated, the whatever. We are the Gentiles, the inferior ones."

Was there no escape from these stereotypes? He was shaking his head sadly. "We live in tribes in this country, and you cannot possibly understand that coming from Canada, where people are equal members of society. Even Europe is now pluralistic. Here we are still living in tribes."

He wiped his brow; I had the feeling this conversation was annoying him.

I asked a question about Israeli and Palestinian Arabs. It was a mistake.

"You speak as though we are different," he said angrily. "I am a Palestinian. I didn't move to Israel, Israel moved in with me. We are at *home* here. We were here before this country was called Israel and we will be here, whatever this place is called, in the next millennia.

"When I hear about the people in the camps in Lebanon eating rats, what do you think that does to me? I have had some arguments with Arab friends over this trial that is going on, this guy Demjanjuk. They say, this is an old story, why are the Jews bothering? I say, the people who suffered this trauma are living here, or their children are here. If your father was tortured, you would want to have a trial too. But our trauma is the trauma of the Palestinians. It is not our fathers but our children who are in those camps."

Silence fell between us.

"I have met a great deal of despair in my travels here," I said finally.

He looked at his shoes with absorbed interest. Several moments passed.

"Not without reason, I think," he muttered.

There was silence again.

"What about your award? Isn't it important?"

He laughed. "It's nice," he said.

"Nice?"

"Well, we never like people to say what we do is bad, or stupid, or worthless. So if people like my work and say thank you, that's nice."

"But not important."

"Important, important...." He pondered the word. "Put it this way. I know that what I write or say is not going to make any difference. So it's nice. Nothing more."

CHAPTER TWENTY-FIVE

The Prophet

Meron Benvenisti was more knowledgeable about the West Bank than anyone else in the country. Since 1982, he had coordinated the West Bank Data Base Project, funded by the Ford Foundation, which examined and reported on all data related to the territory. He detailed his findings in regular monographs and reports that were distributed by *The Jerusalem Post*—with the standard disclaimer about views and opinions belonging to the author and not to the publisher.

Benvenisti examined the economics of the West Bank settlements in terms of what they cost the Israeli government, the patterns of interaction between Jews and Arabs in disputed places such as Hebron, the services offered to both Jews and Arabs, and every other aspect of life and development there.

He was not very popular in Israel—on the left or on the right. He made everyone uncomfortable, particularly as his excellent work could not be discredited.

Benvenisti could trace his roots in Jerusalem back to the sixteenth century. Once, when he was deputy mayor of that city, he fought Jewish religious zealots over the closure of a road that had been paved by Jordanians over Jewish graves. He argued that one must cater to the needs of the living: the road should remain open and any remains found there should be relocated. When he went to inspect the site, he found a very old headstone inscribed with his own family name. Still, he did not change his mind about keeping the road open.

Meron Benvenisti was born in Jerusalem of a Sephardic father and an Ashkenazic mother, a member of a tiny 3 per cent of Israelis who had been born in Israel before 1940 and consequently were old enough to remember the day the Jewish state became a reality. Benvenisti was as intimate with "The Land" as any Jew, but his approach was pragmatic. Since neither the Jews nor the Arabs were planning to give up their claims willingly, he thought any other attitude would only make things worse.

He refused to associate himself with any mass movement ideology, whether of the right or of the left, an act of courage in a country where collective movements of one sort or another formed the basis of society, through youth groups, kibbutz groups, army groups, religious groups, settlement groups, trade unions, and the rest. There were consequences: he was becoming more and more isolated, dismissed by friends and enemies alike.

Benvenisti tried to explain his views in his book *Conflicts and Contradictions*:

> If you accept the fact that the world is composed of opposites, of legitimate contradictions, claims, and counterclaims, and that if one claim is satisfied, others will remain unsatisfied, then in a sense you solve nothing. But you do learn an important lesson.... Few conflicts involve absolute truths; most are between legitimate positions containing relative truths.... Conflicts are more often resolved by the reconciliation of legitimate claims than by the making of value judgments.
>
> All this is elementary, but, alas, not in my environment. My city nurtures absolute truths; my people believe that their struggle involves

absolute justice and so do my neighbors and enemies, the Palestinians. I see everywhere the contrasts, the incongruities.... I suffer from an almost permanent sense of dissonance.

Benvenisti worked out of an office complex with a small reception area and two tiny rooms. His face was leathery and weatherbeaten and a shock of grey hair sprung thick and unruly from his head. His shirt was unbuttoned at the neck—Israeli-style—revealing a mop of matching curly grey chest hair. He was large and physical-looking, like a farmer or rancher...or a kibbutznik.

"I want to ask you about the West Bank settlers," I said.

He inhaled cigarette smoke deep into his lungs and said nothing.

I tried again. "The settlers...."

"Yes. Well, today about 80 per cent of them are Yuppies. From Tel Aviv. It's much cheaper to buy on the West Bank. They don't think twice about it because for them it's already a foregone conclusion that the West Bank will remain Israeli. But that's a political statement in itself. There is a *de facto* annexation. No need to make it official."

He crushed out his cigarette and lit another one.

"If you make it official you have to accept that the situation is permanent, and if it is permanent you have to decide what to do with the people. There is no easy answer to that. So the present situation is the best of all possible worlds: there is an occupation, which means they can have a state within a state—a dual regime. The Jews live under Israeli law and Israeli democracy and Israeli social benefits and Israeli services and everything else. And the Palestinians live beside them under military rule, without political rights."

"I have felt terrible despair among the Arabs I have met here," I said. "And many, many Jews as well."

"Despair is a powerful catalyst," he answered flatly. "If a political solution is not possible there will be other things, probably more violence."

"Does anyone believe in a political solution?"

"Not really. The Palestinians have given up that hope. Some of the Jews keep on hoping, but they are fooling themselves. Everyone knows that the proposed international conference means nothing. Maybe it's even cynical—except for those who need to hope, to appease their liberal consciences."

I gave up on my questioning. Benvenisti's bleakness had caught me unprepared. Was there nothing at all to hope for, in his dark view? Who could live with that?

"A Palestinian told me Israel was right not to return the West Bank," I said. "He said the Palestinians would use their state to attack Israel."

"That's what the Israelis think."

"I said a *Palestinian* told me that."

"I heard you. An attack is a real possibility. That's why the whole so-called peace process exists only in the minds of the peaceniks, and why there really is no such option. That's why the status quo will be maintained indefinitely. But there is a cost."

"I suppose you mean a moral cost," I said.

"Well, a moral cost is only relevant if you think people care. I'm afraid maybe there will be *no* moral cost, because the situation has already deteriorated. The Israelis can feel they are democratic, just that democracy doesn't apply to the Arabs in the Territories because there is an occupation—a permanent occupation. They would not see that as a moral cost at all. I can even foresee a situation where Israelis will not go to the West Bank, and those who maintain the occupation will not be reserve soldiers but professional riot police. The West Bank would be integrated and segregated at the same time. The Palestinians would have some say over improving their sewage system, for example, but no say in political matters—and no vote, of course. That's all the political right really means by autonomy, but if you ask a lot of people they will say that it's very benign and progressive."

But for Benvenisti himself, the moral question was essential.

"For the Arabs, all this is definitely demeaning," he said. His voice was dropping away perceptibly, reminding me of my conversation with the Palestinian journalist Radwan Abu Ayyash. He roused himself. "For the Jews it is also demeaning. For those who do not uphold universal values of humanism, there is nothing wrong with the present situation, of course. But for anyone who thinks that people are born equal, it is a problem. In the long run we are all damaged."

"How many Israelis think like you?" I asked him. I wondered about Hanoch Smith's claim that 50 per cent were doves on most social and political issues.

"There are very many," he replied, "but their problem is that they project everything into the abstract future. They see the danger ahead, but not that it is already here. They talk of a bi-national state as though it hasn't already happened. I say to them, 'We are on the precipice, we are in the middle of the jump,' and they say, 'You are a prophet of doom, you talk about something that may happen one day, but it has not happened yet.' They say the process is still going on, and I say it is too late and things have now gone much too far to be reversed."

He slumped into his chair, averted his eyes, and lit another cigarette. He looked exhausted. I too felt exhausted. Like the struggling liberals he had described, I wanted desperately, almost angrily, to discount this terrible pessimism.

"Why do you do this work?" I asked, finally.

"For myself. Maybe in fifty years people will be grateful that someone recorded this March of Folly. There will be enough material for a future historian. Anyway, when I write in Hebrew there is no response at all. And when I write in English I hear from the wrong people."

"You mean the peace people who think you're letting their side down?"

"No," he said, "I mean the haters of Israel, who use me to attack my country. All over the world I am perceived as the most articulate pro-Palestinian on the West Bank, and that is why people love me so much. But I am not working for the Palestinians. I record the predicament we are all in, and the oppression.... But when I see how they use me, I become antagonistic. I am now *very* upset with the Arabs."

"The PLO uses you?"

"The PLO and some of the Palestinians here. They do not understand how they are abusing me.

"On the other side, the Israelis sometimes call me a traitor. There is a very thin line between dissent and a perception of treason. But never mind. I am doing this research for my own country and I will continue as long as I have the strength."

The press kits. This was what happened when propagandists grabbed hold of good work motivated by personal integrity and twisted it to serve their purposes. Ought Meron Benvenisti to stop his research and writing because the truth-distorters on both sides abused him? He had apparently decided that the cost of buckling under was more than he or his country could afford to pay.

"Will things deteriorate further on the West Bank?" I asked.

"They can't," he replied. "This is it. The two-tier system is already in place. Any change will be an escalation of violence and repression. It is civil war between Jews and Arabs in Palestine—that's how I define it. The conflict is endemic. It cannot be resolved, only managed.

"The reason is simple. There can be only one legitimate collective on the land, because if that is not the case, then neither side has an exclusive right. But the whole basis for this conflict is the belief of each side that it alone has the right to be here. That entrenched logic operates for Israelis *and* for Palestinians. We are mirror images of each other. Nothing has changed in forty years."

We were silent for what seemed a long time. How many conversations like this had I had in the past two months? Conversations that led to a blank wall of despair?

"How difficult is it for you to live with these ideas?"

"Very," he admitted, his voice catching. "But I am as encapsulated as the others, in a different way. Because I am sitting here talking to you, and knowing that it is all too late."

I felt quite distressed. I had fueled my own life on optimism, keeping despair and cynicism at bay as a determined personal credo. But now I wondered if I had come up against a truth I could not deny and remain honest. Had I come all this way to learn that the future looked more bleak than the present, that there was no hope Israel might survive as a society I and hundreds of thousands like me could relate to?

I turned away from him.

"What can I tell you?" His voice was firm and professional again. He stood. I stood.

"Goodbye," he said, and stretched out his hand.

I returned home exhausted and despondent. I wanted to brush off Benvenisti's dire warnings, his Jeremiah-like prophecies. How excessive, *typically* excessive, his vision seemed to be; this country fostered versions of Armageddon, like so many movie scripts. There was Rabbi Kook as prophet for the Gush Emunim–Bloc of the Faithful and their fantasies of holy ground that belonged to them, and only them, by God-given right. There was that putative messiah living in Brooklyn. And now Benvenisti, a latter-day prophet, with his secular rendition of the End of Days.

But Benvenisti's vision was harder to shake off, for several reasons. For one, the accuracy and objectivity of the data he collected were above reproach, and the resulting picture of the occupation was devastating. Secondly, what he said made logical sense. Perhaps the status quo *could* endure indefinitely. No hard decisions about rights and democracy, no mucky analogies with an institutionalized monstrosity like South Africa, which had an officially two-tiered society.

His pessimism was unbearable because it was simply inhuman to abandon hope. Only suicides abandoned hope. I recalled that some people had actually accused Benvenisti of "suicide".

To distract myself, I turned on the television news.

A young soldier had been killed in Lebanon. He was from a northern kibbutz, near Yiftah.

The funeral was without pretension—bare-boned, raw. Soldiers in khaki and members of the kibbutz family stumbled along a rain-soaked road behind a wooden coffin. The boy's parents clutched each other, bent over in their agony. Their son would be buried on the kibbutz grounds.

I clicked off the set and welcomed the black, empty night.

The Israel I had visited since leaving Menachem Perlmutter in Beersheva was a deeply disturbing place. Reality was bad enough, but the fantasies that justified and underscored that reality were more distressing still.

There were two separate Jewish nations living here, each operating according to a different set of philosophical premises. One of them looked back a very long way and justified the means by the end—which was to be messianic redemption. The religious tenets of this nation were absolute and exclusionary, its politics expansionary and not fundamentally democratic.

The other nation looked back a shorter way—no further than the eighteenth-century Enlightenment—and its ideas incorporated a great deal of Western philosophy, including Greek notions of justice, Spinozan ideals of rationality, and those nineteenth-century revolutionary ideals that had underscored the dream of Jewish national independence.

What was one to make of this energetic, stubborn country that lived in a white heat of emotion all the time? Where the Holocaust of more than forty years ago coloured the response to events today; where messianism was a front-page news story and the ultra-religious lived cloistered in a medieval ghetto in the heart of a modern city; where Wild West gun-slingers and religious zealots thought of themselves as God's soldiers defending God's land; where soldiers shot live ammunition at stone-throwing teenagers born in refugee camps?

Yet this was a land that had provided a homeland to Jewish refugees and by its very existence helped ease the suffering of Holocaust survivors everywhere; a land that had accomplished technological miracles in an arid desert, and attempted to integrate a mix of peoples whose only common denominator was that they were Jews and that two thousand years ago they had been driven from this soil.

I was beginning to understand the words of an old friend who had moved here almost twenty years ago. She and her husband had six children, of whom five had now done their compulsory army service.

"I get by by tuning out," she told me. "I can't stay on the roller-coaster, so I go through periods when I don't read the newspaper, or listen to the radio, or watch the television news. This is how I protect myself.

"When something happens to me, I'll have to pay attention. Maybe I'm conserving my resources for that."

It was time for me to return to the source of this country, to David Ben-Gurion. In 1953, when Ben-Gurion had resigned from government and retired to Kibbutz Sede Boqer, he had hoped the youth of Israel would follow him to settle and develop the wilderness desert. More than anyone else, he had represented the original ideals of Israel.

I would visit Sede Boqer.

CHAPTER TWENTY-SIX

The Road to Sede Boqer

The grey, rocky desert of the Negev touched the Judean wilderness in the north and the vast expanse of the Sinai in the south, and descended to the Gulf of Eilat on the Red Sea. Millions of years ago a natural cataclysm had gouged out its ancient limestone crevices. The boulder-strewn topsoil that covered its desert hills was once sand borne overland by Sahara winds.

Ancient secrets lived on in the desert dryness. A century or so before the time of Jesus, a sect of ascetic hermits wrapped parchment documents in linen and hid them in clay jars in desert caves near the salty waters of the Dead Sea, where they lay undisturbed until a Bedouin goatherd stumbled across one in 1947. The Dead Sea Scrolls, now painstakingly restored and conserved, are the oldest known biblical manuscripts in the world.

At a second site not far south of that spot were found documents left by the last tattered followers of Simeon Bar Kokhba, who led the Jews in a suicidal revolt against Rome in A.D. 132–135. Close by, at the mountain fortress of Masada, another band of Jewish fighters called Zealots had also held out against the

Romans; in A.D. 73, when defeat was imminent, the men slew their wives and children and then slew each other by lot, rather than suffer slavery and abuse.

A direct line connected today's spiritual descendants of Masada in their West Bank fortresses to the original Zealots. The years of Diaspora history separating them were set aside as they celebrated a history of heroism and strength.

I drove south through the desert in my rented car. Still unexcavated mounds from civilizations past rose mysteriously in fields, on hilltops, and along the roadside, packed under centuries of sand and soil. Canaanite and Nabataean cities had been uncovered here, and their water-collection and shade-producing techniques were being studied at the Ben-Gurion University of the Negev. The foundations of these cities, high on easily guarded hills, revealed networks of streets, houses, and palaces, linked by an astonishing system of catchment basins, water channels, and deep cisterns.

The highway snaked around desert hills streaked through with strata of pink and blue. Bedouin tents and shacks lined one side of the road. High on ridges, women and children guarded flocks of sheep and goats, while camels gazed imperiously into the distance. On the other side of the road was an army firing-range. Conical tents were lined up in rows, and tanks lined up beside them.

As I continued into the heart of the Negev, the hills grew higher and the wilderness grew more barren, more forbidding, more exciting. How little this must have changed in five thousand years of human habitation!

And there, in the midst of the desert, was Sede Boqer. I pulled into a gravel parking lot at the edge of an oasis of trees and lawns. Hundreds of birds sang as they flitted through the branches. Desert cactus gardens displayed a stunning, large, red flower. Olive groves stretched the length of the settlement, and a desert pine evoked a disconcerting memory of Canada. The box-like kibbutz buildings were sand-coloured—the colour of the Negev.

When Ben-Gurion retired to Sede Boqer, he was moving to one of the least promising places on the surface of the earth. To him, this stark wilderness was a metaphor for the Jews and their necessary regeneration. At the end of the war with Hitler, a people that had survived the decline and fall of dozens of other civilizations over thousands of years was at the lowest point of its history.

"Jewish society needs the Negev and it must bring its people here," he wrote in his *Recollections*:

> This is where a specifically Jewish effort to open the frontiers of the mind and develop the natural capacities of the Promised Land can make its contribution. The supreme test of Israel at this time in its history lies not in the struggle with hostile forces outside its frontiers, but in its success in wresting fertility from the wasteland that constitutes sixty percent of its territory....
>
> The Negev offers the Jews their greatest opportunity to accomplish everything for themselves from the very beginning. This is a vital part of our redemption in Israel. For in the end, as man gains mastery over Nature he gains it also over himself. That is the sense, and not a mystical but a practical one, in which I define our redemption here.

David Gruen was born in October 1886, in the Polish town of Plonsk, during a period of devastating pogroms. While others escaped by fleeing to the West, he dreamed of Zion. In December 1904 he made his decision and wrote to a friend, Shmuel Fuchs.

> When you read this letter, my feet will be treading the land of our forefathers...[for] I have come to one sole decision, that all our young people who seek a serious solution to their lives and desire to bring true succour to their unhappy people which is approaching terrible annihilation—have no other path but to immigrate to the land of our fathers and to dedicate their lives there to the work of renewal!... Here in the Diaspora there is nothing for us, the young, to do, the general stream will sweep us up against our will, and if we do not labour devotedly there, in Zion, then we are lost!

He arrived in Palestine on September 7, 1906, and changed his name to Ben-Gurion, after one of the leaders of the Jewish revolt against the Romans in A.D. 66. The name meant "son of a lion cub".

Throughout his lifetime, Ben-Gurion read, taught himself, and was influenced by the writers and thinkers he admired. When he first arrived in Palestine, he immersed himself in the study of geography, and crossed the entire country on foot; in 1917 he published a book on the subject, *The Land of Israel—Past and Future*.

During these treks, he discovered that there were Arabs in Palestine. The possible presence of other peoples had not figured in the fevered Zionist dream of European youth. He responded with the publication of *We and Our Neighbours*, in 1931, in which he spoke of the need for "free agreement" and co-operation between Arabs and Jews, a theme he would return to over and over again. Ben-Gurion was intent on negotiating with the Arabs, although later on he always answered Arab violations of ceasefire agreements with military reprisals. "You cannot say that this is a people made up of rioters, and that we should not hold a dialogue and conduct negotiations. Nowhere in the world is there a people made up solely of men of violence," he said at a party conference as early as 1930.

Ben-Gurion was attracted to Greek philosophy and its principles of justice, and to Plato's blueprint for a just state. As secretary general of the Histadrut, the combined labour unions of Israel, from 1921 to 1933, he read widely on socialism and revolution and on mass psychology. He devoured the works of Lenin in their entirety and eventually published a book entitled *From Class to Nation*. He studied the historiography of the Jewish people and wrote his own version of that story, *The Jews in Their Land*. He studied Thucydides' history of the Peloponnesian War, the oldest and probably the best examination of both the human and the strategic nature of warfare. He studied Buddhism, which, like Platonic thought, elevated will and reason above emotion.

He studied science and was fascinated by biology and the human mind.

David Ben-Gurion believed that pioneering and settlement would provide a new root stock for Jewish life, and allow post-Holocaust Jewry to recover from the trauma of Diaspora history. The garden—agriculture and development—would permit the new State of Israel to take its place among the nations.

The publication of the 1939 British White Paper, which favoured the Arabs and restricted Jewish immigration to Palestine, hardened Ben-Gurion's Zionism, and for the next decade he led the Jewish community in its struggle against the British Mandate. In May 1948 he became the first prime minister and minister of defence of the new State of Israel, and one of his first acts was to institutionalize the gun. He succeeded (despite bitter controversy) in breaking up the underground militias—the Haganah, the Irgun, the Palmach—and incorporating them into the new Israel Defence Forces (IDF).

"At four o'clock [this] afternoon Jewish independence was declared and the State of Israel was established. Its destiny is now in the hands of our defence forces," he wrote in his diary on May 14, 1948. He saw the IDF as a tool of national unity, educating young people from disparate origins and fashioning them into the new Israelis. The army would incarnate "the purity of arms". It was to be an instrument of national defence only, an agent of peace.

"How important is the IDF in Israeli society?" I had asked pollster Hanoch Smith in his Jerusalem office.

"It is holy," he had replied.

A few metres down the road from Sede Boqer, among the jujube trees, was the kibbutz hut of Ben-Gurion and his wife, Paula. It was a veritable shrine. The letters of "the old man" (as he was affectionately called) were displayed along with such personal belongings as a watch and cufflinks (although, as the world's least formally attired leader, he rarely seemed to need the latter).

The living room had been furnished with utmost simplicity by people who were manifestly indifferent to such things, but the study was a room Ben-Gurion clearly did care about. It was lined with a complete set of the Cambridge Modern History, the Jewish Encyclopedia, the Cambridge Medieval History, Encyclopedia Britannica, the Talmud, several histories of the Jews and of Zionism, Jewish textual commentaries, a collection of French history, a number of books on Egypt and other Arab countries— and a bronze reproduction of Michelangelo's *Moses*. A facsimile of the ordinance creating the IDF and signed by Ben-Gurion on May 26, 1948, hung on his wall, as did a picture of Spinoza.

In the bedroom a photograph of Mahatma Gandhi, clipped from a popular magazine and framed, hung next to his bed.

A little farther down the road, high on a plateau among mountains and canyons, was the Ben-Gurion Desert Research Centre, where ground-breaking scientific experimentation took place (as well as archival study of "the old man's" life). This was Ben-Gurion's dream—to make the garden blossom and produce. But camped along the entrance road was a "pre-military" unit of children of sixteen and seventeen who were there, I was told, to "learn about the desert and the history of Israel's wars".

The garden and the gun juxtaposed once again.

My guide, Yael, led me down a short stony path. We slipped and slid, stepping carefully over desert plants and avoiding crevasses until we reached the edge of a rocky promontory that looked out over the Negev wilderness. Jagged mountains rose from the desert floor in graduated, undulating waves of rock. Some were topped by flat plateaux where ancient Nabataean cities like Avdat, just a few kilometres away, had perched. A tribe of Israel might have paused in this valley; or a Caananite king, a Babylonian soldier, a Greek general, a Roman soldier, or a Turkish caliph. How many thousands of women had laboured in childbirth in this wild terrain? History had not recorded their travails, or the generations of their lives.

Yael brought me back to earth. "There's a military ceremony here this afternoon at the tomb of Ben-Gurion and Paula," she said. "You might be interested."

I most certainly was. At three o'clock I followed a crowd of parents and siblings headed towards the back of the Desert Research Centre, past army checkpoints and several groups of people in khaki who were assiduously brushing their uniforms and combing their hair.

At the end of the footpath an amphitheatre had been hewn from rough stone, facing the concrete tombs of the Ben-Gurions. On each headstone was written a name and three dates: birth, death, and the most important date of all; the year of *re*birth, the year they made *aliyah*, or immigrated to Israel.

Beyond the graves spread an awesome sight. The afternoon sun had bathed the plateaux and peaks in gold, pink, and red. Light and shadow played side by side.

In this land of ideologies, the symbolism of the shrine was inescapable. Ben-Gurion had recognized the eternal quality of this desert: the desert of Abraham, the outpost, the frontier. And this was the message of today's ceremony: Israel, eternal and for ever; Israel, the land of Zion; Israel, the land of the Jews.

A drum rolled. The cadets were about to be inducted into the officer corps. Two soldiers hand-held the blue and white flag.

The class marched in wearing khaki and grey berets. They went through their manoeuvres, they saluted, they stood at ease, and through it all they remained unmistakably Israeli. They slouched. Try as they might, they could not look like the straight-backed military units of other lands.

The amphitheatre benches were filled with proud, noisy families snapping pictures. A dozen parents sneaked under the rope cordon for close-ups.

A new contingent of brown berets entered; we stood. The soldiers unfurled a different flag: the green and yellow flag of the Negev battalion, with the lion of Judah and the tamarisk tree. According to the Bible, Abraham planted a tamarisk in this desert, as a sign that God would bring the Jews to the Promised Land.

We stood again. The soldiers raised the flag of Israel on a central flagpole. Now a lump rose in my throat. In this strange yet disturbingly familiar land, this flag and this ceremony were connecting me to the millennia of history I happened to share with the strangers seated around me.

They began to sing a song called "Jerusalem of Gold", accompanied by a tinny rendition played over a faulty loudspeaker. It was a song that was popular at the time of the Six Day War, about the return to the ancient land, the return to the holy city. Religion, Zionism, history, politics, and the army—all fused into one. How could Israel's problems be separated, or even formulated with any clarity, when everything merged into a single emotional capsule?

"This song is almost a hymn," someone whispered to me.

Emotional quicksand. They played "Hatikvah" and I resonated like a cello string. Music was the great conveyer belt of nationalism, and my reading of history had taught me to be distrustful of it, but here in this Negev amphitheatre "Hatikvah" seemed to have found its rightful place. The parents and children around me sang quietly. I abandoned myself to feeling, and sang with them.

The centrality of the army had never been so visible. Compulsory service at the age of eighteen was a tribal rite of passage, the coming of age in a society where everyone served—for life. Israel was the army and the army was Israel.

The ceremony was over and the soldiers marched out—in their fashion—almost tripping over parents and siblings who rushed forward to kiss them proudly. Little brothers tried on grey berets. A boy of about ten fingered his older brother's gun self-consciously, patently thrilled to be holding the weapon. He turned it over and fondled it lovingly, aimed it towards the sky, and peered through its sights. He too would have liked to be a soldier—and in time, of course, he would be. Indeed, the purpose

of today's symbol-laden ceremony was to help all these people—
the unit of new officers, their younger siblings who would follow
them, and their loving parents—cope with the inevitable next
war and the call-up to the front lines. Without the emotion, the
singing about holy Jerusalem, and the backdrop vision of the
Negev frontier, would these young men march off to the endless
war? Would their mothers let them go?

The army had helped unify Israel. The soldiers had fought
defensive wars, and won. But twenty years of military occupation could only be corrosive. Now young recruits were forced
to police refugee camps, and quell demonstrations, and chop
down olive trees that were the livelihood of peasant farmers,
and defend settlers who often behaved aggressively towards their
Palestinian neighbours. My landlady, Miriam, hoped the values she had taught her daughter would sustain her and keep her
from being brutalized during her tour of duty in the Occupied
Territories. But brutalization was an inevitable outcome of war.

Occupation had transformed both the occupier and the occupied. The abnormal began to look normal. On the West Bank and
in Gaza a dual system of values and rights was now engrained.
Guns were integral to the urban landscape everywhere in Israel,
but now only visitors were disturbed by them. Even more wor-
rying, the very existence of a majority *Jewish* state was being
threatened by vigilante settlers on the West Bank who wanted to
annex territories that were home to a million and a half Arabs
with a very high birth rate who would soon surpass the Jews in
numbers.

Diaspora Jews like myself had somehow been left in the lurch.
For years we had watched and said nothing. Community leaders
had told us that to criticize the policies of any Israeli government
would jeopardize the Jewish homeland, which was built with
the sweat and blood of four generations—and which promised
our own salvation if, one day, another Hitler emerged. I thought
about Menachem Perlmutter's words. In 1945 he had been a man
of dry bones, all his family dead; four decades later he had sat at

his own table surrounded by twenty-six close relatives. "I think Israel was made for people like me," he had said, with utter simplicity.

Still, there was some truth to the claims of the Diaspora conservatives. Israel and the Zionist movement had been sickeningly distorted by enemies; the world's most racist and least democratic countries spoke piously about self-determination for Palestinians while oppressing their own minorities, and the large Arab states were cynical in the extreme.

The Palestinians themselves had missed the boat in the 1920s and the 1930s, and most of all in 1948, when they could have had their own state but opted instead for rejection, armed struggle, and propaganda.

But the damage to Israel seemed devastating to me after two months of nosing into the corners of this country. The Six Day War was starting to look like a Pyrrhic victory. On purely practical grounds, who could be sure the United States would continue paying the bills, to the tune of $3 billion a year? What held many Americans to Israel was a belief in democracy and a common value system—the way Rabbi Laderman's family in Colorado had read the Declaration of Independence as a Jewish document. But the vision of Israel as a democracy that guaranteed rights to all was eroding. Furthermore, as the Cold War melted and President Reagan's term came to an end, the strategic value of Israel as an anti-Communist buffer in a polarized world might diminish.

Pure self-interest dictated a policy change in Israel.

I thought, then, of Danny Rubenstein, the journalist. His personal pain had stayed with me since that day we had lunched together. *He* knew what was happening on the West Bank. Without a peaceful settlement of the Palestinian situation, Rubenstein believed, Israel was doomed. One day the combined Arab forces would be strong enough to overwhelm it, and all the military force the United States could provide would not stem the débâcle. A negotiated peace that included compromise and guarantees was not a sop to the "leftists", as Eliakim Haetzni believed, but a *sine qua non* of survival. Hundreds of thousands of Israelis and Diaspora Jews knew this, but their voices were not being heard.

Like so many others, I was in a painful personal dilemma. Was I supposed to abandon the values I had learned—*Jewish* liberal values—to tolerate or even defend a military occupation that was corroding the very country it was meant to save? Was I supposed to adopt an ethnic chauvinism in which I opposed the oppression of Soviet Jews and black South Africans but "understood" the oppression of Palestinians?

At Sede Boqer and at the Ben-Gurion memorial Israelis lionized "the old man", but all the while his vision was unravelling. David Ben-Gurion had been a pragmatic man who institutionalized compromise. He had promoted the idea of a partitioned state, worked out a *modus vivendi* with the ultra-Orthodox, fought the militaristic, right-wing version of Zionism that eventually came to power with Menachem Begin in 1977.

But compromise no longer seemed to be the order of the day. Israelis might still feel they were under siege, but it was the vision and accomplishments of Ben-Gurion that were truly under attack. The real danger to Israel seemed to loom from within.

On my last night I escaped into tourist Israel at Jerusalem's El Marrakesh restaurant. A large number of tables were occupied by an "insurance incentives" group of South Africans.

There was a show—very professional. The dancers performed Hasidic dances, Israeli folk dances, Druse dances. They sang songs from the many cultures that made up Israel. Then they invited all of us to join in. The South Africans stepped onto the stage to learn the steps, then flew about the room waving bottles of wine to the tune of "Hava Nagila".

It was absurd, of course, but this tourist vision of Israel felt cozily familiar. This was the postcard Israel of something called "Israel Day" in the Diaspora, the Israel of music, song, and dance. It was the dream of pioneers who never grew old or lost children in the war or struggled with pangs of conscience—or seethed with rage. It was the fantasy of a longed-for plurality where Druse Arabs and Hasidic Jews and Zionist kibbutzniks danced separately and together, moving in and out of each other's lives with dream-like grace; a fantasy world in which there were no angry Palestinian youths with nothing to lose, no frightened parents watching their children go off to war, no bitter disputes over which Jews were really Jews, no Holocaust survivors still suffering after forty years, no funerals on muddy kibbutz roads.

I shut my eyes tightly and imagined home.

Epilogue

I returned from Israel a few months before the uprising broke out in late 1987, but as the reader will doubtless infer from my experiences there, I was not in the least surprised by events. By spring of that year, the Occupied Territories were ready to explode. The uprising appears to have been a reaction to despair, acted out in the main by adolescent youths—wildly, randomly, and with little in the way of an accompanying political strategy. At this writing their rebellion is not over yet; but sadly it does not seem to have helped whatever peace process may have been under negotiation. If anything, already rigid positions appear to have hardened, and there has been an immediate backlash from influential radicals on both sides against all compromise proposals.

Beyond the inestimable tragedy of destroyed lives, Israel has lost hundreds of millions of dollars in tourism and export revenues, and the good will of strong allies in the West. It cannot afford any of these losses.

I am convinced there will be other *intifadas*, with graver and graver consequences, until a just compromise is reached—one that recognizes the legitimate security fears of Israel and the national aspirations of both Jews and Palestinians. I am equally convinced that until that day arrives, Israel will remain the country of *The Garden and the Gun.*

Erna Paris
Toronto
July 1988

Bibliography

Aviad, Janet. *Return to Judaism: Religious Renewal in Israel*. Chicago: University of Chicago Press, 1983.

Ben-Gurion, David. *Jews in Their Land*. London: Aldus Books, 1966.

—.*The Land of Israel—Past and Future*. Tel Aviv: Davar, 1931.

—.*We and Our Neighbours*. Tel Aviv: Aiyanot, 1956.

Benvenisti, Meron. *Conflicts and Contradictions*. New York: Villard Books, 1969.

Bettelheim, Bruno. *The Children of the Dream*. New York: Macmillan, 1969.

Bransten, Thomas R. (ed.) *Recollections of David Ben-Gurion*. London: Macdonald & Co., 1970.

Bulka, Reuven P. *The Coming Cataclysm*. Oakville, Ontario: Mosaic Press, 1984.

Elon, Amos. *The Israelis: Founders and Sons*. New York: Holt Rinehart and Winston, 1971.

Gavron, Daniel. *Israel after Begin*. Boston: Houghton Mifflin, 1984.

Grose, Peter. *A Changing Israel*. New York: Council on Foreign Relations, 1985.

Halabi, Rafik. *The West Bank Story: An Israeli Arab's View of Both Sides of a Tangled Conflict*. New York: Harcourt Brace Jovanovich, 1982.

Halkin, Hillel. *Letter to an American Jewish Friend: A Zionist's Polemic*. Philadelpha: Jewish Publication Society of America, 1977.

Katz, Samuel. *Battleground: Fact and Fantasy in Palestine*. New York: Bantam, 1973, updated 1985.

Mergui, Raphael, and Philippe Simonnot. *Meir Kahane: Le Rabin Qui Fait Peur aux Juifs*. Lausanne: Editions Pierre-Marcel Favre, 1985.

O'Brien, Conor Cruise. *The Siege: The Saga of Israel and Zionism*. New York: Simon & Schuster, 1986.

Paris, Erna. *Unhealed Wounds: France and the Klaus Barbie Affair*. Toronto: Methuen Publications, 1985.

Perlmutter, Amos. *Israel: The Partitioned State. A Political History Since 1900*. New York: Scribners, 1985.

Shipler, David. *Arab and Jew*. New York: Times Books, 1986.

Teveth, Shabtai. *Ben-Gurion and the Palestinians*. New York: Oxford University Press, 1985.